My Wild Ride

The Untamed Life of a Girl with No Self-esteem

By Susan Bump

Copyright © 2013 by All Star Press

All rights reserved. No part of this book may be used; reproduced, or transmitted in any manner whatsoever without permission in writing from the publisher or author except in the case of brief quotations embodied in critical articles and reviews.

Edited by Richard J. Nilsen

Cover photo by Dave Cantrell

First Printing: August, 2013

ISBN#978-1-937376-24-6

Library of Congress number 2013948247

This book is based upon actual events, persons, and companies. However, the names used herein and numerous characters, incidents, locations and businesses portrayed have been changed. Any similarity of those fictitious characters, incidents, or companies to the name attributes or actual background of any actual person, living or dead, or to any actual event, or to any existing company, is entirely coincidental, and unintentional.

DEDICATION

To Karen Levine, who changed my life.

CONTENTS

Chapter 1:	The Farm	9
Chapter 2:	Montour Falls	14
Chapter 3:	Gary	18
Chapter 4:	Paquara Ranch	24
Chapter 5:	Gary Again	27
Chapter 6:	Santa Ynez	30
Chapter 7:	Two-year-old Sale at Hollywood	42
Chapter 8:	Santa Anita	50
Chapter 9:	Del Mar	58
Chapter 10:	Walter and The Farm	62
Chapter 11:	Santa Ynez	69
Chapter 12:	Anza	80
Chapter 13:	Santa Ynez Again	85
Chapter 14:	Belmont and Canterbury Downs	91
Chapter 15:	Home Again	95
Chapter 16:	Centurion Farm	104
Chapter 17:	Argentina	113
Chapter 18:	The Gardner Ranch	119
Chapter 19:	Santa Ynez	126
Chapter 20:	My Wedding	139
Chapter 21:	My Honeymoon	143
Chapter 22:	Home Again	146
Chapter 23:	Trainer's Test	149
Chapter 24:	San Luis Rey Downs	153
Chapter 25:	Bonsall	161
Chapter 26:	Ramona	163
Chapter 27:	Free at last	181
Chapter 28:	Lake Hodges	191
Chapter 29:	Florida	200
Chapter 30:	Pomona	212
Chapter 31:	Pala	215
Chapter 32:	Rainbow	226
Chapter 33:	Lake Hodges Again	234
Chapter 34:	Valley Center	250
All Star Press Publications		287

Chapter 1

The Farm

I am the daughter of the town drunks in a small town in upstate New York and this is my story.

Life started off well enough. In the beginning there wasn't even a hint of the chaos that would eventually swallow us all.

My brother, Scott, was a year older than me and I worshipped him. He was always our fearless leader. We had complete freedom and played for hours in the cornfields with our dog, Missy. Dad worked and was gone most of the day and Mom just turned us loose on the farm. There was no better place for two little kids to grow up.

My earliest memories of my Mother are how often I disappointed her. She wanted a daughter who would play with dolls and wear dresses and that was never me. I played guns with Scott and climbed trees all day. At the end of the day I was as dirty and tired as any little boy would be.

On his fifth birthday Scott got his first bike and taught himself how to ride it. I ran along beside the bike thinking I could catch him if he fell. It didn't take him long at all to learn how to balance and pedal, but braking was a problem. He didn't know that the bike had brakes so he would run into the side of the barn when he wanted to stop. This always ended in a crash on the gravel driveway and then he would calmly get up and put his bike away. He never cried or complained.

Scott started school in the fall and I was devastated. He was my only friend and playmate and now I was alone for hours. Our old farmhouse had a huge picture window where I would sit in a chair all day waiting for a glimpse of the school bus that would bring Scott home. Mom would tell me to sit and wait for Scott and I thought that if I didn't watch for him he would never come home. My days were long and sad and I hated sitting still and waiting all day, but I couldn't risk never seeing Scott again.

I spent hours daydreaming about having a pony to ride. Not just short little daydreams, but the ones that last all day and turn into dreams at night. Even back then I was obsessed with horses.

When I was five years old and ready to start school we moved to a housing development in Binghamton. All of the houses were brand new, in neat rows with perfect lawns. Scott and I really missed the farm and our days in the cornfields. We didn't like Binghamton at all and wanted to go back to the country.

I didn't fit in with the other girls in the neighborhood. The only game they ever played was Barbie and I hated it. Mom would insist that I play Barbie with the little girls and even make me change into clean clothes and wipe the dirt off my knees. There were five of us, all about the same age. We would sit in a circle and make a pile of Barbie clothes in the middle and then take turns choosing an outfit for Barbie. My Barbie collection was extensive and I knew that was the only reason I was invited. I could only play this game for about five minutes and then I would stand up and announce that I had to go home now. I didn't want to ruin their game, so I would leave them my Barbie and all of her clothes. I didn't want them anyway and would have been happy if they just kept my collection.

When I arrived home without my Barbie and her wardrobe Mom would be furious and march me back down the street lecturing me on taking better care of my doll. She never understood how I could give away Barbie and her entire wardrobe. I never understood how dressing a doll could be fun. Why should I care what a stupid doll was wearing? The line between us was already clearly drawn.

Mom and Dad were very happy in our new house and they loved being part of a neighborhood. The neighbors were mostly young couples with children and very social. It seemed like there was a party every weekend. I think this is when they started drinking.

Mom didn't seem to care much for me and I understood that I wasn't who she wanted me to be. She was beautiful and loved pretty clothes and having her hair done. In her dreams I am sure that her daughter wore dresses with white gloves and drank tea. My hair was so bleached from the sun that it was white and I was usually dirty from playing with the boys. I always hated getting dressed up and much preferred my old comfortable jeans and a well-worn T shirt. I ran as fast as the boys and climbed trees better than they could. I watched the other young mothers hug and kiss their children and wondered what it felt like.

School wasn't going very well at all, in fact I hated every minute of it. I was very shy and had no friends and it was painful to be inside all day. On the playground the boys would chase me and tear the sash off my dresses. I thought they hated me and I would run for my life, but they always caught me and tore my dress. Mom made me wear patent leather Mary Janes that were stiff, uncomfortable, and not good to run in. No wonder Mom didn't like me; she had to mend my dresses nearly every day. When I came home from school she would be so disappointed and angry to see me with a torn dress once again. I faulted myself for my lack of speed. I thought that if I had yellow hair instead of white hair maybe they would leave me alone.

One day on the playground I was determined that the boys wouldn't catch me and I ran like I had wings. I managed to escape, but I fell and landed hard on the pavement, skinning one knee to the bone. The school nurse called my mother and I knew that I had let her down again. Mom was instructed to take me straight to the doctor's office since the wound was too deep for the nurse to clean. I tried to assure them both that I was fine and needed no care and I was very sorry. The nurse didn't seem to understand why I was so sorry and I didn't try to explain.

After the doctor cleaned and bandaged my knee and gave instructions that I was to not to bend it for a couple of days we went home. Mom put a dozen board games on the foot of my bed so that I would have something to do and not bother her. Since you can't really play board games by yourself, I just stayed in bed all day and looked at the walls. Sad and lonely, I escaped to my daydreams of riding my own pony. Over the hills I galloped, faster than the wind.

When Dad came home he was furious that Mom had confined me to bed and ignored me. They had a terrible fight and I knew that it was my fault. Later when the fight was over Dad carried me outside and put me in lawn chair in the yard. This was far better than being in bed, but I was scared that he would forget to bring me back in before dark.

Mom and Dad were fighting more all the time and Scott and I learned to be invisible. We desperately wanted to go back to the farm, to a time when there was no fighting. We didn't understand how their moods shifted so quickly and unpredictably. One minute they would be happy and laughing, and then all hell would break loose. We quickly learned how to lay low, be quiet, don't exist. My mantra became 'shh, be quiet, don't exist.'

Mom was no longer able to hide her feelings about me. She wanted a daughter who would wear pretty dresses and play with dolls and she got me instead. I was a huge disappointment and, in her opinion, not even pretty. She was forever telling me it was a pity that I was so plain. I hated my white blond hair and wished it would at least turn yellow. The only attention I got from her was when she said, "Shh, Susie, be quiet." I knew that she would never like me, and I understood that something about me made me unlikable. It wasn't her fault, there had to be something very wrong with me.

Riding home on the school bus I watched with longing as other kids got off the bus and ran into their mother's arms and got hugged. I thought if I could fix what was wrong with me maybe my mother would hug me too. She had never hugged me before, but I hadn't given up hope yet.

Most of Mom and Dad's fights were about me. I cried all the time because I was so unhappy. Mom said it was normal for little girls to cry for no reason and that it would be best to ignore me. Dad would accuse Mom of not taking care of me because good mothers didn't have miserable daughters and then they would fight. The fights would rage on for hours.

I was just a bad kid who couldn't figure out how to completely disappear. Since the fighting was about me it had to be my fault. The fights were always worst at the dinner table. I couldn't eat when they were yelling. No one understood why I couldn't eat so I would be sent to my room as punishment for not eating. Most of what was happening made no sense to me. I would chant in my mind 'shh, be quiet, don't exist.' If I let my body sway with the chant I could go away in my mind to a place where there wasn't any yelling. I was forever riding my imaginary pony, galloping free, with the wind in my hair.

I don't know how Scott handled the chaos because I was so wrapped up in my own despair. I was five years old and I wanted to be dead.

When I was six years old, my sister Betsy was born, and then Ray was born a year later. Now it was even easier for Mom and Dad to ignore me. I wasn't allowed to ask questions or make noise, so I became the silent one. The best thing I could do was to sit very still and not speak. I was aware that my existence was barely tolerated. They would all be happier if I could die.

I was determined to take care of my sister, Betsy, and not let anyone yell at her or hit her. Since she ended up being Dad's favorite, I need not have worried. His eyes would light up when she walked into a room. Since I loved her so much I wasn't jealous, but I didn't understand what she had that I lacked. If I asked for something the answer was no before I even finished asking the question. If Betsy needed something Dad would smile and open his wallet. Eventually I quit asking and got Betsy to ask for me. She instinctively knew when to approach Dad for the best results. Saturday morning after the first drink and before the third drink became her target zone.

Ray was seven years younger than me and he was always Mother's favorite. She loved him in an obsessive, unhealthy way that even as a child I could see wasn't good. All through school Mom did Ray's homework for him and he barely learned the basics like reading and writing. As he got older his girlfriends did his homework for him. He was a good looking, easy-going boy and had lots of friends.

Chapter 2

Montour Falls

We moved to a small town in upstate New York when I was eight years old. I loved our old red brick house in a beautiful neighborhood with fields and a creek bordering our property. I was free again to climb trees, run through fields and sit by the creek for hours, but now I played alone. Scott and I were no longer close although we were both struggling to survive. With everything so new and exciting, I felt like I had been given another chance to be happy. Our new neighborhood had lots of kids my age who welcomed Scott and me. We played team sports every day in the summer and played in the snow in the winter.

Scott and I learned to pretend that our family was just as good as the other kid's families. We got really good at keeping the family secrets. If Scott was bruised from a beating, he would say he ran into a door and I would nod my head in agreement.

Mom was beginning to act peculiar, and I tried hard to ignore it. She would drink wine and smoke cigarettes all day and stare out the kitchen window like she was in a trance. If I spoke to her she wouldn't hear me. When she wasn't staring out that window, she would be watching her 'stories' on TV. Every day from 11:00-4:00 she would smoke, drink wine, and watch TV. If any of us kids needed something between 11:00 and 4:00, it was just too bad. We were not to interrupt her 'stories' for any reason.

One day I was out playing with the neighborhood kids and we were having a snowball fight. For some reason they had chosen a different kid to gang up on each day that week and now they were ganging up on me. Instead of having two teams fighting each other, everyone threw snowballs at me. The snowballs didn't hurt physically but they wounded my soul. I didn't understand why they would gang up on me and ran home in tears. When I arrived home breathless and crying, the door to the house was locked. I was banging on the door, desperately wanting a mother who cared about me to open the door and be a mother. Instead, my mother opened an upstairs window and yelled at me to go away. This was my life.

I already knew that Mom didn't love me and now I knew that I wasn't even as important as a soap opera. I thought I was garbage. At that time I didn't know what self-esteem was, but looking back I know I had none. I don't matter, I don't exist, I wish I was dead, were my prevalent thoughts.

Mom had her first nervous breakdown when I was in sixth grade. I remember it was the middle of the night. Scott and I were watching through my bedroom window as she screamed in the front yard until an ambulance took her away. The paramedics wrapped her up in a straitjacket and I didn't know what it was. Dad told us that she was sick and in the hospital and would be gone for a long time. It was a classmate of mine who told me that my Mother was in Willard, a psychiatric hospital. I could tell by the hushed tone of my classmate that I should be ashamed of this.

Dad took us to visit her several times but we weren't allowed out of the car. The four of us would sit in the car and look at the outside of the old red brick building with barred windows. I wanted to see the sick people on the other side of the bars, but I could only see shadows. There was always an eerie silence inside the car while we waited in the parking lot. We were all intimidated by the prison-like hospital. Sometimes Mom would come out and speak to us and bring us some silly craft project that she had built, but usually not. I accepted that she wouldn't want to talk to me but didn't understand why she wouldn't even speak to Ray.

I don't remember missing her at all, but eventually after months of being away, Mom came home for a few weekend visits and then was home for good. She seemed very fragile now and I wanted to help her. Maybe if I was really good, she would learn to like me.

The drugs she was taking turned her into a cardboard person. She was there on the outside but might as well have been a cardboard cutout of a person. She still drank her wine and sometimes for an hour or two would have a spark of life. Occasionally she could even think of something kind to say to me. Other times she was mean, mostly to Scott, and I was sure she hated him. I felt fortunate that she didn't hate me. She sure didn't like me, but that was better than being hated. I would console myself with the thought that at least she didn't hate me.

Dad always had rules for us and most of them didn't make any sense. The windows had to be cleaned with Windex every Saturday morning inside and outside even if they weren't dirty, and that was my job. After doing the windows, I had to clean the mirrors in the house, and they were always dirty. Mom and Dad were both chain smokers and smoke would hang heavy in the house. When the morning sun tried to shine into the living room windows, you could see heavy layers of smoke. The mirrors were always covered in black soot from smoke. The white ceilings had turned dark gray.

Scott and Ray both had asthma and took medicine so that they could breathe. Mom was always especially concerned when Ray had an asthma attack. There were many days that I couldn't breathe either but no one noticed. On the worst days when I couldn't sleep, because my lungs and throat ached after hours of wheezing, I would sneak into the bathroom and take some of Ray's asthma medicine. I would pretend that I got up to get a drink of water and quietly open the medicine cabinet while the water was running, so that no one would hear me. I was always scared that I would get caught stealing Ray's medicine, but I had to breathe.

Scott was the target of most of the physical abuse. I was still trying to make sense of it all. I have always had this idea that if I could figure something out, even if it was crazy, I could accept it. As hard as I tried I could find no logic behind the attacks on Scott. I became very, very, sad and spent hours crying, hiding in my closet or sitting by the creek. I cried in solitude like my heart was broken. I wanted to be dead.

One night the attack against Scott was more brutal than usual, and I was hiding in my closet shaking and crying as Scott begged Dad to leave him alone. The beating continued for what seemed like forever to me, as I berated myself for not being brave enough to do something. Missy, our dog, was old now, but she was brave enough to at least try to break up the fight and would bark at Dad when he hurt Scott. If I was just braver I could do something to help Scott instead of hiding in the dark. But I wasn't brave; I was just a scared little girl hiding in a dark closet. I was nothing. A plan came to me that night as

I was crying and Scott was screaming. I realized that if I could hate Scott like Mom and Dad did, then I wouldn't care if they beat him. It was like flipping a switch, my emotions were gone. There would be no more hiding, no more crying, no more feeling.

I was far from happy but I could maintain now. The new Susan had been born and she was tough as nails. Inside I was seething, on slow boil, and I would occasionally erupt with a show of temper that scared even me. I survived my childhood in this mode and left home when I was seventeen.

Chapter 3

Gary

When I was seventeen, my world almost came crashing down on me. I had my first real boyfriend, Greg, and was basking in his attention. It felt so wonderful to be noticed for the first time and I was in heaven. I would borrow his jacket even when I wasn't cold just to wear something that smelled like him. I replayed our conversations over and over in my head, amazed that someone wanted to talk to me.

I knew nothing about sex and the risk of getting pregnant. My life experience was limited to what I saw on TV, where women always seemed to be trying hard to get pregnant.

Greg wanted to have sex and I wanted his attention, so I said yes. After having sex only four times, I got pregnant and wanted to die. I told Greg that I was pregnant and he disappeared. So, now I am seventeen, pregnant, alone, and planning my suicide.

I had a horse that I rode every day and I was walking to the ranch and crying when a man stopped and asked me if I wanted a ride. His name was Gary, and I knew who he was because he was in a rock band that had played at our school dances. He asked me what was wrong and I told him my sad story. He took me to Planned Parenthood to confirm the pregnancy and then loaned me $150 and drove me to Buffalo, New York for an abortion. I was weeks away from being eighteen and lied about my age. It was all very easy and I thought Gary had literally saved my life. I would have killed myself before I told my parents I was pregnant or went through with a pregnancy.

Gary and I stayed together for five years and most of it was hell on earth. At first everything was fine between us. He was the lead guitar player and singer in a rock band and I got to tag along to practices and gigs. He and his friends were all at least six years older than me and their lifestyle was very different from what I had known. They were free spirits, and laughed, danced, drank, and did drugs.

Gary and I built a tiny cabin in the woods on a farm that Gary's friend owned. We had no electricity and no running water but it was cozy and I felt safe. I had two dogs, some cats, and my horse to care for. We had a Franklin wood stove for heat and as much wood as we needed close at hand. It wasn't easy to drag the wood in and chop it up, but I enjoyed feeling self-sufficient. The farm was paradise for the dogs. We let them run free and they would hunt all day and come home at night, tired and happy.

Everyone we hung with smoked pot but most of it wasn't very potent. We usually smoked our own homegrown and sometimes better quality weed from Mexico. I liked weaker pot because I could smoke more of it and I enjoyed the taste and smell as well as the high. I became a hippy and a vegetarian, smoked pot all day, wore patched faded jeans and T shirts, and threw away my bra.

Gary was a drug dealer and I thought that was really cool. After being a goody two shoes for my first seventeen years I became cool. I was ready to experiment with any drug that was available. High was good and the higher the better. LSD and whites were my favorite. I was desperate to try heroin, but in our little town it was unavailable. Anything that could make me high was acceptable since without the high life was quite dreary indeed.

I still looked like an innocent young girl at eighteen, so it was my job to carry the drugs. Back then everyone wore jean jackets and the chest pockets were the perfect place to hide drugs. One of my pockets would be for LSD and the other for pot. During a gig the band would take breaks and we would all go outside to the van and get high. Because I was Gary's girlfriend and the keeper of the drugs, I had some status for the first time in my life.

After trying Quaaludes, codeine, and my mother's tranquilizers, I found that downs were not my drug of choice. I loved speed and could eat white crosses all day. When I would smoke pot and take whites, the high was almost as fun as LSD. Since I had always loved nature, I would hike in the woods for hours on speed or LSD. The thought of being part of the world and relating to people while high was terrifying. I always planned my days very carefully to avoid coming in contact with people. I had some perfect days tripping on acid and walking for hours and hours through the woods, crossing streams, sitting by waterfalls. Usually Gary and I tripped together, and by the end of the trip, might go our separate ways. I will never forget the peace I found in nature and LSD. The streams, trees, fall colors, and waterfalls were all gifts from the Universe and when I was high, I could really enjoy them.

I was starting to see that Gary wasn't the happy guy he wanted the world to know him as. His mother was an alcoholic and had abused him horribly. Gary liked to drink and take downs, a powerful and dangerous combination. The first few times I saw his temper flare, I tried to pretend it wasn't happening. We would be sitting at our little table in the cabin eating dinner and suddenly he would start yelling and throwing things. Since we had so little, the throwing and breaking of stuff really upset me. We had only two bowls to eat from and he broke one. Our only light was an oil lamp and he broke that. My respect for Gary dwindled and I began to fear him.

Since I was accustomed to unpredictable behavior, I took it all in stride, never thinking that there could be a better way to live. I was well versed on laying low until the rampage was over, and then pretending that it didn't really happen.

I was very unhappy living with Gary, but had no place to go. Thoughts of suicide filled my days. I felt like I had jumped out of the frying pan and into the fire. At eighteen I had very little hope for happiness or a future. I would spend hours planning my death and then berate myself for not being strong enough to actually follow through.

Gary and I had a strange relationship. I still didn't like sex so he slept with other women, but that didn't bother me. We were never open about this. I knew it was happening and I was just happy that he left me alone.

Gary was very jealous and was always imagining that I was interested in other men. One unusually hot summer day, I had walked to our favorite swimming hole three times by myself to swim. The swimming hole had a beautiful gentle waterfall with a ledge you could sit on and actually be behind the cascading water. I was alone sitting on the ledge, enjoying the falls and the warm water, when Gary came charging down the trail enraged. He made as much noise as a horse would have galloping down the trail, and his face was beet red. Someone had told him that a handsome friend of his had been at the swimming hole all day. He assumed I was cheating on him. When I saw the fury in his eyes I knew that he was literally out of his mind. He quickly realized that he was wrong since I was alone, and still accused me of cheating on him. This was crazy. I couldn't have been any more innocent of his accusations.

It wasn't long after this that Gary became abusive with me. His band wasn't doing well and we were doing so many drugs that there wasn't much profit in the drug business. Somehow it all became my fault. If he had not loaned me money for an abortion, he could have bought a pound of weed and doubled his money and wouldn't be broke now. I heard this story so many times that I believed it. Yes, I was bad, I got pregnant and then I fucked up Gary's life, when he only wanted to help me.

One day we got into a horrible fight in front of my sister. Gary slapped me and I tackled him. We both were rolling and fighting on the ground. I hated him so much for hitting me in front of my sister that I wanted him dead. In my twisted mind it was acceptable to hit me, just not in front of anyone. I reached out on the ground and picked up a rock and had every intention of bashing his brains out. I was imagining what brains would look like coming out of a cracked skull. He was a useless, mean, lazy, abusive piece of shit and I thought he should die now. Just as I was about to kill him, God stepped in and I had an asthma attack. I absolutely could not breathe. I dropped the rock and grabbed my throat while making horrible choking, gasping sounds. That was my first and only serious asthma attack, and I later thanked God for intervening. Gary didn't know how close I had been to killing him, but my sister saw it all. She never said a word.

My life continued to spiral downward. I still had my horse and rode every day. I think this is what kept me sane. In the saddle I was balanced, focused, and in command. I could gallop in the hills with the wind in my face and be free. On the ground I was a mess. I hated my life and I hated Gary, most of the time I just wanted to be dead. Gary became more and more violent and I just got tougher. He would slap me so hard it would knock me out of my chair, and I would just get up and continue my sentence, as if nothing had happened. I knew he was an alcoholic and especially mean when he drank and did drugs, but I stayed with him. Oh, there were times that we broke up and I moved home for a while, but I always went back to him, like a moth to a flame.

Gary had become a poor excuse of a man, mostly feeling sorry for himself because his band wasn't getting any gigs. The band was really not very good, in fact, they sucked. The guitar players and drummer would compete to play the loudest and Becky, the lead singer, who was their only saving grace, would be singing as loud as she could and you still couldn't hear her. She was so talented and couldn't be heard. Becky was the girlfriend of the bass player, Troy, and she was living her own drug/abusive boyfriend nightmares. She finally left the band and Troy. As she was driving away, Troy grabbed her arm out of her car window and bit her, like a mad dog from her hand to her shoulder. These people were my world and I did fit in here. With the exception of Becky, we were all drug loving misfits.

After four years of living in this dreadful hell of a life with Gary and company, I finally got the courage to leave him. I rehearsed in my head a thousand times what I would say to him. Finally when I couldn't stall another day, I was ready to leave. I had been in Buffalo visiting my Grandmother, and although I never spoke to her about Gary, I had ample quiet time to reflect on my miserable life. The day before I was to return home and break up with Gary, I got a phone call from a friend telling me that Gary was in the hospital and had cut off his fingers with an axe. My first thought was 'shit! Now I can't break up with him.'

When I arrived home Gary was out of the hospital with his hand bandaged. He told me that he had been doing acid and goofing around with a friend and an axe, and two fingers of his left hand had been cut off. The doctor had sewn his fingers back on, but the prognosis wasn't good. He would be lucky if the fingers stayed on and didn't get infected, and full use of his fingers probably wouldn't happen. Of course Gary was devastated because he couldn't play guitar and now would never be a rock star. He kept telling me that he knew I would probably leave him, and I assured him I wouldn't. He would tell me that he was going to die young, maybe soon and I hoped it was true. I thought the only way out was for one of us to die. Gary was so depressed that he couldn't even sell drugs and we were penniless.

In the summers I earned enough money to feed my animals by giving riding lessons, but we were in the dead of winter and most people don't ride horses during a New York winter. My animals had never missed a meal, and that wasn't going to change. I found a job in Ithaca, thirty miles away, as a waitress at a Sheraton hotel restaurant. Two girls from my town already worked there and could usually give me a ride to work, and when they couldn't, I hitchhiked.

I was the worst waitress who ever lived. I was so shy that when I walked up to a table to take an order I would blush and stammer, "Hello my name is Susan, can I take your order." Once I got the order, chances were about 50/50 that I would totally screw it up.

On Sundays there was a self-serve buffet and all we waitresses had to do was offer coffee to the customers. One Sunday morning I had a complete meltdown after only two hours of saying, "Would you like more coffee?" I started crying and couldn't stop. The other waitresses were more than kind as they whisked me off to a back room, sat me down, served me coffee and let me cry it out. Finally when I had calmed down, they asked what was wrong and all I could answer was that I couldn't say, "Would you like more coffee one more fucking time because I would scream."

The coffee was really only the straw that broke the camel's back. One of the girls who drove me to work was a girl I went to school with, dumb as a post, flunked the 5th grade, yet she was ten times the waitress I was and she had a car. There were many days when she got off earlier than me and wouldn't wait even a few minutes to give me a ride home. On those days I would hitchhike thirty miles in my waitress dress in the cold and snow. I didn't have a winter jacket and was wearing my little sister's old jacket with sleeves that barely covered my elbows. On a good day, Gary would let me wear his old Army jacket and at least my arms were covered. I was a complete and utter failure.

Somehow I got through that winter and in the spring I started giving riding lessons. Gary was selling drugs again, but couldn't play guitar. He could barely move the two fingers that had been sewn back on. He had spent most of the winter sitting in a chair smoking pot. Now that the weather was warmer, he moved the chair outside and continued his long sit. Even his drug friends noticed that he rarely left the chair.

Chapter 4

Paquara Ranch

One day my horse was being shod and the shoer asked me what I was going to do with my life. I answered that I only wanted to work with horses and since there weren't any horse jobs I was going to do nothing. My answer amused him, and he replied, "Is that so?" He told me of a riding school in Pennsylvania that was looking for help. I still didn't have a car, but somehow I talked Mom into driving me 60 miles to the ranch for an interview. I had threatened to hitchhike if she wouldn't take me and it worked. She didn't know that I had been hitchhiking since I was fourteen.

The ranch was beautiful, with an old white farmhouse, and a brand new twenty stall barn. An old dairy barn had been renovated and was now a bunkhouse. The pastures were huge with lush summer grass and a herd of happy school horses.

The ranch hired me as student staff, and I moved in. I gave riding lessons to beginners and helped care for the school horses in exchange for room and board and five hours of riding lessons for me. It was fun giving lessons to kids and adults. The adult groups had their lessons in the evenings and it always felt like a social event.

At first I loved the ranch because horses were finally my life. Mary, the barn manager, made sure that all the school horses were well cared for. She had charts and lists for everything and ran the school horse barn like a racing stable. Stalls were cleaned early each morning, and the shedrows were always raked. If a horse got hurt he became top priority. We always had a list of horses who needed twenty minutes of cold water hosing on a leg or a hoof soaked in hot water and Epsom salt.

There were usually two or three other girls who worked as student staff. We all lived together in the bunkhouse. We rode, cared for the school horses, and gave lessons all day. The work was hard and the days were long, but it was fun. We were all aspiring young horsewomen and were capable of working twelve-plus hour days.

The owner of the ranch, and our leader and riding instructor was Reggie. He was married to Jane, a wonderful lady from a wealthy family in Philadelphia. The ranch had been a wedding present from her family. Jane was a schoolteacher and left the ranch to teach every day, but would usually ride with us when she got home. She wasn't as horse crazy as the rest of us, but she was a damn good rider.

We had some fun times at Paquara Ranch with three hundred acres and miles of beautiful trails. As student staff I rode at least five hours a day on trails and in lessons. Sometimes we would all go for a 'ride.' Reggie would lead, and we would follow on crazy fast gallops through the windy trails, up and down hills, crossing streams, jumping downed trees. I had ridden wild on my own but never in a group, which was even more fun.

In the fall we would take the ranch truck and look for abandoned apple orchards. We filled feed sacks with delicious apples and then dropped them off in town to be pressed into cider. There is nothing like fresh apple cider from old apple trees.

Sally was hired after me as student staff and she hated the ranch. She was overweight, not fit, and consequently, struggled with the physical work that we did. She especially hated helping with firewood. We supplied our own firewood from the acres of nearby trees, and she couldn't do it.

In an unusual act of generosity Reggie decided that Mary, Sally, and I should travel to Oklahoma to watch the World Quarter Horse Show. He gave us his truck, and we drove from Pennsylvania to Oklahoma to the biggest Quarter Horse show in the Country. The road trip was fun even though we didn't have much money.

Sally saw this trip as her escape plan and once we arrived in Oklahoma we barely saw her. She met a cowboy the first night and told us that she wasn't returning to Pennsylvania with us. Mary, always practical and responsible, tried to talk her into coming back to the ranch, but Sally was long gone.

Reggie was an old school style instructor and was very negative and critical. His style played into my low self-esteem issues and we clashed often. Reggie never praised my riding or encouraged me in any way. Without positive reinforcement I was beginning to think that I had no potential.

One weekend the ranch hosted a riding clinic with an outside trainer who did appreciate me and thought I had talent. Susie Carpenter was positive, happy, and fun and kept asking Reggie where he had found me. Several times on the P.A. system she said, "Reggie, where on earth did you get this girl." I rode several horses in the clinic and they all were perfect. One of my mounts was a Thoroughbred off the track, and Susie told me that I had done an especially good job riding him. My heart and soul were hungry for praise and recognition. I was in heaven that weekend, feeling like the belle of the ball.

After the clinic Reggie was quick to put me back in my place. It only took a few snide comments for me to feel useless again. I decided that the visiting instructor was kind, but only felt sorry for me, so I discarded her opinion about my riding

One day during a lesson Reggie decided that I should only use my legs to make my horse move forward and forbade the use of a whip. Unfortunately my mount that day was Domino, an Appaloosa with completely dead sides. Reggie ordered me to make him trot, and I couldn't get him out of a walk. I kicked and squeezed and chirped to him but he would not trot. Reggie asked me what was wrong with me, that I couldn't even make a horse trot. I thought about it for a second and realized that everything was wrong with me. I was useless on a horse and that is why I couldn't make him trot. My pride prevented me from crying in front of Reggie, but I got off Domino and walked him back to the barn.

I was completely crushed. I was convinced that my dream of being a horse trainer was stupid since I couldn't even make a horse trot. It was time to grow up and forget about horses. I left the ranch in despair and couldn't even look at a horse for many months. I sold my horse and looked for a real job.

Chapter 5

Gary Again

Gary and I were together, but it was now a secret. We had officially broken up when I went to the ranch, but when I came back we started hanging out again. I was living back home, but sneaking out to see Gary.

I found a job as a teacher's assistant at my old high school and saved almost every penny so that I could leave this town and never come back. The job wasn't fun and I counted the hours until the school day was over, but it was only temporary and my ticket out of here.

After three months Sally called and said she could get me a job at a Quarter Horse breeding farm where she was working in Oklahoma. I had saved enough money to buy an old car so I gave three days' notice, quit my job at the high school, and was on my way to Oklahoma in a week.

What I didn't tell anyone was that Gary was going with me. Looking back, I still can't fully grasp how very strong the negative bond between us was.

Gary and I arrived in Oklahoma, and I started my job at Reeve's Ranch. We shared a trailer with Sally and it was rough from the start. Gary had long hair and the cowboys in Oklahoma didn't approve of hippies. I don't think he tried very hard to find a job. I was making more than twice the money I had earned in New York.

Having my friend Sally as a witness living in the same trailer, and the fact that I had a paycheck I could count on, made me feel a little stronger. I finally realized that I didn't need or want Gary. Every day when Sally and I went home for lunch, I would ask him how the job search was going. One day I asked my usual question and he slapped me, knocking me and my chair over backwards. Sally was horrified and told him to leave and never come back. I was embarrassed that anyone had seen how Gary really treated me. Usually he hid his aggression until we were alone.

In the middle of that same night Gary came back to the trailer. He had a key, let himself in, and went to my bedroom. He sat on the floor and cried. He was drunk and I am sure he had done drugs too, because he was really messed up. The hunting knife that he always wore on his belt was in his hand. He was pointing the knife at his stomach, threatening to stab himself if I wouldn't leave with him. I wanted him to kill himself and be gone, so I could go on with my life. When he realized that I didn't care if he was dead, he stopped crying, stood up, and threw the knife at me. I was in bed and the knife stuck in the mattress less than an inch from me. I screamed and Sally called 911, but Gary ran out of the trailer and was gone before the cops arrived. How I wish I could say this was the end of Gary and me.

Sally and I eventually both left the Quarter Horse Ranch and rented rooms from a girl she had met who worked construction. She got us jobs painting at a new apartment complex. I wasn't strong enough to handle the big ladders and nearly broke several windows. I quit before they fired me.

During this time I met an older guy at a bar who seemed to be quite taken with me. We went out a few times and talked on the phone and then he invited me to travel with him to Abu Dhabi. I was ready to go anywhere with almost anyone so I said yes. Sally was sure that he intended to sell me as a sex slave, and she and I had some big arguments. I was intent on going and she thought I was a naïve fool. I now think that she was probably right. In any event my man never arrived on the day that we were set to travel (thank you God!).

I was very depressed and hung by the phone waiting for a call that never came when Gary reappeared. He was sorry that he had been a jerk, had a job in Wyoming, and wanted me to join him. I had no reason to stay in Oklahoma so I said yes.

We arrived in Wyoming and moved into a rented trailer with Gary's best friend from New York. They both worked at a dam site in the wilderness. I was bored, but I hiked all day and smoked plenty of pot. We stayed only a few weeks when Gary and his best friend got into a big fight and we were kicked out.

We still had the old car we had driven from New York and decided to take a road trip heading west. We arrived in California in the summer and I found that I was a true beach person. I loved the s, and the ocean, the wind and the beach people. The sound of the ocean was like music for my soul.

Chapter 6

Santa Ynez

Gary and I drove up and down the coast of California just hanging out for a month. One day we pulled off the highway in Santa Ynez to buy gas. The Santa Ynez Valley was breathtakingly beautiful with its soft rolling hills and miles of horse fencing. I decided to look for a job and stopped at the first farm we came to. They didn't need help, but directed me to Silent Oaks Farm, a Thoroughbred farm in Los Olivos where a rider had been injured the day before.

Silent Oaks Farm hired me on the spot. Since I had no address and no phone number they had to take me now or never. They put me on a racehorse that was lame and told me to ride him around a small round pen and then asked me if he felt okay. I replied, "No, in fact he is lame on his left front leg." I was in!

I started work the next day at Silent Oaks as a rider. Every rider was given a riding list with the names of the horses we were to exercise each day. I was so excited I couldn't speak. When I got on the track with my first horse, I knew that my life had finally begun. All the years of misery were suddenly just history. Now I had a life. I rode and rode and rode. The other riders weren't as addicted to riding as me and they would give me their horses to ride. Since we were all on salary, they were very happy to share their mounts.

Eventually the rider who had been injured returned to the farm and she was not at all pleased that I had been hired. We were introduced and she wouldn't even say hello to me. Jane was the head rider and it was her job to make the riding lists. Since I was very green and just learning to gallop racehorses I was no threat to her, but she seemed to hate me anyway.

The trainer was Paul Hall, who was a quadriplegic from a racehorse accident. He had a motorized wheelchair and a sunny spot in the courtyard, where he could watch the horses train on the track all morning. Paul and I got along well and I respected him as a horseman. He told me that Jane was jealous of me which I couldn't understand since she was ten times the rider I was at that point. It never dawned on me that Jane might think I was prettier than she was and that was her problem with me.

Jane sought revenge on me through her power to create the riding lists. It started off harmless enough with every horse that wasn't very good looking ending up on my list. Whenever such a horse arrived at the farm, the riders would all tease me that another ugly horse came in for me. This did not bother me at all since I loved riding and they were all beautiful to me. They didn't understand that I was living a life I hadn't even dared to dream. Who would have thought that Susan Bump from Montour Falls could come to California and ride racehorses?

Jane kept the pressure on and cranked it up a notch giving me a horse to gallop who was a wobbler. Paul explained that a wobbler is a horse with a disease that affects him neurologically and causes him to stumble and fall. He told me that if I was uncomfortable riding the horse I could take off him. Silly me saw this as a challenge and I galloped the horse. Thank God he never went down on the track with me. No reputable farm would train a wobbler since they are dangerous and there is no chance they would ever make it to the races, but I didn't know that then.

Millwood Richards was the owner of Silent Oaks Farm and every fall when breaking season started he hired a cowboy to break the horses. The cowboy would break them in the round pen, take them to the track a few times, and when they were safe, they would go on the riding lists for us. I asked Millwood why we couldn't break our own horses and he said we were all too pretty. I was so naïve that I took this as truth. Years later when another trainer asked me why I wasn't breaking horses I repeated this story to him and he laughed his ass off.

Bob was the cowboy horse breaker for the farm, and he was doing a wonderful job. All of the horses that he broke and then passed on to us were well behaved. He invited me to a concert and I happily accepted the invitation. The day of the concert he got bucked off a big red colt and hurt his neck. Being a cowboy he didn't pay much attention to his injury, and the concert plans were still on. We started out in his truck and only drove a few miles when he said he was in serious pain and would have to go home. I was disappointed and tried to be compassionate by not sulking too much. I hate to admit that this was the depth of my compassion, but I really wanted to go to that concert.

It turned out that Bob had a broken neck. Poor guy, he had a broken neck and a sulky, self-centered date! That was the end of breaking season for him. He was replaced by another cowboy.

The big red colt was called the Unconscious colt since Unconscious was his sire. Jane put him on my list and I am sure that she thought this would get me out of her life. The colt didn't like the track so Paul decided to send him on trail rides instead of making him track. I was in heaven, actually getting paid to ride a big beautiful colt on trail rides. I would take some pot with me, tie my helmet to the western saddle and have fun. The colt was always nice to me.

One day I was heading back to the farm after a trail ride, high as a kite with my helmet still tied to the saddle. The farm vet, Dr. Sands, was behind me on the driveway to the farm and busted me. The helmet cover had fallen off my helmet. He stopped and picked it up and asked me why my helmet wasn't on my head. I told him I was only trail riding and didn't need a helmet.

Bob was a respected horse breaker, and it was known around the Valley that an Unconscious colt had broken his neck. This horse was now considered an outlaw. Dr. Sands asked me if this was the Unconscious colt who broke Bob's neck and I said, "Yes, this is him but he likes me." Dr. Sands knew that Jane put me on the horse and he knew what her plan was. He promised not to rat me out on not wearing a helmet if I never tied it to the saddle again. I am sure that he and Paul had an interesting discussion on how the outlaw horse of the Valley ended up on my riding list.

Gary and I were together when I started working at Silent Oaks Farm. We were living out of our car and at night we would find different places to park so we could sleep. I was embarrassed about my living situation, so I lied to anyone who asked and said we were camping at Gaviota Beach, and that I loved to camp. My co-workers at the farm thought living at the beach was bad and I wondered what they would think if they knew the truth. After my first month of work, I was offered a room in the barn with the stipulation that Gary could not join me. I was thrilled! A room of my own and no Gary! Paul offered me the room and I could tell that he was sure I would turn it down without Gary. I said, "Thank you, can I move in today?" and he reiterated that Gary could not live with me. I said, "Good. I wanted him gone anyway." The look on Paul's face said it all. Suddenly he understood my situation and saw through my lies. I think he was happy to help me.

I moved into my room immediately. It was only a bedroom with an adjoining bathroom in the training barn, but I was very happy to have it. The down side was that the bathroom was in the barn and used by the grooms, so it was always filthy. The grooms who used this bathroom had very different cleanliness standards than I did and it was impossible to keep it clean. I never took a shower without my flip flops on. Still, I was thrilled to be breaking away from Gary and getting deeper into a life with Thoroughbred racehorses.

Gary looked for a job in Santa Ynez, but with his long hair, he was as likely to find work as he was in Oklahoma. Much of my paycheck went into the gas tank of our old car so that he could drive around looking for work. I became increasingly bold with Gary. At the end of each working day he would pick me up and we would go to the beach. The first thing I would do is look at the gas tank hoping that there was enough gas to get us to the beach and back and then quiz him about where the gas had gone. I would be so happy riding all day and then at 4:00 go back to the war zone. Finally Gary gave up looking for a job and decided to hitchhike to Louisiana to work on an oil rig. I don't think I had ever been so happy to see someone leave.

With Gary gone, I was able to save some money and I bought a small motorcycle from another rider. For the first time in my life I felt free. I had a job, a place to live, and transportation. I began working through lunch so that I could leave the farm earlier and have more beach time.

I became a regular at a nude beach just past the Gaviota State Beach, only a fifteen minute bike ride from the farm. Most of the other beach people were older gay men and they looked out for me since it was unusual for a girl to go to a nude beach alone. At first I thought that these nude sunbathers looked very comfortable but I could never do that. One day when I realized the significance of the men being gay, and that they probably were not very interested in my body anyway, I took off my bikini top. It felt so good to feel the sun on my bare breasts that I finally really understood nude sunbathing. It wasn't about sex or being an exhibitionist. Nude sunbathing was about being comfortable and enjoying the sun. It wasn't much longer until I just had to feel the sun on my entire body and my bikini bottoms came off. Soon I was swimming, walking, and playing volleyball, with the other nude beach people.

I was having so much fun with life for the first time ever and I was twenty-two years old. Up until now I had been treading water, sometimes frantically, waiting for my life to start. I knew my wait was over. Freedom is what I had craved all these years and I had it now. I fed on it and became stronger and stronger.

Gary came back from Louisiana a few weeks later and we had a terrible fight. He barged into my room at the farm late one night, all fucked up on drugs and alcohol. He was in a rage yelling at me because he had found the unused concert tickets from my date with Bob in my trash. He sprayed a bottle of red wine on my walls and ceiling and broke a lamp. He threw me against the wall, but I wiggled loose and ran outside. I hid behind a tree so that I could think and come up with a quick plan. I had to decide if I was going to take a beating silently to ensure that the farm didn't find out that Gary was here, or put an end to this now. He found me hiding and threw me against the tree. When I fell to the ground and tried to get up, he kicked me. It was this kick that made something inside me snap. I was a rider, I had a job and a place to live, and Gary was not going to fuck this up for me. I got up and ran for my life. Gary was so messed up on drugs and alcohol that it wasn't hard to outrun him. I was not going down easy and finally willing to fight for myself. I couldn't take this anymore. I was no longer the loser who could be kicked and beaten. The thoughts 'I have a job, a place to live, a bike, and freedom' went round and round in my head as I ran.

I ran about a quarter mile to where the grooms lived in trailers and knocked on the first door I came to. Louis answered the door, and I knew he would help me. I was breathless and all I could say was, "Help!" He was the biggest, friendliest, groom that I worked with and he hit Gary once in the face and knocked him out. Louis called Millwood Richards, the police were called, and Gary was arrested. I was so scared that I would be fired for causing this mess that I couldn't stop shaking. Everyone thought I was shaking because I was afraid of Gary. I couldn't tell them that I was used to being abused, and I was shaking because my future at the farm was in jeopardy. Instead of firing me, Millwood helped me and I was shocked. I was not expecting kindness and was so ashamed of the sick ugly drama that I had been in the middle of.

The next day a police officer came out to take a statement from me and he asked if I had anything that belonged to Gary. Gary had left a box of clothes with me when he went to Louisiana and I gave it to the cop. They wanted to make sure that Gary had no reason to come back to the farm. What I didn't know was that there was a bag of weed hidden in the box that belonged to Gary. Anyone who knew me would know that I would never ever give a bag of weed to a cop, but I am sure Gary thought I did it to get even with him. At long last Gary was out of my life. It took me a while to feel safe and enjoy my freedom, but I got there.

With Gary gone my whole perspective on life began to change. Life no longer was a struggle to survive. I had peace, shelter, wheels, and an income. For the next few months I galloped horses and went to the beach and barely spoke to anyone. When I was galloping on the track I became one with my horse. I loved to feel the wind in my face. To be in control of big, powerful, and beautiful racehorses who liked me was the most amazing feeling. I was somebody…finally.

Working through lunch was a gift that allowed me to get to the beach an hour earlier. On days that there were still horses on the hot walker at noon, someone had to stay to watch them and then put them in their stalls when they were cooled out. I was always a willing volunteer and would sit on a stone bench in the sun near the walker in awe of my good fortune.

On days that I wasn't needed to work through lunch, I would ride my motorcycle for an hour. Santa Ynez had so many beautiful country roads lined with old gnarly oak trees that I could choose a different road every day. I loved to feel the wind in my hair and on my face, and no one could make me wear a helmet.

There were three riders besides Jane and me that summer. Carl and Billy were young high school boys and Darlene was Jane's best friend. Paul lived on the farm and every day for lunch Jane, Darlene, and Paul, watched *All My Children* at Paul's house. Jane tried to make a point of omitting me from this great event and would make a big deal out of asking Darlene and Paul if they were ready to watch their show. They never invited me and it mattered not at all since I hate soap operas and TV. What did hurt was Jane making such a point of not including me. Always the master of hiding my feelings, I would smile, get on my bike and ride.

I started to get very lonely even though I was happy. I didn't expect anyone to want me as a friend especially after the ugly and public fight with Gary. I knew the horses really liked me and I wanted that to be enough.

Paul had a yearling filly that was very well bred but small. He wanted to bring her out of the yearling filly pasture early to feed her up in hopes that she would grow before breaking season. Her sire was Youth which made her the Youth filly and she became my project. With Paul's coaching I taught her how to go on the hot walker, to be groomed, and to wear a blanket. At night I always read books and I began to take my book to my filly's stall to read. She would be sleeping and I would quietly enter her stall, curl up next to her, and read for hours. I think she must have been very lonely too, knowing that her friends were still out in the pasture. During the day when I walked past her stall, she would nicker at me to come in. I always took a minute to go in and pet her. When it was her turn to be broke she was very difficult and wouldn't go forward. The cowboy breaking her said she was the worst of the bunch. Jane blamed me for spoiling her.

In the fall before breaking season started, Tina was hired to ride. Suddenly I wasn't the greenest rider on the farm. Tina was shunned by Darlene and Jane so we became friends by default. After a few quiet months of solitude I was ready to rock. Tina and I started going to Anderson's bar in Buellton on Saturday nights. I have never been comfortable around groups of people, especially when they are drinking, but I was so lonely that I gave it a try. What I quickly learned was that if I was one of the drinkers I didn't mind hanging with them at all. It seemed like all of the horse people in the Valley were either at Anderson's or the only other bar in the Valley, the Maverick, every Saturday night. There was always music and dancing and I had fun. Tina and I weren't earning much money and were always broke, but if we had just a couple of dollars to buy our first drinks the men at the bar would buy for us after that. Sometimes we would have five or more drinks lined up on the bar paid for by different men. We drank, we danced, and we got silly. Oh, to be young and carefree! This was all new to me, and I loved it.

Tina didn't get along very well with the Mexican grooms at the farm. More than anything she did, it was her attitude that was offensive. The crew had always been nice to me and we were all friends, so I didn't really understand her attitude. Coming from a small town in upstate New York where we were all white, I had never experienced racism. I think Tina's racism bothered me even more than it hurt the grooms.

The Mexican grooms were a group of young, good natured, hard-working guys and much to my delight they didn't get mad, they got even with Tina. The riders all left our boots and helmets in the office at the end of the day. First thing in the morning we would be getting dressed to ride and Tina would scream. Somehow a dead mouse would be either in her boots or her helmet. One morning she found her boots half filled with urine. Paul put a stop to the pranking after Tina tied one of the dead mice to the zipper on his jacket, but the revenge didn't stop there.

When we were in the round pen on a horse and ready to come out to go to the track, we would shout for someone to open the door please and then ride out. There were days when I would be on the track and could hear Tina screaming "OPEN THE DOOR" for fifteen minutes. When I came off the track, she would still be screaming and several grooms would be standing near the round pen laughing. I would put my horse away and let her out.

One day Tina got bucked off a young horse in the center of the courtyard. She didn't get hurt physically, but it always bruises your ego to get bucked off in front of everyone. Tina had a rather ample butt and her nickname was bubble butt. She left the imprint of her ass in the dirt in the center of the courtyard. The grooms drew a circle in chalk around the imprint and kept it intact all day. Poor Tina must have wondered whose side I was on because I laughed as loud as the guys.

Tina wanted us to be tight like Jane and Darlene, but I wasn't interested. She was fun to ride with and drink with, but that was enough for me. I never invited her to the beach with me because that was mine and not to be shared. I still went to the beach every day, even if it was cold and windy. By now I knew all the coves and had favorite spots for windy days. When it was cold I would huddle in a cove and let the sun warm me.

I called home to tell Mom and Dad how well I was doing a couple of times a month even though they didn't seem very interested. I rationalized that since they weren't horse people they just didn't get it. They called me twice to ask for money. They had lost their fuel oil business and needed money to pay the mortgage. I was earning $600 a month and gave them $350 to cover the mortgage twice. It felt good to be needed by my family for the first time, but the second time that they asked for money it didn't feel as good. I was saving money to buy a car and didn't want to be still on my motorcycle when the rainy season started. The weather was changing, getting colder, and I wanted the comfort of a car. The third time they asked for money I said no. They tried hard to guilt me into changing my mind but I stood firm. When I hung up I cried my heart out and felt like a selfish bitch, but there was a part of me that knew I had made a good decision. I knew I had to distance myself from them or they would milk me dry and never look back.

The next phone call from home was to inform me that Scott had suffered a nervous breakdown and was in a psychiatric hospital. Scott and I had not been close for years but news of his breakdown sent me spinning. I knew why he had broken down. My only surprise was that he had kept it together as long as he did. They beat him until he broke, as I watched and didn't help. I cried for days but never when anyone would see me. I needed to take a giant step back from this sick family and save myself. No one in California knew about my family so my secret was safe. I couldn't help Scott without giving up my life. I wasn't prepared to do that.

The rainy season finally began and I got caught in a downpour on my motorcycle, not fun. I had $1,800 saved and was ready to go car shopping. There was an MG Midget advertised for sale in Santa Barbara for $1,800 and I fell in love with her the first moment I saw her. I wasn't expecting much because she was old, a 1969 model, but she was beautiful. She was a lovely shade of pale yellow with spoked rims, a padded roll bar, and in mint condition. Without a moment's hesitation I named her Nelly. Nelly and I had adventures that few would dare to dream or live through.

Nelly ran like a top and was unique and adorable. Paul told me I could park her in the vet clinic at night, which was behind the main training barn. Every morning before the riders arrived, I would move my car out of the clinic and park in the main parking lot. After ten days of doing this, Jane told Paul in front of the other riders that Susan had not spent a night in her own bed since she bought a car. She was basing this on the fact that she saw me drive into the parking lot early every morning, but Paul set her straight. I am sure this incident made her hate me even more. There must have been lots of mean remarks behind my back because soon everyone at the farm was telling me that Jane was jealous of me and that I should watch my back. I wasn't very concerned because I only wanted to ride.

Nelly was a sign of my growing strength and independence. With Gary gone and very little contact with my family, the feeling of freedom was like a drug that I couldn't get enough of. Eventually freedom wasn't enough and I wanted wild ass fun. I threw common sense out the window and proceeded to make up for lost time.

One Saturday night Tina and I went to Anderson's to drink and dance. As usual, drinks were lined up on the bar for us. The farm vet, Dr. Sands, had a brother, Tommy, who worked at River Edge Farm, a huge Thoroughbred farm close to Silent Oaks Farm. He was really cute and all of the girls at our farm flirted with him except me. I was still shy around men and didn't like sex, so there was no reason for me to flirt. Tommy was at Anderson's that night and we drank and danced. I mentioned that I had heard that there were always bar fights at the Maverick and cowboys were often thrown through the large front window, just like in the old West. Tommy offered to accompany me to the Maverick in hopes of witnessing my first bar fight. I insisted on driving Nelly and once we were on the road, I asked him if he thought I could scare him. When he said no (he was a cowboy and had to say no) the race was on. Nelly could easily do 105 mph but my favorite speed was 102. I liked to fly but know that I still had a little bit more. After a few miles we were entering the town of Solvang and Tommy was sure I would slow down to drive through town, but I didn't. He had to admit that he was scared. At that point I was already showing off so much that I couldn't stop. I told him not to worry because we had a roll bar. I drove on through Solvang still at 102 mph and entered Santa Ynez.

We were only two blocks from the Maverick when I ran a stop sign and a cop pulled me over. Nelly had a powerful sound system and I was listening to a new Allman Brothers Band tape that I had just bought. It was cranked up loud so that I could hear it through the wind with the top down. The cop asked me nicely to turn the music down and I said no. I told him that this was a new tape, my favorite song, and he would just have to wait. At this point he recognized Tommy and said, "What are you doing with her?" Tommy was one of those people who would probably go through life without ever getting a speeding ticket and the very idea that he was with a girl who was bad-ass was unbelievable. Tommy shook his head and apologized to the cop for my bad behavior and explained that we were on our way to the Maverick, only fifty yards away. The cop let us go and I never did turn that music down. When Tommy got out of the car he swore that he would never get in a car with me driving again for as long as he lived and he hasn't.

I must admit that what I considered fun at this time in my life was way over the top. Tina wanted to go for a ride in Nelly one beautiful Sunday afternoon so off we went. My New York license had been revoked because I didn't pay a ticket and I had not yet applied for a California license. I also had not had a chance to insure or register Nelly yet, so I was more than a little illegal. My plan was that if a cop tried to pull me over, I would make a run for it. At least I would have some fun before I went to jail.

Tina and I were heading out of Buellton and sitting at a four-way stop. I did stop, but there was a semitruck entering the intersection, and knowing how quick Nelly was, I knew that I could just barely dart in front of him. I did just barely dart in front of him and he blew his big truck horn at me (I thought he was so rude) so I flipped him off. I hadn't noticed that a cop was sitting at the same intersection and he tried to pull me over. I told Tina to hold on because we were going to make a run for it. Adrenaline was coursing through my veins and I was ready for the ride of my life. Unfortunately Tina wasn't. She screamed at the top of her lungs and grabbed the steering wheel so I had to pull over. I was so mad at her. It was my car, my rules, and she had no say in anything. The cop was very friendly and didn't even ask for my license and registration. He asked me if I knew how little my car was and that I would have no chance of surviving a crash with a semitruck and then he let me go. Tina was shocked into silence as she saw for the first time that I was a free spirit with no boundaries and no respect for the law. I am sure that she thought I was seriously crazy that day.

Chapter 7

Two-Year-Old Sale at Hollywood Park

Breaking season on Thoroughbred farms begins in September when the horses are yearlings. Back in the 1980s there was only one two-year-old in training sale in Southern California and it was held at Hollywood Park in March. Most of the horses we were breaking at Silent Oaks Farm were being prepared for this sale. In January all of the sales horses, along with their riders and grooms, would ship to Hollywood Park for the last three months of sales prep. This was the highlight of the year for the riders and only the best riders would be going to Hollywood Park. I was still new and only riding the homebreds so it was unlikely that I would be needed at the sale. This was fine with me since I was having so much fun in the Valley.

I had finally saved enough money to move out of my little barn apartment. Tina, Darlene, and I rented a three bedroom house in the country. Darlene only had time to move in and she was off to the sale. My move in was easy since I had only a few clothes and nothing else. I bought a waterbed on credit and Tina had a stereo so everything was great. Led Zeppelin and ZZ Top were my favorites back then and the louder the better.

Two weeks later Millwood called from the sale and wanted me to ride at the track. I was absolutely thrilled and on the road within hours, headed to L.A. I was so proud that I was a rider that I put my helmet over the emergency brake in the center of Nelly to use as an armrest and hoped that other drivers could see it and realize that I was a 'rider.' It was a beautiful sunny day to travel and I made the most of it, smoking pot as soon as I was out of the driveway of Silent Oaks Farms. I thought I was as cool as one can be in my Nelly with the top down, and instead of using an ashtray, I would hold the joint in the air to let the wind blow the ashes off.

Paul had given me directions to Hollywood Park, but I have always struggled with directions. I have absolutely no sense of direction. In fact I have such a strong case of no direction that I call it geographic dyslexia. I may have been enjoying my road trip a little too much as I completely missed L.A. and drove another two hours to San Diego before I realized I was lost. I did eventually find Los Angeles and

Hollywood Park and arrived late in the evening with bloodshot eyes from smoking pot all day. Millwood knew I was stoned and when he asked me why my eyes were so red, I tried to keep a straight face as I lied and said it must be the smog.

Hollywood Park was filled with racing stables, many of which were sales barns like ours. Most of the sales barns put their riders up in a nearby hotel, but Millwood was the last to do this. Millwood stayed at the hotel but the crew all lived in tack rooms in the barn. A tack room is a twelve by twelve room with a cement floor and a window. When Darlene showed me my room, I was a little shocked but took it in stride. My room was filthy and completely empty except for the garbage that had been left behind. I had borrowed a sleeping bag from a friend so I slept on the cement floor in my borrowed sleeping bag.

Jim Gardner was the foreman of our barn. The first morning we met, he asked me if everything was okay and I told him everything was fine. My second night at the track Darlene invited me to stay in her room because she at least had a rug on her floor that I could sleep on. Jim found out that I had nothing, no bed, and not even a rug, and was furious that Millwood would treat me like that. I tried to tell him it wasn't Millwood's fault that I didn't have money for a bed or a rug, but Jim wasn't buying my story. He said that if Millwood paid us properly this would not be an issue. He had two mattresses on his bed and he gave me one.

My dream had come true and I was riding at the track only five months after I started galloping. I loved being on a mile track. The farm track was only a half mile with tight turns that you had to slow down for. This mile track had wide, banked turns that you could lean into.

Racing stables are very different from farms. At the farm riders often do more than just ride. It is not unusual to help the grooms by tacking up horses and holding them for baths or even raking the barnyard. At the track riders only ride. We each had two sets of tack, and we would set the tack in front of the stall of the horse we were riding next so that it would be ready when we got back from the track. Everyone is in a hurry at the track since training hours are from 5:00 a.m. to 10:00 a.m. and then the track closes. It is easy to get an attitude when you are treated like you are suddenly too good to help a groom. We would ride about ten horses each morning, clean our tack, and then be done for the day.

I discovered the local beaches and spent most of my free time at Manhattan Beach. I loved all beaches but this was not my favorite because of the airplanes that flew overhead to nearby LAX. I noticed that most people talked louder as the planes flew over and I vowed not to compete with the noise of the planes. If I was speaking and a plane flew over, I would be silent until I could speak without raising my voice. This was my silent protest.

It didn't take me long to meet like-minded people on the beach. Tye was an artist and lived in an abandoned church at Redondo Beach. We quickly became friends and smoked pot and snorted cocaine on the roof of the church. This was my introduction to cocaine and it quickly became my drug of choice. Fortunately for me, it was very expensive and I didn't have access to it except through Tye.

When I left the Valley I had been warned over and over that Inglewood was very dangerous. The safest place to be was on the backside of Hollywood Park. Since everyone I knew told me this, I believed it to be true and I planned on being very careful.

One day on my way to the beach a tire on Nellie went flat. I was on a busy street and managed to pull over to the curb and get out of traffic. I was directly across from a nude bar and thought that I was probably in terrible danger. This must be a bad part of town because a nude bar wouldn't be in a good part of town. All of the warnings I had heard came to mind and I was scared and started to cry.

I had a spare tire but didn't know how to change a tire. This was before everyone had cell phones. I was parked in front of a car dealer and I walked in and asked to use their phone. They were very nice and asked me what the problem was. I told them that I needed to call AA. I thought that the Automobile Club was called AA, and since I was a member, they could change my tire. When the kind people at the car dealership heard that I needed to call AA and saw me wiping tears off my face they jumped in to help. They offered to change the tire for me and brought me a glass of water and then sat with me until my car was finished. I stopped crying and couldn't get over the kindness that these strangers in Inglewood showed me. It was weeks later when I told a friend my story that I realized that they thought I needed to call Alcoholics Anonymous and this was why they were so kind to me.

I met Gypsy, a rider and a free spirit at Hollywood Park, and we became friends and drug buddies. She had a motorcycle, was only here for the sale, and then would be traveling cross country on her bike alone. I thought she was so cool! Gypsy and I would smoke pot in the ladies' jockey room and never worried about getting caught. We were too cool to care.

Gypsy and some other riders I met were all being paid almost double what Millwood paid his riders and they were living in a hotel instead of in a tack room. I was still thrilled to even be at a major track and money wasn't important to me, but I was beginning to get a clear picture of how Millwood Richards operated.

As we got closer to the sale, the riders were told that we would be working in the afternoons to help show horses. At a Thoroughbred sale, trainers and owners are free to walk around the barns to look at horses. The consignors would rather have a pretty girl show the horses than a Mexican groom. It was all about the show. Pretty girls brought the horses out to show, a short girl would show the small horses so that they would look bigger. Millwood was known for his crew of blond-haired blue-eyed girls and I fit the bill. I would ride for free, but working in the afternoon really cut into my beach time and no extra pay was offered.

I protested silently by taking many quick trips to the ladies' jockey room to get high. The ladies' jockey room had nice showers and bathrooms, so when questioned, I would say I went to the bathroom. It didn't take Millwood long to realize what I was doing since my eyes were always red and he demanded that I ask for permission to go to the bathroom. My reply was something like "yeah right."

I had met an older man from South Africa on the track who was devastatingly handsome and seemed interested in me. He was an assistant trainer for a big racing stable and I couldn't keep my eyes off him in the morning on the track. He told me later that one of his riders always noticed and would tell him that girl is staring at you again. His name was Robin and he soon proved to be a good friend. He had a girlfriend so we were never to be more than friends. He didn't approve of the way Millwood was taking advantage of his riders. We worked twice as hard for half as much money as the other sales riders. Robin gave me the courage to quit Richards and start riding as a freelance rider at Hollywood Park.

I had become increasingly disillusioned with the Richards stable. Jane was even bitchier than normal and rumor had it that Millwood and she had sex in her tack room every year at the sale. I heard this rumor so often, I think it was true. Maybe this is why she saw me as a threat. She need not have feared since I had always been repulsed by Millwood. The first time I met him at the farm when he reached out to shake my h, and I had involuntarily backed up two steps.

Millwood called me into his tack room office one morning to talk. He told me that I had progressed very fast, and was becoming a solid rider in record time, and that if I stayed on through the sale he would find me a job as a head rider. This sounded good except for the fact that his farm is the only farm that has a head rider. Most farms have a trainer, an assistant trainer, a foreman, and riders. It would create too much strife to put one rider above the others. I didn't know this until I talked to Robin. Robin warned me that Richards wasn't to be trusted and that I needed to look out for myself.

Near the end of the sale all of the two-year-olds are shown on the track in formal previews. Most of the horses breeze 1/8 or 1/4 mile and some only gallop. This may be the most important step in selling a young racehorse at a two-year-old sale. If you blow the preview, the horse won't sell well.

Riders all dress in stable colors for the preview and Richards riders wore white jackets with gold MR on the back. The horses and riders would all be perfect for a day. Although I loved riding on the track, I was still very shy and didn't want anyone watching me ride, so I was not looking forward to the previews like the other riders were. There were only two horses on my riding list to preview and they were galloping, not breezing. I was sure I could do this but I was sick with stage fright for days before the preview.

On the day of the preview Millwood called me into his office to explain that I was needed to stay at the barn and show horses during the preview and would not be riding in the previews. He went on and on about how important this was to him. An idiot could have seen through his lies and I felt mortified and furious that he would treat me like an idiot. I have always been a lover of truth, even blunt, painful truth. If he had just said "That because I had been galloping only six months, I wasn't ready to preview a horse," then I would have agreed and been relieved.

I was so hurt and mortified that I went to Robin's barn and asked him for advice. He said I should quit the prick and start freelancing tomorrow. My plan was to run. I wanted to get in my little car and just drive somewhere far away, maybe Texas. I had heard from other riders that Texas had a race track near a nice beach. Robin talked me out of Texas, told me he would get me a nice tack room in the new barns and help me find horses to freelance starting tomorrow. Robin's good sense prevailed and the next morning I got on ten horses as a freelance rider. Robin told me which barns to go to, and like magic they all said "Yes, we have horses for you to ride this morning." Ten horses is a good morning even for an established rider so I was on top of the world.

Later that morning when I was taking my very few belongings out of the dreadful tack room that Millwood had given me I spoke to Darlene. She had been on the track that morning talking to Millwood, when he informed her that I had quit. He was worried that I would starve because I was in no way ready to ride at the track. Just then she saw me on a beautiful horse being loaded into the starting gates. She said, "Excuse me but isn't that Susan in the gates?" She told me that his mouth dropped open and he shut up fast.

One of my new mounts needed to jump out of the gate that morning and when the trainer asked if I had ever jumped one out of the gates, I couldn't say no. The truth would have been career suicide for a new rider at Hollywood Park. The last thing a rider would ever do is admit that she was green. There are at least three gate men working at the starting gate and when the head starter asked me if I had ever been in the gates, I knew better than to lie to him. He was kind and showed me how to grab mane, put loops in my reins so the horse could stretch his neck without me hitting him in the mouth, stand up and fly! Damn that was fun! Robin had been watching me all morning and he said I did great.

Robin and I had a bond in that we both loved horses, but in a way different than most people. I didn't know it then but we both had similar backgrounds, coming from extremely dysfunctional families. He told me a few stories of the abuse he endured as a young boy and they chilled me to the bone. I think that when children are severely emotionally or physically abused, we become super sensitized, and that makes us exceptional horse people. Robin and I could both look at an unhappy horse and know what his problem was and how to fix it. Robin was especially good with young fillies. When he walked down his shedrow, his fillies would all stick their heads out of their stalls from behind the webbings and stretch their necks out to be petted. I have never to this day seen a stable so filled with love.

Robin went to the racing office and got me a tack room in the new barns as he had promised. He put me in a room next door to his best rider, Mike, so he could look out for me. Although I didn't need anyone to look out for me, I did appreciate the gesture.

Once the sale was over and all the sales barns went home, Hollywood Park went back to normal off-track training. The exercise boys were all very nice to me and this pissed off the exercise girls. If they had only known that I didn't even like sex and had no interest in their men, maybe they wouldn't have seen me as a threat. My days went back to galloping in the morning and beach in the afternoon. I spent evenings with Tye smoking pot and snorting cocaine.

I thought Tye and I were friends and it was fun to get high with him on the roof of the old church. The view of the ocean only two blocks away was beautiful and even more so after a line of coke. One day he decided that he had given me enough of his coke and pot and that I should put out or get out. I got out. Because he was blunt and honest there were no hard feelings.

I loved earning my living galloping horses. It was still mind boggling to me that I was getting paid to ride. A lady trainer, Carol Cash, offered me a salary job riding for her and I took it. She was a wonderful woman and really looked out for me. When you are new on the track and not a solid rider yet, it is important to ride safe horses. Green riders end up getting hurt needlessly, far too often. I wasn't very strong yet and sometimes a horse would run off with me. The other riders all told me not to worry about it because everyone gets run off with. The horses get so strong, especially when they are ready for a race, and it takes either finesse or strength to hold them back. I had neither yet. Carol was very patient with me, and if I got run off with, she would just say that horse was too strong for you so we will let Raymond ride him. Raymond was the other salaried rider and he gave me lots of good tips.

I loved talking to the exercise boys about horses. They would answer all of my questions and offer helpful hints. No one ever seemed to take life seriously. They thought my fears of being a bad rider who couldn't hold a tough horse were ridiculous. They always had interesting and funny track stories to tell. I fit in better with the boys than the girl riders, who didn't like me.

Chapter 8

Santa Anita

When the Santa Anita race meet ended, Santa Anita became the off-track and Carol shipped her stable across town to Arcadia. She had been wonderful to work for so I was happy to go with her.

Santa Anita had a much prettier backside than Hollywood Park. Old pepper trees lined the dirt roads and early in the mornings they would be full of singing birds. Years before someone had turned some domestic rabbits loose, and now there were beautiful rabbits living under the barns.

I still lived in a tack room but at least it was a nice room in our barn, number 106. Carol had hired another girl rider and her tack room was next to mine. Inger was from Poland and even though she was a good rider, no one would hire her. I had seen her walking around the backside in boots and breeches. Because all of the riders wore jeans and boots, she was too different to hire. She was very poor and had brought her boots and breeches from Poland and didn't have jeans to ride in. Carol was responsible for getting Inger started on the track. When she hired her and gave her mounts, the other trainers got a chance to see that she could ride. She had been an alternate on the Polish Olympic team and was a damn good rider.

Inger and I got to be good friends. I didn't know then that riders are cutthroat and you can't have real friends on the track. I would soon learn this lesson from Inger.

Before I left Santa Ynez to go to the track I had gone out a few times with the farm vet, Dr. Sands. On my days off I drove two hours back to the Valley and would spend a day and a night with him. Bill was twenty years older than me, a respected veterinarian, and a very handsome man. I had no idea why he wanted to hang with me, but we had fun. We would hike in the mountains behind Santa Barbara and find hidden swimming holes. Just to prove how tough I was, I would swim in freezing water and pretend it felt good. I really liked Bill, but I really had no clue how to have a relationship. On top of that I couldn't feel that Bill cared for me. His actions showed that he liked me but I couldn't feel it. I still didn't like being touched and didn't like sex, but

Bill was able to convince me to sleep with him. It wasn't ever bad, but it wasn't ever good either. I had built walls around my soul and my body that were made of cement.

Bill and I were together for several months and I was still seeing him when I met Scott, a racetrack vet at Santa Anita. I had seen him driving his vet truck on the backside but we had never spoken. Being painfully shy still, I sure wasn't going to be the first one to speak.

One morning Carol put me on a filly I had known at Silent Oaks Farm. America's Laurel was a three-year-old filly who had a bad habit of flipping over. This is a very dangerous habit and can kill a rider. Paul had worked out a system to handle this filly so that she wouldn't be tempted to flip. Carl, one of the high school boys, always rode her and he got on in the round pen for safety reasons. If she flipped in the round pen, at least the rider would probably survive because there was no roof to hit your head on and the ground was soft. The trick with this filly was that she had to be walking when the groom legged the rider up, and she didn't want anyone on her head. The second the groom threw you up, he had to turn her head loose. This method worked and she trained for months at Silent Oaks without ever flipping over. When she shipped in to Carol at Santa Anita, Paul was sure to send her with detailed instructions.

On this particular morning America's Laurel was scheduled to work 5/8ths of a mile in company. I was really excited because 5/8ths is a nice long distance to work, and going with company ensured that we would go in the time that Carol specified. I was still getting my clock in my head so company made that part easy. Because I was so excited, I completely forgot that this filly likes to flip and can't have a groom on her head. When the groom legged me up and didn't turn her head loose, it took her a fraction of a second to flip over in the shedrow. I hit one of the beams on the ceiling with my forehead. I was knocked out cold with blood streaming down my face. When I woke up a few minutes later my first thought was that I had fucked up big time. I knew that this filly flipped, I didn't follow the protocol that kept her safe, and now she was probably hurt and the morning was ruined for everyone.

I don't remember how I got there, but I was sitting in a chair in Carol's office with the vet cleaning out a gash on my forehead and arguing about going to the hospital for stitches. I heard the wail of the ambulance sirens and was so embarrassed that I had caused all this commotion. I refused to go in the ambulance because I could walk and drive myself to the hospital if I decided that I wanted stitches. Carol and the vet just laughed at me and told me I was going to the hospital and to just shut up. I remember the vet asked how I had ended up with a gash on my forehead even though I had a helmet on. Carol's reply showed such insight into me. She answered that the cool riders never use their chinstraps. She knew that I was hanging with the guys and had to be cool. I heard the vet say, "I bet she will wear her chinstrap now" and Carol replied, "Probably not."

I ended up with a bad headache and fourteen stitches in my forehead and this is how I met Scott. He was new at the track and working for Dr. Sage, who was our stable vet in Carol's barn. The day that I got hurt a security guard picked me up at the hospital and brought me back to Santa Anita. That afternoon I wasn't feeling very good so I hung around our barn, which was unusual for me. On a good day I would either drive across town to go to the beach or go hiking in the mountains above Santa Anita.

I was sleeping in my tack room when I heard someone ask where the blond girl who got hurt that morning was. Inger knocked on my door, all excited, to tell me that the young cute vet was looking for me. I couldn't even imagine that a young cute vet could be interested in my welfare, but I went out and talked to him. He examined my stitches and told me the doctor had done an excellent job and I would barely have a scar. He invited me to go with him and pick up drugs at Western Medical in Arcadia. I had nothing better to do so I joined him and then came back to Santa Anita and watched him treat some horses. I don't know how he ended up in my tack room that night, but I do remember that we only kissed, and kissed all night long. I felt like I was with a long lost friend and I didn't want him to leave, ever. He spent the next five nights with me in my tack room and then Security told him he had to park his vet truck in the parking lot if he was staying all night. Up until then, Security had looked the other way and hoped that he was treating a horse all night. They finally asked Carol what was wrong with the horse that needed a vet for five nights and our secret was out.

Scott had been living at his parent's house in Orange County because money was tight since he was new on the track. He decided that he would rent a house and we could live together. One thing that I always loved about Scott was the way he could make things happen. Six days after we met we were living together. Life was good!

The move was easy for me because I only owned a bed and a few clothes. Scott bought a designer couch, a washer and dryer, and a refrigerator. We were complete.

Dr. Sands had given me a Dalmatian puppy and I had a kitten. We all felt very cozy in a real house. The house had a nice yard for my puppy and the streets around us were fairly quiet for city streets.

Scott was fun and always high energy. When we were first together, he went on hikes with me. We would drive to the top of Santa Anita Ave., park at Chantry Flats and hike for hours. I think he did this only to please me because he didn't seem to enjoy hiking. He was always ready to go home, and like a child, would ask me if we could go home now after hiking only a few miles.

On the surface our relationship was perfect. Scott was sweet, kind, fun, and he was crazy about me. I didn't tell him anything about my past because I was ashamed. If he knew that I came from a trashy alcoholic family I thought he would leave me. I still didn't like sex and that drove Scott a little crazy. After our first night of passionate kisses there was nothing else.

Scott was always trying to fix my life and make it better and this really annoyed me. He didn't like me riding on the track and always worried that I would get hurt. The year before I came to the track an exercise rider who had two young children and was married to a vet friend of Scott's, had died in a horse accident on the track at Hollywood Park. Her husband was a track vet and he saw her dead body on the training track. Scott knew how dangerous riding on the track was and he didn't want me there.

I still smoked pot and did a few other drugs. Scott was okay with the pot but didn't like me doing Quaaludes or cocaine. He liked jazz music and I liked hard rock. He wore nice clothes and I wore old jeans. I accepted our differences but he couldn't.

I was trying to be a free spirit still and having difficulty being free in Arcadia. Cities have always made me feel weird, and as a result, I got depressed. I couldn't handle all of the noise, people, red lights, and rules and I fought back. My driving rules have always been unique. I feel that since I am a highly skilled driver, the rules of the road do not apply to me. That first year with Scott I got thirteen tickets, mostly for speeding and running red lights. Part of breaking the rules was throwing the tickets away and some of them went to warrant.

One night I was driving home from running errands and I stopped at a red light, looked both ways, and then drove through it. There was an oncoming car but I knew that Nelly could safely dart in front of it. This ended up being a bad move on her part. I always blamed Nelly when my plans didn't work. The oncoming car was a cop. He arrested me for outstanding warrants and I spent the night in El Monte jail. I remember thinking don't they know who I am? I am a super driver with superior skills and a hot car, and I should be allowed to drive as I please.

Scott finally bailed me out at 5:00 a.m. and by then I was furious. I could see the humor in being in jail for the first five hours, but after that it wasn't so funny. One of the cops who arrested me was nice, but everyone else in the police station acted like a pig. When we arrived at the police station he called for a woman officer to search me. When she saw me she said, "That is a girl?" I had short hair, big muscles from galloping horses, and was wearing jeans and a puffy goose down jacket. The friendly cop told her that I was a very nice young lady. She didn't do much of a search at all and barely checked my pockets. Her attitude was nasty and it was all I could do not to call her a fucking bitch. I grew up being treated like dirt but this was even worse. After I was booked I was taken to a cell with two other women who looked like hookers. They didn't speak to me and one of them had taken my blanket. If I had not worn my down jacket that night I would have been really cold. When Scott finally arrived to bail me out instead of thanking him I asked him what the fuck took him so long. We were still inside the police station and he grabbed the neck of my jacket and asked me if I would like to go back inside. I managed to mumble 'no.'

Bail was cash only and this was before ATM machines. Scott had spent the night calling the other track vets to borrow cash to make my bail. He was mortified, to say the least.

I tried to explain that I can't do cities and it is really hard for me to live in Arcadia. I needed to hear the birds sing and have trees around me, not pavement. Scott didn't get what I was saying. I knew that I was often a disappointment to him. I still only wore jeans and T shirts, and he wanted me to get dressed up and wear makeup. I didn't even own any makeup and wouldn't have known how to apply it. He also had an issue with my short hair. Because I galloped horses and wore a helmet every day, short hair was practical and it suited me. Poor Scott, we went round and round and the more he pressured me to make changes, the more stubborn I became. I even cut my hair shorter and dyed a little tail pink in the back.

One morning I arrived at Santa Anita to gallop my horses in Carol's barn and the horses were gone, all of the stalls were empty. I found Carol in her office crying her heart out with her head on her desk. She told me her assistant trainer, Raymond, had gone to her owners behind her back, and convinced them all to move their horses to Lou Carno's barn, where he was now the new assistant trainer. I knew the track was cutthroat but this was low. Carol was liked and respected by everyone and ran a tight barn.

Robin was at Santa Anita and he found me a job working for a big-time trainer, Reggie McAnally, that same morning. I much preferred riding on the off- track because it was more relaxed than the track that was holding a race meet. I didn't like the pressure and hustle and bustle of the main race meet tracks. Cuba was McAnally's assistant on the off-track and he was fun to work with. He would put me on as many horses as I could ride and laugh when I was so tired that I was nearly falling off. He would ask me if I was tired yet and I always answered "No, do you have another horse for me?" Riding was like an addiction and I couldn't get enough.

My riding was going well at Santa Anita that spring. Besides getting on horses for McAnally I rode for trainer Justin Fanning, and a small barn with an old Irish trainer, Pete McAlear. Pete was in his 70's and such a nice man that he didn't belong on the racetrack. Every morning we would greet each other with a happy, "Good morning, how are you?" And he would reply "Everything is good here, just keeping the wolves away from my door" in his thick Irish brogue. He would tell me how many horses he had for me that morning and I would tell him what time I could come back and get on them.

Freelance riders usually ride for several barns, and besides staying on the horse and keeping him between the rails, you had to be on time. There was nothing worse than making a horse and trainer wait for a rider who didn't show or was always late. I was always on time, usually stayed on, and so far had kept them all between the rails.

One morning Pete had seven horses for me and I told him I would rearrange my schedule and be at his barn earlier than usual. When I arrived at his barn on time he told me that my friend, Inger, had already taken all of my horses out. I thought that I must have screwed up on a horse the day before for Pete to take me off his horses. I asked him what I had done wrong and he said nothing. Inger had come by his barn early and told him that I was too busy to take his horses out that morning, and that he should put her on my mounts. I told him it was a lie, and he just rolled his eyes and promised me mounts for the next day.

Silly me, I had thought that Inger and I were best friends. She was dating trainer Adam Lagets, who lived in a very nice apartment with a beautiful pool near Santa Anita. Every morning after the track, she would invite me to the pool and we would swim and sunbathe until afternoon. When we needed a break from our long siesta by the pool, we would go to David Copperfields', a bar near the track frequented by race trackers, and drink pina coladas until it was time to go home. I would never have stolen her mounts and expected the same from her.

It was old Pete who clued me in about how cutthroat the backside is, and that you could never have a real friend on the track. I told Pete that if I ever had to take off his horses I would inform him early enough not to mess up his morning. I remained friends with Inger, but I never trusted her again.

As summer drew closer all the riders were anxious for Del Mar to start. From July through the beginning of September the Del Mar meet was on and everyone looked forward to it all year. The beach was only blocks from the track, and I heard countless stories about beach parties and riders swimming in the ocean every afternoon. The trainers, riders, and vets, rented houses for the meet and the grooms and hot walkers lived on the track.

Chapter 9

Del Mar

Scott was determined that we would go to Del Mar. He said that he didn't care if he starved, he would not miss his first Del Mar. Money was tight because he wasn't yet established on the track. He would have to pay rent on the Arcadia house while we were in Del Mar. Scott's mother was his biggest fan and best supporter and she organized our Del Mar accommodations for us. She had a small trailer that we could borrow for the first month. The second month we would be house sitting in an enormous house owned by a friend who would be out of town for five weeks. I could take my cat, Miss Muffet, but not my dog, so I was going to stay behind with Raven. Scott's mom wouldn't hear of it and she took my dog for the summer. We all shared the humor of living in a trailer court for the first part of Del Mar and a mansion for the remainder of the meet.

The beautiful Del Mar grandstand. Photograph by Richard Nilsen

I had been getting plenty of mounts at Santa Anita and assumed that I would do well at Del Mar. This was not to be. Since I had been riding on the off-track, most of the main track trainers didn't even know me. Every morning I would put on my boots and helmet, put my stick in my back pocket and go from barn to barn asking if they needed help. They all said no and I was devastated. It didn't take much for my low self-esteem to kick in and I became very depressed.

I continued to make my rounds of the barns every morning and eventually Tom Barrera's barn put me on some horses. It wasn't until two weeks later that I met Tom, who was a big name in racing because his father Laz was very famous. Tom had some serious drug problems, and most mornings, couldn't even make it to the track.

Tom's assistant, Devon, hired me. May was Tom's girlfriend and she also galloped horses. May was known for her big mouth and one morning I overheard her (because she was yelling) telling Devon that, just because he wasn't going to fuck me, did not mean that I couldn't ride in that barn. She screamed at him, "What are you, a fucking dog in heat!" The day before Devon had mentioned to another trainer that he planned on nailing me and he was laughed at and informed that I was living with Dr. Leeth. He had intended to fire me that morning and this is why May had come to my defense. I was mortified and didn't want to be near that barn so I quit the next day.

I didn't have a very good summer at Del Mar that year. After I quit Barrera's barn I gave up on a riding job for the summer and became a beach bum. I didn't have any money so I was a beach bum, literally. The stories I had heard about the riders hanging out at the beach all summer were only stories. I was there every day, all day, and I rarely saw anyone from the track.

One day I did run into a rider, Alexis, and she invited me to her house to see her new litter of puppies. I told her I would love to see her puppies and asked her where she lived. She told me she lived next door to Dale, a trainer at Del Mar. This meant nothing to me since I barely knew Dale and didn't know where he lived. When I told Alexis this, she got a real catty look on her face and told me that she knew I had spent the night with him at his house the evening before. I never did see those puppies and wondered how many men claimed to have slept with me that I wasn't aware of.

I was really missing my Dalmatian, Raven. The beach wasn't much fun without her. She always swam with me and could body surf in the waves. When she wasn't swimming she would chase the beach birds or sit with me. My beach days were long and lonely and I was miserable.

Del Mar finally ended and we picked up Raven and went back to Arcadia. The Pomona race meet was on. I didn't want to ride on a 5/8ths mile track, so I got on a few horses at Santa Anita instead.

One Saturday after I was finished galloping and had the next day off, I decided that I needed a road trip and called Tina in Santa Ynez. She was happy to hear from me and said I could spend a night with her. She planned a night of bar hopping for us and told me to get there soon.

Scott and I had not been getting along very well and I really needed to escape, at least for a couple of days. I left him a note, packed a few clothes and was ready for an adventure. When I had Nelly loaded, I turned the key and she wouldn't start. I continued to try to get her going since I had to leave now, and she caught on fire. She was parked only three feet from a garden hose so I quickly put the fire out. Now I was in tears and still had to get to Santa Ynez.

Failure was not an option. I put a few things into my beach backpack, walked to the highway and started hitchhiking. Within a few minutes a nice man picked me up. I looked much younger than my twenty-three years, and he thought I was running away from home. He gave me $10.00, which I tried to refuse, but he wouldn't hear of it, and told me to go back home. He dropped me off in Ventura. My next ride was a man who was doing speed and had some for sale. I spent my $10.00 on speed and was dropped off at Tina's apartment. Tina and I did go out bar hopping that night but it wasn't as much fun as it used to be. I visited Dr. Sands on Sunday and hung with him for a while and then took a bus home.

Back in Arcadia my life was a mess again. Nelly was dead, Scott was ignoring me, and I needed a job. It seemed like when Scott was sure that he 'had me,' I became a possession, and then he mostly ignored me. Scott was very social and always wanted to go out to the restaurants that the race trackers frequented. Since I am not the least bit social, this was always very difficult for me. We argued a lot in those days, usually about my clothes or my drugs. Scott wanted me to be the girl who wore makeup and dresses. I didn't even own a dress or makeup and didn't plan on changing. I couldn't articulate my thoughts that if I wore makeup I would be plastic, like so many other city people. I was fighting for my right to be me, even when I wasn't at all sure who 'me' was.

Chapter 10

Walter and the Farm

I was still getting on a few horses at Santa Anita when a trainer, Valerie Peterson, asked me if I would like to ride at her ranch in Chino. I jumped at the chance and Scott drove me out to the ranch that very afternoon. The ranch wasn't very pretty and Chino was ugly, but when I arrived, I felt like I belonged there. I looked down the long row of eucalyptus trees that lined the driveway and knew that they would become very familiar to me.

The trainer was an old man in his seventies, Walter McCally, who became my mentor and best friend. The beginning was a little rough and I didn't realize then what a huge impact Walter would have on my life. Walter only met me, shook my hand and said, "When can you start?" I told him that my car had just died and I needed a couple of days to find a new car. Since so many race trackers talk shit, Walter heard shit. Scott had promised to co-sign a car loan if I found a job and he was ready to sign. His only stipulation was that the car had to be a BMW. I had never even heard of a BMW, but was in no position to argue. We found a nice, used BMW the next day, and I was back at the ranch in two days ready to ride. Much to my dismay Walter had hired another rider. I was almost in tears as I questioned how he could do that when I said I only needed two days to find a car and here I am two days later with a car. He told me that riders always talk shit and he didn't think he would ever see me again. He saw the despair in my eyes and told me that there were enough horses for two riders and he hired me.

Mike was the other rider and we didn't get along from the start. He was very heavy to be riding racehorses and loud. I could tell that Walter didn't like him much either. Walter was very quiet around the horses. Most of the horses we galloped were babies, just yearlings being broke. Walter would do the groundwork, Mike would get on for the first few rides, and then they would be mine. I got bucked off a lot that first year. Walter and Mike's relationship deteriorated and Mike became even less friendly to me. We took the horses to the track in sets, and I struggled to stay cool and ride with Mike. He loved to mess with me in a mean-spirited way. We had a half-mile track that was bordered by two dairy farms and often the dairy workers would be very close to the track and spook the horses. Mike would tell them to make more noise around my horses and try to get me dumped. After I got dumped a few times, I told Walter what Mike was doing and he told me that good riders just smile and ride through fire. In other words, shut up and ride!

Eventually Mike even got on Walter's nerves and he was fired. That left about twenty horses for me to break. Walter told me that I would break the last twenty and I told him I couldn't. When he asked me why I couldn't break the horses, I told him that Millwood Richards had told me that I was too pretty to break horses. Walter laughed so hard that tears came to his eyes, and then he said that he didn't think I was all that pretty and shouldn't worry about it. That sounded good to me and I was more than willing to learn how to break horses.

The first month at the farm Walter didn't teach me anything. He only observed my riding and kept his thoughts to himself. I had learned at the track that you never admit that you are green so I wasn't about to show Walter how little I knew. Of course now I know that Walter could see right through me and was only waiting for me to ask questions. Finally after getting bucked off many, many times I started asking questions. I would walk back to the barn hanging my head after getting dumped once again on the track and ask Walter what I had done wrong. He would say very slowly, "Well, the first thing you did wrong was to get on." In order to get a real answer from him, I would have to agree, and then ask 'what did I do wrong' after that. This opened the door to a flood of knowledge on horse breaking that Walter was very willing to share. He had been waiting quietly for me to ask him to share. From then on every horse, every day, became a riding lesson and I was in heaven. The horses all loved Walter, and I wanted to relate to every horse on that level. I was galloping twenty horses every day, getting paid well, and riding under the best horseman I had ever met.

There was only one horse that first year who didn't buck me off and that was only because she never tried. Her name was Avigation and she was my favorite. She was a big beautiful chestnut filly by Windy Sands and her mother had been a multiple stakes winner. I was in awe of her beauty and felt honored to ride her. Walter knew she was very special and always warned me not to fight with her. Since she was happy to do whatever I asked of her, we had no reason to ever fight. Avie and I were best friends.

In January Scott was invited to attend a Veterinary Conference at Lake Tahoe and insisted that I accompany him. Walter gave me the week off and found another rider to get on my horses for six days. Scott said the trip would be fun and I could ski all day and attend the cocktail parties with him at night.

I bought new skis and ski clothes and was ready to rock. I knew that the cocktail parties would be painful, so I bought a gram of cocaine and brought that with me too. I spent hours putting together several outfits to wear to the parties. They had to be perfect, comfortable, not sexy, and warm. I was so shy that I didn't want men to look at me, but I didn't want them not to look at me either.

We checked into the Hyatt Hotel at Tahoe and I went straight to the gift shop to buy a mirror and razor blade to cut up my coke. Scott saw me in the shop and joined me. Poor Scott was so green when it came to drugs that when he saw me buying razor blades and a small mirror, he loudly asked me why I needed a razor blade and mirror. Some of the other vets were in the gift shop and they all turned to look at me, waiting for the answer. I knew my cover was already blown. I turned three shades of red and quietly told him, "Just because."

The skiing was wonderful, weather was great and Tahoe was beautiful. I skied until I nearly dropped from exhaustion. Scott had never skied before but he gave it a good try. We goofed around like children and I pushed him down several times while he was learning to snowplow. We would both end up falling down in the snow and just lay there and laugh.

The cocktail parties were hell. I went to the first one without cocaine and just sat in a chair, wishing I could leave. I was surrounded by friendly veterinarians and their wives and girlfriends and I had nothing to say to anyone. I sat in a corner hoping that no one would notice me. Parties had always been painful for me and I avoided them. If I could have been invisible and been allowed to only watch the party, I would have enjoyed it. As it was, I was visible and sitting there watching the party worried that everyone could see that I was a misfit, a social disaster. I escaped early and went back to our room. When Scott came in later I could tell that he was very disappointed in me.

The next day I again skied all day and went to a party that night. This time, much to my surprise, Scott insisted that I do a line of coke before the party. I was not even prepared for the difference coke would make in me in a social setting. Suddenly I wasn't the wallflower, the weird girl who sits in the corner with nothing to say and blushes if anyone speaks to her. I fit in, I could speak to people, I could even mingle and sip a glass of wine. In order to stay this way I needed to sneak away about every half hour and do another line of cocaine but no one seemed to notice. Scott was very pleased with my performance that night. The wife of the head of Veterinary Dept. at UC Davis had taken a liking to me and we chatted about dogs and horses all evening. Scott was proud of me finally. I still heard the "Now, if you could just wear some makeup and let your hair grow longer"...but it didn't hurt like it usually did.

When I returned to the ranch after our ski trip, Walter said all of the horses had been perfect except Avigation, who had bucked the rider off every day. I was so flattered that the 'big mare' only wanted me to ride her. She thought I was special.

Walter and I had become good friends quickly and I loved his wicked sense of humor. If he hadn't been fifty years older than me we would have made a perfect couple. As it was, he turned our age difference into a joke. I often took him grocery shopping, and instead of making a list, he liked to walk through every aisle with his cart. When he came to the aisle with condoms, he would stop and pretend that he was having a hard time decided which ones to buy. He would be waiting for the perfect victim and when a reserved middle-aged woman would walk by, he would loudly ask me which condoms I wanted this time. We would always get a look of disgust from the shocked shopper as I blushed.

His other favorite grocery store prank was to pretend that I wanted to buy cigarettes. Walter and I both hated cigarettes. While we waited in line, he would fake an argument with me and then he would loudly tell me, "No, absolutely not and I am not telling you again." When we got to the cashier he would tell her that his grandson (me) wanted him to buy cigarettes for him but he wouldn't do it. The cashiers would always say, "Good for you!" and then give me a look of disdain.

Walter and I continued to train this first group of babies until May when they went into Santa Anita. Valerie and Walter both wanted me to go in to the track with them, so I went to Santa Anita in the mornings and the ranch in the afternoons. The horses were all perfect on the main track and I was as proud as I could be. My horses never made a mistake, never bucked or did anything silly, and never even missed a lead. I knew I couldn't have pulled this off without Walter. I glowed with pride whenever anyone asked who broke these horses.

By summertime, ranches are dead quiet and riders all start planning for Del Mar. I wanted to go to Del Mar again with Scott, and Walter was fine with the idea, but Valerie protested. Walter understood that I put 110% effort into breaking horses and I would burn out at that pace without a break. Valerie was a total control freak and could be impossible to get along with. Since I can't do rules that make no sense to me, I gave my notice, told Walter I would love to come back in the fall for breaking season, and then went to Del Mar with Scott.

Valerie Peterson was Walter's ex-wife and he knew her better than anyone. He warned me more than once not to get on her bad side. When they had been married they both worked at the ranch and the owner was Ned Peterson. One day Walter found his wife Valerie with Ned having sex on a horse blanket in the round pen. Since Walter had a young daughter with Valerie, he felt he had to stay and was made ranch manager/trainer. Valerie married Ned and became the ranch owner. This is a typical racetrack story. It seemed like everyone was sleeping with everyone else, and it didn't matter if they were married.

I went to Del Mar and had a good summer. Scott rented a nice little beach house. I went to the beach every single day and stayed there all day long. I had some money saved and I had my dog, so life was good. We went out to dinner almost every night and came to an agreement that one night Scott would choose the restaurant and the next night I would. He always chose fancy and expensive places and I managed to find cute little vegetarian restaurants.

It was important for me to stay fit because I was sure Walter would want me back in the fall. I ran on the beach in the morning and went to aerobics classes in the afternoon.

Near the end of Del Mar, Walter called and told me that if I wanted to ride for him at the ranch he needed me now. I drove up to Chino early the next morning and was on my first horse at 7:00 a.m. Later that week Walter's best friend, John, told me that Walter had been fighting for me for weeks and finally told Valerie that he would quit if I wasn't hired back as his rider. It felt so good to see someone go to bat for me like that. Walter and I were the perfect horse breaking team and only an idiot would have broken us up. Unfortunately, Valerie fit into that 'only an idiot' category.

That second year with Walter went much smoother than the first. I learned how to stay on the young horses when they bucked and then took it a step further and didn't let them buck. Walter was a true horse breaking genius and could do anything with a horse. His most important lesson for me was that if a horse trusted you, he would gallop through fire for you. Every horse, every day, was a lesson that I soaked up like a sponge. I finally had a teacher who knew I was worth teaching. I always had a zillion questions and Walter always had all of the answers. I was worried that I was asking too many questions and would annoy him, but he welcomed my questions. I had to know why his plans worked and why other plans wouldn't work and what would happen if you did this instead of that, and on and on I went. I had to know!

Scott and I had very separate lives although we lived together. I would get up early and be on the road by 6:15, six days a week, and be in bed by 7:00 p.m. Scott was asleep when I left in the morning, and I was usually asleep when he came home at night. In the morning, instead of saying good morning to Scott, I would say see you tomorrow. On my Sunday off I liked to go to Clocker's Corner at Santa Anita in the morning and watch horses train and then hike in the mountains. Although this was an odd relationship, it worked for me. I wanted to be the 'best' horse breaker in the West and needed to put all of my energy into breaking horses.

There were a few times that I was pretty sure that Scott was cheating on me but it was always easy to ignore. Once I found a long brown hair in the shower and Scott and I were both blond. He said his cousin had been at our house and taken a shower. He didn't have a cousin with long brown hair who visited us. Another time I was getting a haircut at the Mall near Santa Anita and saw him enter David Copperfield's Bar with a pretty girl. I walked in and said, "I am Susan, who are you?" Scott was angry and told me she was his bookkeeper. His bookkeeper was Edith, a wonderful 70 year old woman, not a pretty young girl. I was so focused on breaking horses that nothing else mattered to me.

For the next three years everything was pretty much the same. I broke horses with Walter for eight months of the year, took a week off to ski in the winter, and my summer off for Del Mar. At the end of every summer Walter would again threaten to quit if I wasn't hired back, and every year I went back.

It was becoming harder for me to live in the city, and by now, Scott was totally ignoring me. One night he came home from the track and walked right past me in the living room like I wasn't even there. I might as well have been part of the furniture. I started telling Scott that I wasn't happy but he didn't hear me. After five years with Walter, I was ready to go out on my own and Walter agreed. He had taught me all that he knew. We stayed very close until he died.

Chapter 11

Santa Ynez

I really needed to get out of the city and back to Santa Ynez. Dr. Tim O'Sullivan, the owner of Clear Springs Ranch, offered me a job riding at his ranch in Buellton. Since Tim was only rarely at the ranch and the main house was empty, the job offer included a room in the main house which had a pool and racquetball court. I told Scott I was leaving and left on the best of terms. He even gave me his gas credit card to take with me.

Clear Springs Ranch was a disappointment from day one. When I arrived at the ranch, the trainer, Ryan, informed me that I would not be living in the main house. Instead, I would be staying in a dome house that was in the middle of the barn area. Although this was not what had been promised, I went inside and looked around. The place was filthy and not fit for humans. Mouse and rat droppings were everywhere and my bed had a huge urine stain on the mattress.

I spent the first night in my car and the next day searched for a place to live in town. The first house I looked at was a roommate situation with two other girls, just a few miles from the ranch in Buellton. Kathy and Kelly welcomed me and my two Dalmatians, Raven and Emily Jane, and we moved in that same day.

My job at Clear Springs Ranch wasn't going well, and not at all what I had expected. Ryan, the trainer, had married Darlene, my old riding mate from Silent Oaks Farm and they had a two-year-old child. Darlene had become a cocaine addict and was paranoid and bitchy most of the time. Her young son was miserable all morning because they locked him in the house alone while we were all on the track.

I had never seen so much coke and at first it was fun. We had six riders and we would all tack up and walk around the barn until everyone was ready, and then go to the track in sets. While we were waiting someone would shout, "Whoa back" and we would all stop and pass a bullet around and each have a snort of coke.

One day we were all coked up and one of the young fillies stopped the hot walker. Horses quickly learn that if they pull back on the walker, it will stop. It is really not a big deal, and if someone chirps or gets behind the horse, they will move forward. Ryan took a girth off a saddle, walked up to the filly and hit her in the face. I was horrified and when Ryan saw the horror on my face, he calmly explained that hitting her in the face was the only thing that worked. I was sick and quit the next day.

I called Scott and told him I had quit Clear Springs Ranch, and he assumed I would be coming back to him. I had no intention of going back to the city and the next day I was hired at the Oakview Ranch in Solvang.

The Oakview was a step up from Clear Springs Ranch and there were no drugs. I was one of two riders, the other was Lisa. The grooms were both girls and the four of us got on well. The owners, William and Jill Nelson, weren't around much and that was good. William was a retired horse shoer, and Jill came from a family with money and didn't know a whole lot about breaking horses.

Lisa wasn't a bad rider but she wasn't very good either. I got on all of the more difficult horses, and because we were paid the same, I would let Lisa clean all of the tack. Tack is cleaned daily at racing and training barns and the best riders are usually exempt. Lisa could either accept this or start getting on some of the more difficult horses, so she chose to clean tack.

Jill and I didn't get along because she knew so little about breaking horses and I was a threat. She would come into the barn and decide that all the bits had to be three holes too tight in the horse's mouths. The other girls would nod and smile and comply, but I just couldn't. As soon as Jill was out of sight, I would adjust my bridle properly so that my horse would be comfortable. The girls would tell me that I couldn't do that because Jill said…and I would reply that Jill isn't here now is she?

One day I was riding a very athletic young colt who was good at bucking and had bucked Lisa off several times. When I felt him thinking about bucking, I doubled him so fast his head spun. Doubling is bending a horse around super tight in a tiny circle so that the horse can't run or buck. It is not mean or cruel in any way, and quickly gives the rider the upper hand in a smooth and quiet fashion.

Jill was in the arena with me, sitting on her pony. Although she had limited intelligence when it came to breaking horses, I thought that even she would be impressed by my smooth move. Instead, she yelled at me to turn him loose. I tried to explain that he was going to buck, had bucked Lisa off the last three days, and I had the jump on him. She told me he wasn't going to buck. I explained that although she hadn't seen it, he had stiffened his jaw, raised his back, and his next move would have been bucking like a bronco. She explained like she was teaching me, that I was wrong, he wasn't going to buck, and anyway, all I had to do was keep him in a straight line because horses don't buck hard in a straight line. I couldn't even believe my ears, "because horses don't buck hard in a straight line." Anyone who has ever seen a rodeo knows that horses buck very hard in a straight line. Her ignorance and her attitude were more than I could take so I got off the horse and handed him to her. I told her that she should probably lose about fifty pounds and ride him herself.

Scott and I were in contact when I told him that I had quit my job at Oakview. He again wanted me to come home. I was so much happier in Santa Ynez than I had been in L.A. that I just couldn't go back. We were both dating other people and officially broken up by that time. We didn't actually verbalize that we were seeing other people but we both knew it. I was fine with Scott dating other women and hoped that he would find a woman who had long hair, wore dresses and make up, and made him happy. Intuitively I knew that he couldn't handle me dating other men so I never talked about it.

I was still living with Kelly and Kathy, and although the three of us couldn't have been more different, we all got along. Kelly was an aspiring artist and an art teacher in Lompoc. Kathy ran the family business, a kite store in Solvang. Kelly and I were drinking buddies and danced at the new cowboy bar, Zaca Creek, in Buellton every Saturday night. I have never liked cowboys and they don't like me. They are threatened by my skills as a horsewoman and they hate short hair. Kelly was from Colorado and loved cowboys. She would dance all night at Zaca, and then take a cowboy home with her.

I was only without a job for a few days when I was hired to ride at Mandysland Farm. This was by far, the most beautiful farm I had ever seen. The stalls were huge, twelve-by-twelve, with a solid wall only to chest height and then brass bars to the top. The horses were all treated like royalty. Stalls were bedded knee deep with straw and kept immaculate. The mares with foals had double, twenty-four by twelve foot stalls. There was a three-man crew that caught the young foals in the stall with their moms each morning and cleaned their baby butts with warm soap and water and then dried them with soft white towels. After breakfast, the mares and foals would be led outside together and turned out for the day in a beautiful grass pasture with oak trees for shade. It was quite a sight to watch as the well-bred mares and foals were turned out all at the same time each morning. The mares would watch proudly as the group of babies ran and played.

I got on well with Brian, the trainer, and the only rider, George. It was March and most of the young horses had already been broke, so our job as riders was easy. We conditioned them on a small training track so they would have some level of fitness when they shipped in to the track. We also had some impressive older horses from big stables who had been laid up and were now starting back in training. I have always gotten a special thrill when I have the opportunity to ride a stakes horse. At Mandysland I had the honor to ride Lord Grundy and Nepal who both became stallions after their racing careers.

Brian, George, and I became buddies and all drank together on Saturday nights. Work was fun and we goofed around all morning. By noon we were finished riding and went our separate ways. I still went to the beach everyday but Brian and George weren't beach people. George did go with me a few times but he wasn't comfortable at a nude beach.

Mandysland Farm paid me well and I could afford to join the only health club in the Valley. The Club was new and very nice. I worked out, played racquetball, and went to aerobics classes every day after the beach. I met Steve at The Club and we were instant friends. He was a surfer, loved to play racquetball and go on bike rides. He was everything Scott wasn't. We played hard from the moment we met.

Kathy was getting weird at home and it wasn't so nice to live there anymore. Her parents owned the house we rented, so she had rank on Kelly and me. She was a few years younger than us and had young, obnoxious, beer-drinking, cigarette-smoking friends. She had been inviting them all to our house to drink and play quarters. This was hard for me because I loathe cigarette smoke and I always went to bed early so I would be fresh to ride in the morning. Kathy played the drums and the last straw was when she and her friends started jamming in the living room. The music they played was so bad that you would have to be as drunk as they were to listen to it. It was time for me to go.

Steve invited me to live with him and I jumped at the chance. He owned a small condo in Solvang and had a roommate who didn't approve of me. The roommate was a born-again Christian and didn't think Steve and I should be together, since we weren't married. The few times that I met him at the house he was always sitting at the dining room table reading the Bible. He moved out as soon as I moved in.

Steve and I clicked like magic. I would ride at Mandysland in the morning and then, depending on the weather, Steve and I would go to the beach, bike ride, or go to The Club. Sometimes we did all three. I never had so much fun with a guy. This is what I had been waiting for, a man who would not only pay attention to me but actually have fun with me. We were like two kids playing all day.

Steve came from a very wealthy family who owned a pipe store in Buellton. We occasionally saw his Mother at The Club and she did not care for me at all. Steve and I would always try to hide from her, but she busted us all the time. Before she even said hello, she would ask us why we were not working. I was always in the clear because I had worked at Mandysland before I played all afternoon. She didn't think that Steve worked hard enough and she would grill him. As soon as he could escape her, we would dash to the beach or go on a bike ride.

My days and life were nearly perfect and I was very happy. There was one problem in the background that was threatening to become big. I had told Scott about the situation with Kathy and that I had rented a room at Steve's house. I was paying rent to Steve so this part was true. I left out that Steve and I were falling in love.

Scott started acting crazy. Steve had an answering service on his home phone and Scott would call thirty-five times a day asking for me. I didn't know what to do. The truth would kill him, but the lie wasn't much better. Scott sent a certified letter to me at Mandysland from an attorney demanding custody of my Dalmatian, Raven. Raven was my pride and joy and I loved her with all my heart. When things were bad in L.A., I started training her, joined a dog school and showed her in obedience shows. She was a top dog and won most of her shows. My other Dalmatian, Emily Jane, was also very good and won her share of shows. I was known at the track for my beautiful, well trained Dalmatians, and was rarely seen without them.

Although I knew that Scott only did this to hurt me, instead of fighting him, I gave him Raven. It killed me to part with my dear friend but I knew that, if I could defuse this mess, he would come to his senses and return her to me. Everyone knew Raven was mine, as we were inseparable.

Scott bought a Bonanza Beechcraft twin-engine plane and had been taking flying lessons. I later learned that this particular plane is nicknamed the Dr. Killer. Scott loved to fly, and if he didn't have anywhere to go, he would take off and just fly circles. He always wanted me to fly with him and I tried a few times, but I get sick in planes and throwing up isn't fun for me.

Scott flew from El Monte to Santa Ynez and picked up Raven while I managed to show no emotion as I handed her over. I told him that I understood he needed her more than I did right now and please take good care of her. I knew he would take care of her because he loved her too.

My plan worked and two weeks later he called and wanted to bring Raven back to me. He said she wasn't happy and needed me. I was overjoyed and he flew her up the next day. I met them at the airport, picked up my dog and went home to Steve. Oh how I wish this could have been the end of the craziness!

Scott got more erratic and continued to call Steve's house twenty to thirty times a day. Steve and I were outside all day playing and when we got home the answering service would report that Scott had again called all day. One night, very late, there was a knock on Steve's door. Scott had never been to Steve's house and I was shocked to see him at our door in the middle of the night. Steve answered the door with a shotgun in his hand. This had suddenly gotten very sick and ugly, and it was all because of me. I had still not been able to tell Scott that Steve and I were a couple. Scott walked into the house with Steve holding a shotgun and looked around. He assumed the guest room was mine and asked me to come out and talk with him. I had to get him away from that shotgun so I said yes.

We went to his hotel room and talked all night. He told me that he had been seeing a psychiatrist and was on prescription drugs because he had to have me back. I explained that I can't live in the city, that I was miserable, whenever I was alone I cried. He said he didn't like the city either and he didn't like being a vet and wanted to quit. He wanted to buy a place in the country and be a family again with me, Raven, and Emily. I was so torn that I didn't know what to do or say, so I did nothing. I agreed to fly with Scott to Paso Robles and look for property. We spent the next day in Paso and looked at a few places and then flew home. We were flying close to the coast and in the evening the marine layer was thick and we couldn't land in Santa Ynez. Instead, we turned around and flew back to Santa Cruz, landed safely and rented a car. Scott was a good pilot.

I didn't even know what to say to Steve and he didn't ask any questions. It was like the three of us were caught up in a bad, drama-filled, theatrical play, and had to see how it would end. Steve and I still had fun and played all day, but it wasn't like before. We were strained and trying not to show it.

The next week I had an overwhelming feeling that I had to see Scott. I didn't want to drive two hours to L.A. so I stayed busy, galloped horses at Mandysland, and went to the beach, and still couldn't get Scott out of my head. Instead, the feeling grew even stronger and I couldn't shrug it off. Finally I told Steve I had to see Scott and I had to leave now. He didn't try to stop me.

I arrived unannounced at Scott's house in Arcadia and he was thrilled to see me. We had a long heart-to-heart talk that I will never forget. He told me that while we were apart he had been dating other girls who wore dresses, heels and makeup, and had found them to be plastic. He wanted me back because I was real. Finally he understood that the gifts, a bike, a racket, and a volleyball I had given him for birthdays and Christmas were hints that I needed him to play with me. He was sorry that he had hurt my feelings by ignoring me and wanted to start over. We agreed to start over and hugged with incredible passion. I will never forget that hug for it was to be our last. We both had loose ends to tie up and planned on meeting the following weekend. Scott would be picking me and the dogs up in Santa Ynez and flying us to a dog show in El Monte. He had never been to one of our dog shows and was anxious to remedy that.

I went home and told Steve that I felt I owed Scott at least an honest try at a relationship since he was willing to even give up being a veterinarian for me. Steve wasn't happy but he didn't argue. On Saturday when Scott was due to fly in, Steve went surfing with a friend in Montecito and planned to spend the night far away.

Scott called at noon to say there was a problem with the plane, but mechanics were working on it and he would take off soon. By late afternoon I could feel that something was wrong, but I didn't want to go there. I stayed very busy and tried to lose the sick feeling that was getting stronger. At 8:00 Scott still hadn't arrived and I understood that my world as I knew it was about to end, but I wasn't ready to deal with that just yet. Instead, I went to bed and slept for a couple of hours. When I woke up I called the police and asked if there had been a plane crash between El Monte and Santa Ynez. I knew the answer before I asked the question. Instead of saying yes or no, the cop asked for my address. Within a few minutes there was a knock on the door and it was a cop. He asked if I was alone and I said yes. He then asked if he could come in and I said yes. He told me that a plane had gone down at El Capitan ranch, outside of Santa Barbara and the pilot was dead. Like a robot I thanked him for coming here with the news. He asked if I should call someone and I said yes and walked toward the phone. I lifted the receiver but was shaking so hard I couldn't dial. The cop took the phone from me and called Steve at his friend's house and spoke for me, since I could no longer speak.

Steve arrived an hour later from Montecito and thanked the cop for sitting with me, and not leaving me alone. I had been sitting like a robot in the living room still unable to feel anything or speak. As soon as we were alone Steve put his arms around me and I collapsed in tears. I cried for hours, sitting on the couch with Steve and he never left me. Raven and Emily were near me, hiding under a table and shaking.

My sister and her boyfriend Bret arrived from L.A., and I wasn't very pleased to see them. Steve didn't really understand our relationship and had wrongly assumed that I would want my family near me.

After crying for hours, I felt drained and suddenly decided that I needed to choose what to wear to Scott's funeral. I stood up and told Steve that I needed to decide what to wear, and then pack my car for the drive to L.A. Steve, Bret, and Lizzie looked at me like I had lost it but Lizzie helped me put my outfit together. I chose a dress that had been Scott's favorite, and then stuffed some jeans and T-shirts into a backpack and was ready to go. I needed to be alone. Like a wounded cat, I always looked for a dark quiet place to hide when I was hurt.

The drive to L.A. was unbearably painful. The radio kept playing Shaka Kahns' song, *Through the Fire*, and I could picture Scott's plane on fire, his legs burning off. Some details had come out about the crash and I knew that his legs had been burned off.

I had called Scott's mother and told her that her son died when he crashed his plane on his way to see me. We had agreed to meet at his house in Arcadia. I knew that it was all my fault and I expected the family to hate me. I hated me too.

When I arrived at Scott's house, I was the first one there. I went to his closet and wrapped myself in his bathrobe because I wanted to smell his scent. I sat on the floor of the closet, wrapped in his robe and cried buckets of tears.

Scott's mother, father, and two sisters arrived. I could feel their pain, and I knew I was the cause of it. His older sister, Martha, had never liked me and warned Scott to get rid of me, and she had been right. She couldn't look at me. Scott's mother had loved me because

Scott did, so she tried to be kind. We were all too stunned to speak and only cried together. Martha abruptly stood up and went walking around Scott's house grabbing things that she wanted. She picked up several small things and then a big brass tray for firewood and was saying, "I want this and this and I always loved this." I found my voice and asked her if she could please leave everything as it is for just one night. I planned on spending the night in Scott's house and I needed just one night before it all changed. Scott's mother made Martha put everything back and then announced that I should choose what I wanted first. I insisted that I didn't want anything except for the house to stay the same for one more night. They agreed and soon everyone left. I was alone again so I wrapped up in Scott's robe and cried my heart out. I thought that I would never be able to stop crying.

Steve called the house and was concerned that I was alone. He insisted on sending Lizzie and Bret to be with me but I told him I didn't even like them, so please don't. My sister and I had been close when she moved to L.A., but when she met her boyfriend Bret she didn't need me anymore. Bret was bone lazy and a drinker whose dream was to be a model. Lizzie had been going to school in Santa Monica and studying to be an Interior Decorator until Bret decided she should quit school and be his makeup girl. Unfortunately Bret never got any modeling jobs because he wasn't very good looking and tended to be overweight. Bret saw me as a threat and created an uncomfortable distance between my sister and me.

Steve had a surfer friend in L.A. who I had met, and he asked him to drive to Scott's house and see that I was okay. He was a nice man and arrived to find me in Scott's robe over my clothes listening to the same Bob Gruesen song over and over. *Mountain Dance* by Bob Gruesen had been Scott's favorite song and I had to hear it again and again. I found a book that Scott had given me about Dalmatians. Scott had added captions and footnotes to the book and made it all about me, Raven, and Emily. I couldn't let the book out of my hands and I couldn't stop listening to *Mountain Dance*. I knew that I looked crazy with the robe over my clothes and the book tightly clenched in my hand. My heart was shattered and the pieces were breaking away fast.

I slept in Scott's bed that night and could still smell his scent on the pillow. I did more crying than sleeping because I couldn't stop thinking about our last hug, our last conversation, our plans for the weekend. The guilt was already consuming me. I knew in my heart that this was entirely my fault. A good, young, handsome veterinarian was dead because of me.

Scott's family returned in the morning and started taking things. Even though I didn't want anything it was killing me that Scott's belongings were being dispersed. Scott's mother Barbara again asked me what I wanted but I only asked for a few of his albums, the stereo, and his bathrobe. They began taking his house apart while I sat and cried. We were all crying.

Two days later a memorial service for Scott was held in the Paddock at Santa Anita and a huge crowd attended. A minister had asked me for some anecdotes and I told him the story about Scott giving a homeless man $20 and a bottle of wine the day before Christmas because he was in the dumpster behind Trader Joe's. The minister used that story in his eulogy. I was in the front row with the family and when the minister stopped talking, I stood up and started to walk away. As soon as I was at the edge of the crowd I took off my heels and ran away. I knew that Scott's death was my fault and I didn't want to see the blame in everyone's eyes. I was ashamed of the raw emotions that were welling up inside of me. I had never hated myself more.

I drove down to Chino because I had to see Walter. I had to be with someone I could trust. When I arrived, Walter opened the door and I blurted out, "I killed him! He loved me and I killed him." Walter and I sat down on his couch as I collapsed in tears, and he reached out and held my hand. We sat that way for hours while I cried and I felt comforted for the first time. He told me that it wasn't my fault, but I knew he was wrong. Walter thought that I should get busy and break some horses. He knew of a ranch in the high desert town of Anza that needed help breaking about fifty head of horses. He made the call and they wanted me to start the next day.

Chapter 12

Anza

I have never liked the desert and didn't like Anza at first, but it grew on me. Anza Valley Thoroughbred Farm was a huge 200 acre farm that was fighting bankruptcy. They had over 150 horses and many of them were not healthy. Since they hadn't been wormed in a long time many of them got colic and died.

Ruth was the farm manager and she was doing the best she could since she really cared about the horses. Her plan was to get the young horses broke so that they could be sold and then put that money back into the farm. She showed me a pasture of yearlings, a pasture of two-year-olds and a pasture of three-year-olds that were all unbroken. This would be my project. She trusted me enough to leave me alone and understood that I needed my space.

I started with the three-year-olds and we brought all fifteen of them into the training barn. I began working with them the same day. There were a few horses already in training and almost ready to ship into the track.

We had a skeleton crew at Anza because there wasn't much money for salaries. Besides Ruth, Robert was the maintenance man, Rod was the shoer, and Albert was the foreman. There had been a rider but the night I arrived he had been in a knife fight and left the ranch. As I pulled into the ranch, I saw two men fighting with knives and wondered what I had gotten myself into now.

I lived in the main house with Ruth, while Robert and Rod shared another ranch house. Anza was a tiny desert town with only a gas station and a few small stores. The grocery store was like an old time general store and sold everything. I bought a pair of chaps in the grocery store. The nearest 'real' grocery store was forty-five minutes away either in Hemet or Temecula.

The farm bordered an Indian Reservation and this posed its own set of problems. One day I had been checking fences with Robert and had my dogs with me when a drunken Indian stopped his car, got out and took a shot at my dogs. I was enraged and ran towards the drunk screaming at him. Robert grabbed me, apologized to the drunk, and warned me that the Indian would shoot me next if I didn't shut up and I should keep my dogs close at all times. Robert didn't know that shooting me would have been a gift.

I was still terribly sad and missed Scott so much it was almost unbearably painful. My pain was on a level that I had never imagined possible. I would cry during the day whenever I was alone, go to bed early and wake up many times during the night with my pillow soaked from tears that I cried in my sleep. The dogs were even worried about me. Raven and Emily had always been a big part of my life. We talked, played, competed at dog shows and trained. Now I only fed them.

I had so many horses to break that I worked all day. I was doing an okay job but not even close to what I was capable of. My thoughts were focused on my misery, and I couldn't give the horses the focus that I normally did without effort. I refused to wear a helmet. When Ruth quizzed me, and she tried hard to leave me alone, I cited the warm desert temperatures as a reason not to wear a helmet. The truth was, I wanted to get bucked off hard, land on my head and die so that I could be with Scott. Some days I could think of nothing other than that I wanted to be with Scott. It was like a broken record in my head, I want to be with Scott, I want to be with Scott.

When I finished riding for the day I would take a break and sit on the dock of the ranch pond. My beach chair was set up there permanently because it was a good place to cry. One day Robert walked out on the dock and I was crying so hard I didn't hear him approach. He told me that Ruth had shared my story with the crew before I arrived and everyone was instructed to give me my space. I had been in Anza for a month and Robert thought it was time to talk to me. He was really cute and very kind, but also simple and uneducated. His grammar made me cringe. We became friends and I occasionally watched a movie at his house in the evening instead of crying with my dogs. I felt us getting closer even though he wasn't the type of guy I would date. Scott had been very intelligent and sophisticated and Robert just wasn't.

Sunday was my day off and I would usually make the long four hour drive to Santa Ynez on Saturday night to visit Steve. I missed the Valley and Steve and wanted my old life back. When I arrived in the

Valley on Saturday night a wave of pain would overwhelm me and I would go to bed, turn off the lights and draw the shades. I only got up to feed the dogs and would go back to my darkness. On Sunday I would drive back to the ranch.

The guilt I felt for killing Scott was eating me up. I thought that Steve should feel guilty too since he played a part in killing Scott, and I told him this. He disagreed and tried to pull me out of my depression. He argued with solid logic that a sane man would not have been calling me thirty-five times a day, or arrived at his house in the middle of the night. I argued back that of course he wasn't sane after I fucked him up. We went round and round and eventually it became too painful to be near Steve. I was wishing he had died instead of Scott and it became difficult to even look at him.

I didn't want to be with anyone and thought I deserved to suffer alone and then die. Robert was very inviting and kind and really wanted me to start sleeping at his house. He had a way of holding me in his arms that made the pain stop for a while. My new M.O. was 'total honesty.' I was never going to lie or withhold information again that could hurt or kill a man. In line with this I told Robert that I was totally messed up right now and wanted desperately to be dead. If he still wanted to spend time with me knowing this, he also had to understand that while I might hang with him in Anza, when I was ready to leave the Ranch he was not the type of guy I would take with me. I knew this sounded heartless and cruel but I had to be honest. I couldn't risk killing another man.

I began spending some nights at Robert's house. Although I wasn't interested in sex I did like sleeping in Robert's arms. He was strong and had an incredibly tight and fit body. Most nights I would still cry all night and he would hold me.

For the next five months I broke horses all day and then slept in Robert's arms at night. Instead of going to Santa Ynez on Saturday nights, Robert and I would go to Del Mar and walk on the beach. It was a long, sixty mile drive to the beach, but it always made me feel a little better. I would hop onto the back of his motorcycle and take a cold bottle of Bailey's Irish Cream to drink on the way.

I had been honest with Steve and told him that I could never be with him again because we had killed Scott. I was still completely sure that Scott was dead because of me. Steve was hurt but he accepted my decision.

Robert and Rod liked to party and usually had beer and cocaine at their house. I started doing coke with Robert and it helped me to stop crying. The emotional pain that I felt was so intense that I thought I would probably kill myself soon. I had killed a man and for that I should suffer and die. I just wanted it to be soon.

In the past when I had done coke it was always for fun and never when I was riding. Now I did coke to get through the days without crying. I would take a little vial of coke to the training barn most mornings and do a line every two or three horses. I noticed a difference in the horses right away. Horses had always liked me and now they didn't. Days that I was high on coke the horses knew it the second I got legged up. My butt would only touch the saddle and I would pick up the reins when I would feel them tense up. It was like they were thinking, "Oh shit, not her again" instead of the usual, "Oh this will be fun." They would then walk out of the barn cold backed and ready to buck. I got bucked off several times on the hard ground between the barn and the track. I knew why.

On a day that I wasn't doing coke the horses were kind to me and happy again. I felt that they were willing to forgive me over and over. This made me cry even on coke.

My friend Robin from the track came to visit one day and was appalled at how I had deteriorated. I didn't hide the coke from him and was surprised that he preferred to lecture me, rather than get high with me. I had gotten really skinny from being depressed and from coke and I knew I was riding for shit. Robin said my riding was worthless and that I needed to get my act together. I didn't care what he thought.

I had been in Anza for six months now and I could see the beauty in the desert. It was so still and quiet, with a unique beauty. When I left the ranch to go anywhere it was hard to adjust to noise again. Anza was dead quiet. I realized now that it was the best place for me in these six months after Scott died. If I was ever to find peace again I needed silence now.

The horses were all broke and the ranch was going downhill fast. All of the horses were still fed twice a day, but salaries weren't being paid and we were more like volunteers than workers. It was time for me to go.

Chapter 13

Santa Ynez Again

I called Steve and told him I wanted to move back to the Valley and set up my own horse breaking business. He understood that I wasn't coming back to him, but he helped me anyway. Steve knew everyone in Santa Ynez and told me to call the Gardner Ranch. Old Peggy Gardner was the ranch owner, and she agreed to rent me a small house and stalls in the training barn. I called some of my old contacts and lined up seven horses to break. I knew I should have been ecstatic, but I was at best, a little less sad.

I said goodbye to Robert and left Anza thinking that for once I had been totally honest with a man so this would be smooth. I was wrong.

Scott's mother Barbara and I had always gotten along well. She was more like a mother to me than my own mother was. If Scott and I were fighting about something silly, I could call her and she would always be on my side. She would start our conversations with, "What did that butt hole do now," and we would both laugh. When we were taking Scott's house apart she insisted that I take the antique oak dining room set because she knew that Scott and I had found it on a trip to Tahoe together. She also gave me a racehorse print that was beautifully framed. She called when I was in Anza and told me that someone in the family had expressed interest in the print and she wanted it back. I didn't care about the print and told her to take it, but I felt like I had been stabbed in the back.

When I moved back to Santa Ynez I hated my little house on the ranch at first. It was dirty and needed paint, and I knew Scott would think that I was a real loser for living like this. The walls were filthy white and badly stained with fly shit. I sat down on the floor and cried, thinking I had truly hit rock bottom.

Barbara came to visit and loved my house. She was like an artist pointing out all the positives of this little house, like the open beam ceiling, huge living room, cozy bedroom, and three big closets. She had ideas for paint, lamps instead of bare bulbs in the ceilings, and cute wallpaper, and this gave me hope. It was good to see her, but we made each other sad, and were never to speak again.

My client's horses that needed breaking were shipped in and I was in business. It was surprisingly easy to gather seven horses to break. My plan was to offer a super low day rate and make just enough money to cover expenses and pay myself to ride. I figured that at least I would be riding for myself and wouldn't have to ride for an idiot. On paper this plan worked. I set up accounts with the feed store, tack shop, shoer, and vet. The only tack I needed to begin with was one exercise saddle and one bridle. I bought this on credit and ate peanut butter for two months to pay for it quickly.

I sent my bills out at the end of the first month and didn't get paid as quickly as I expected. My funds were scary low, as I counted out change to my last pennies for a can of cat food. On one of our trips to Del Mar on Robert's motorcycle, I had found two yellow kittens at the tack shop and I took them home in a bucket. Andrew and Sherman were my little boys, and the Dalmatians Raven and Emily, were my girls. They all had to eat.

I realized that I would have to do some freelance riding to insure cash flow and I found some small farms in the Valley that needed help. I rode my horses early, often at 4:00 a.m. in the moonlight, and then left to ride my outside horses.

Gail Balzer was the trainer/manager for a small farm in Santa Ynez and I rode for her. She had older horses coming back from lay-ups and they were all easy to ride. Gail and I got along fine and being a rider herself, she knew to give me my space. I think I needed my space more than other riders did. I liked to be real quiet and 'feel' what was going on with a horse. If someone was chattering to me or telling me what to do, I lost focus and got flustered.

Just down the road from Gail was another small farm that needed a rider. The trainer was Carol and she and I didn't always get along, but she paid me in coke so I could tolerate her. Every two weeks on payday she would give me an eightball of coke.

I wasn't doing coke on horses or during the week, but Saturday nights were still fun in the Valley. By Saturday night I would be so tired that I needed coke to even get myself out of the house. I was only twenty-seven years old and not ready to stay home every single night alone.

One Saturday night I had made plans to meet Brian and George from Mandysland at Zaca Creek Bar because Brian had a friend he wanted to set me up with. I did a line of coke, put on some clean jeans, and was ready to go.

Brian's friend, Richard, was smart, good looking, and fun, and we hit it off immediately. The four of us were drinking and laughing when suddenly the entire bar got quiet. I looked up and saw Robert from Anza staring at me like he wanted to murder me from the doorway of the bar. It reminded me of a Western movie when the bars always get dead quiet just before a brawl. Richard quickly got as far from me as he could. For all he knew I was a drama queen and had set this up. Robert entered the bar and I looked around for help and caught the eye of the bouncer. Robert asked me to go outside and talk to him, but I refused. I told him that he wasn't my boyfriend and that he should leave now. The bouncer escorted him out. The night was no longer fun and Richard wanted nothing to do with me so I went home.

Robert was waiting for me at the ranch. He really wanted to think that I was 'his' and he was ready to fight for me. I was angry now and reminded him that I had been totally upfront with him from day one. He begged me to change my mind, but I stood firm and he finally drove off into the night. I was never to see him again.

The following week my new friend, Richard, called and wanted to see me. I think Brian and George had been able to convince him that I wasn't a drama queen. We started spending time together and it was nice to have a man in my life. Richard had found his Mother hanging dead in a closet when he was eight years old and he understood pain.

When Richard and I started seeing each other I was still very sad and missing Scott. He lived in a tiny dark apartment in a renovated barn and drove a new Saab. He let me drive his car and the turbo power impressed me to no end. My house was nicer than his apartment but he was allergic to my cats, Andrew, and Sherman so we rarely went there. I didn't like his dark apartment and was afraid I would become more depressed in the dark.

Richard had two friends, Elliot and James, who he worked with in Lompoc. They were all engineers at the naval base, and on Saturday nights they drove to Santa Barbara to listen to jazz. They included me in these outings and we always had a little coke for the night. We had fun together and it felt like my life was slowly getting back to normal.

One Saturday night Richard and James were out of town so Elliot and I went to Santa Barbara without them. We had more coke than usual and when the bars closed we weren't ready to stop partying. We went to my house, woke the dogs up, and took them for a hike on the Gardner Ranch Mountain. When the sun came up I fed all my animals and we decided to go for an early morning beach walk. By the time we got to the beach we were running out of energy after being up all night, so we took off our clothes and slept. It was a beautiful warm sunny morning and we were at my favorite nude beach so there was no reason not to take my clothes off. Elliot was cool and we were just drinking buddies. We slept for a few hours enjoying the warm sun on our naked bodies.

When Richard returned later that day and asked how jazz in Santa Barbara had been without him I told him that Elliot and I had a great time. I wasn't prepared for Richard to be furious that Elliot and I had gone to the beach together. Nothing happened and Richard believed me, but he didn't know how he could work with Elliot now that he had seen me naked. I looked good naked so where was the problem? I thought Richard was being ridiculous and we broke up soon after this incident. He had been perfect for me when I was so depressed, but when I started feeling better we weren't such a good match.

My horse breaking business was going well and all the horses were progressing nicely. I even got a few more horses in from local clients so things were looking up. I loved having my own barn and it was a happy barn.

The Gardner Ranch was the best place for me to be at the time. It was an old ranch on 5000 acres that included the Gardner Mountain. Peggy Gardner, the owner, was in her late 70s and a delightful woman. She was slender and frail but went for long walks on her ranch every morning with her old Australian Shepard, Cinqo. She was a morning person like me and always greeted me with," Oh isn't it a glorious morning." Peggy was a sweet and wonderful woman who loved life and her ranch. I wanted to be happy and feel joy like she did.

Months after Scott's plane crash I was talking to a friend about how guilty I still felt. He asked me why on earth Scott would fly drunk. I replied that he was an exceptional pilot, was instrument rated, and would never fly drunk. My friend told me he had seen the story on the front page of the Santa Barbara New Press and Scott's blood alcohol level had been very high. He died drunk.

I still couldn't believe that Scott had crashed drunk, and so I called Steve for verification. He told me that yes, Scott was flying drunk, and that everyone had thought it best to keep this from me. If they had only known the guilt that was eating me up could have been lessened by knowing that Scott was drunk, I am sure they would have told me. The relief I felt on hearing this news was like a warm wave splashing over me. I didn't make Scott drink and fly. That was his choice and I could not be held responsible. I still missed Scott and always would, but maybe I wasn't 100% responsible for killing him. Maybe someday I could even forgive myself for the role I had played in his death.

In May my horses were all well broke and had shipped out to the track. The farms in the Valley almost shut down in the summer because there are no horses to break. Breaking season begins in the fall and ends in the spring when the babies ship in to Santa Anita.

When I worked for Walter I earned enough money to have a fun-filled four month vacation every summer. Those days were gone. I had earned enough to stay afloat but needed to work through the summer to keep things going. The very idea of galloping at Santa Anita was painful. I didn't want to be around people who knew me at the track. I had taken several trips to Santa Anita to hustle horses to break and I hated it. Several men on the track were more than a little suggestive offering me 'anything' I might need now that Scott was dead.

The worst pig of a man to 'offer' his services was bloodstock agent Chuck L. I had met him several years before at Walter's ranch and I knew that he was married. He was very flashy in a cheap sort of way, wearing gold chains and too many rings. He asked me to drive down to a farm in Norco to look at his yearlings. I arrived on time after a three hour drive, looked at his horses and asked when he wanted to send them to me. He invited me to lunch to discuss the details. I got in his car and as we drove out of the ranch he stopped at a dilapidated trailer, got out of his car and told me to follow him. I asked him why and he said, "Well you didn't think I was just going to give you the horses did you?" I didn't break his horses. I wanted to break his face.

Nikie Holloway was manager for Cave Creek farm in the Valley and she had sent me five horses to break. She could drive me crazy, but she was good pay. There were strings attached to these horses and I was obligated to be Nikie's friend and party with her. She wanted to go out drinking with me one Saturday night and I couldn't say no, but I could make sure it wasn't fun. The Buffalo was a new cowboy bar close to the ranch in Buellton, and so we decided to start our night of drinking there. Billy Gardner, Peggy's son, was at a table with at least ten friends and he asked us to sit with him. They were already quite drunk and Billy liked to tease me, so he told me that Steve had told him some private things about me. I knew Steve wouldn't do that so I told Billy he was full of it. Billy insisted that he had and wanted to share the 'secrets' with me. Finally I told him he could whisper what he thought he knew. He leaned across the table and whispered to me that Steve had said that I shave everywhere. This wasn't true and I knew Billy was only trying to embarrass me. It worked. I was mortified that Billy would even talk to me like that so I picked up his drink and threw it in his face. This only made him laugh so I picked up all twelve drinks on the table and threw them in his face. This pissed everybody off and they started chanting "86 her! 86 her!" Within seconds the bouncer told me leave the bar and escorted me out. Nikie thought I was crazy and swore she would never go out with me again.

Chapter 14

Belmont and Canterbury Downs

I was worried about money and needed a plan for the summer. A trainer who had been one of Scott's favorite clients had a string of horses at Canterbury Downs in Minnesota and needed riders. Canterbury was brand new and had not held their first race meet yet. My old friend Sally lived in Minnesota, two hours from the track. If I could think of this as a working vacation maybe it would even be fun. My plan was to ride at Canterbury for a month and then go to Belmont Park in New York for a month. I had called Rick Violette, an old trainer friend in New York, and he said I could ride for him all summer.

I had horses lined up to break in the fall so couldn't give up my little house at Gardner Ranch. The cats and dogs needed a safe place to live while I was away. My old roommate Kelly was looking for a place to live so we worked out a deal. I would pay all of the rent and she would take care of my animals. Kelly was a born-again Christian now and I thought I could trust her. I was wrong.

It was a long drive to Minnesota and I listened to sad songs and cried most of the trip. I finally arrived at Canterbury Downs and I was impressed. Everything was beautiful and well designed. I was riding for Chuck Telefaro, a good trainer who was an old friend of Scott's. It was nice to be somewhere that everyone didn't know my story. I would ride for Chuck in the morning and then make the long drive to Sally's ranch in the afternoon.

Sally had married a veterinarian and lived on a twenty acre farm in a small town in northern Minnesota. She had a covered, heated arena to ride in, though she seldom rode. She had her own breaking business but wasn't about to break horses by herself, and had not been able to find anyone to do it for her. I needed more work so I agreed to break five backyard horses at her ranch. They were easy and I had them going well in thirty days.

The long drive from the track to Sally's ranch was killing me so I decided it was time to go to New York. Rick Violette had been calling me from Belmont and needed a rider immediately.

The drive to New York wasn't half bad. I only got lost once in Pennsylvania and found myself in an Amish town. I had never seen Amish people in their buggies before so it was a good place to be lost.

I arrived at Belmont ready to rock. Rick had some nice horses from his big owner, Alfred Vanderbilt, one of the wealthiest and most successful owners in the history of the sport. His stable was medium sized with about thirty horses. He had three other riders, and I became fast friends with his best rider, Susie. She had been on the New York tracks forever and knew everyone. She was recently divorced from a trainer on the track. If she even spoke his name she would change from fun Susie to Susie the viper. She had caught him having sex with her best friend in her bed and she was filled with hate and rage.

Susie made me her social project. I was feeling ready to date again but wanted to take some of the risk out of dating a race tracker. That is where Susie jumped in. Because I was the new girl at Belmont I attracted plenty of attention. Whenever a man asked me out I would reply that I would let them know tomorrow and then ask Susie. She was invaluable and shared her information about several big name trainers. One was a pervert and another abused his girlfriend in a tack room. The list of seriously ineligible men went on and on.

Finally, Alex Wilson, a trainer from Irel, and asked me out and Susie said yes. Alex and I hit it off from the day we met. He was funny, silly, handsome, rich, and loved to party. Within a week I had given up the room I rented near the track and moved in with Alex.

Alex and I had a blast. He bought cocaine in huge rocks and we never ran out. Every night we went to a bar with several other trainers and drank lots of drinks and talked lots of shit. I was the only girl in the group, but Alex wanted me there.

Soon the girlfriends of my drinking buddies got curious and joined us at the bar. They disliked me on sight and I didn't really care. They were typical racetrack bitches and saw me as a threat. I had grown used to this ill-founded concept and sometimes fought back.

One night at the bar trainer Darron White's girlfriend, Sheryl, lost her purse. She was the leader of the little group of bitchy girlfriends and had been the nastiest to me. I still wore jeans and T shirts even when I was out, and she looked at me like trailer court trash. She was always well dressed with gobs of makeup and perfect nails. She was frantically looking for her purse when I told her that Alex had taken it. I told her not to worry because he only wanted the makeup that was in the purse. Alex and I were the only ones laughing but we nearly fell off our bar stools. The lines were drawn that night and I became public enemy number one.

I found it hard to party all night and gallop horses in the morning so Alex suggested that I quit riding for Rick. I only had two more weeks until I should be heading home and Alex wanted to take me to Kentucky for the yearling sales. He told me not to worry about money and I didn't. I had been sending most of the money I earned home to Kelly to pay all my bills and buy food for the animals.

We flew to Kentucky with a big group of trainers and their wives and girlfriends. From the dirty looks that the women gave me I knew they didn't like me even though most of them had never met me. It didn't matter much to me. There was a layover in Ohio and we all trooped into the airport bar. We had just time for one drink and we all got up at the same time to go to our plane. I was wearing a pair of short khaki shorts with small unsafe pockets. Alex had given me the vial of coke to carry even though I told him that my pockets weren't safe. They were designed at a bad angle and things always fell out. Alex and I were almost out of the bar when a trainer's wife from our group saw my coke vial on the floor. From across the bar she yelled, "Susan, Susan, did you lose something" and held the coke vial in the air. Alex and I had been partying hard and I was so fucked up I took the vial and said, "Thank you." A sober person who gave a shit would have denied that the coke was hers.

Alex expected me to be busted for cocaine when we landed in Kentucky, but nothing ever happened. The yearling sale was one big party for us, and I don't even remember those two days in Kentucky.

We flew back to New York without an incident, and then it was time for me head home to California. Sally wanted me to drive to her farm in Minnesota where she had rented a tow package for my little car, and she would then drive us back to California in her big dually truck. She had a two year son, Kyle, who would be joining us and it sounded like fun to me.

I planned to get cocaine under control and drive to Sally's straight. Alex had offered me coke for the road, but I said no thank you. We said our goodbyes and Alex was at the track when I packed my car and hit the road. I really had decided not to do coke on the road, but the thought of all those miles and a subpar stereo made me waffle. I knew where Alex's stash was hidden and I helped myself to a generous portion. I left him a note that he had been raided.

My trip back to Minnesota was fun. I was high and listened to happy music all the way there. When I arrived Sally was packed and ready to go, and we left the following day. It was a luxury to sit in her new truck and be a passenger all the way to California. Sally loved to drive and always had a nice truck.

Chapter 15

Home again

We arrived at the Gardner Ranch, and I had been looking forward to showing Sally my cute little house. I had taken Barbara's advice about redecorating and completely painted and wallpapered, so now my little house was adorable. When I opened the front door and walked in, I was shocked. Kelly knew I was returning and I was right on schedule but the house was a mess. She had tacked her born-again Christian shit on the walls, and instead of a quaint country cottage, my house looked like a religious fanatic had taken over. It was dreadful and I was so embarrassed. Although she was an artist, nothing was framed, and most of the pictures she had put on the walls were torn from books or magazines and had ragged edges. She had porcelain angels on my shelves. I explained to Sally that this was not my shit, and I didn't live like this.

My dogs and cats had survived the summer and were so happy that I was home. I had missed them all terribly. We hugged and played for hours and then they wouldn't let me out of their sight for days. I was to learn later that Kelly mostly ignored them while I was away and Hector, my neighbor, had been caring for everyone.

Kelly knew that I was bringing a friend home, and I assumed that she would have found another place to stay. Instead, it was obvious that she planned on staying in my house. My living room was huge, but Sally, Kyle and Kelly all had to sleep on the floor or couch because I didn't have an extra bed. I still thought of us as friends so I didn't tell her to leave. That came later.

Sally planned to stay for two weeks. She didn't understand that I would be busy getting ready for breaking season and hustling horses. Sally had always been low energy and overweight and she expected me to help her with Kyle. Her brain quizzes for the little guy were an alternative to playing with him. I had never agreed to baby sit and since she had nothing else to do it was easy to leave her kid to her.

The Del Mar yearling sale was on and I needed to be there. It was a four hour drive from Santa Ynez to Del Mar and I didn't invite Sally. I couldn't hustle clients with her and her child in tow. My original plan was to go round trip in one day.

After the sale a group of race trackers invited me to Bully's, a well-known party bar in Del Mar. Inger and several other people I knew were all drinking and having fun. Although I had planned on only one drink before heading home, I ended up getting as shit faced as they all were. I called Sally to tell her I wouldn't be home until the next morning.

When I arrived home Sally was angry and in her truck ready to go back to Minnesota. I think that she expected more of me than I could give.

Now I only had to get rid of Kelly and I would have my house back. When I left for my trip two months before the house was well stocked with animal food, paper towels, light bulbs, and toilet paper. All Kelly had to buy was her own food. Since I trusted her, I had left her signed checks to pay bills as they came in. I had been sending her most of the money I earned at Belmont Park to deposit in my checking account. This was born-again Kelly, so surely she could be trusted.

I was counting on my checking account to have at least a $3,000 balance to get me through until my horses came in, but the money wasn't there. I went over my checkbook and saw that Kelly had taken $100 out of my account on the day that I left, even though she was well stocked. As I went over my account I saw several bounced check fees. She had bounced checks to the shoer, the feed store, and the veterinary supply store. I broke out in a sweat. I could only think, "What the hell!" My money was gone and the bills had not been paid. I was furious and scared. I wouldn't be earning any money for at least another two weeks and was nearly out of dog food. And Kelly, the thief, was still in my house!

I went over my ledger and checkbook countless times and still came up with a $0 balance. As far as I could figure I was missing about $3,000 and had a stack of unpaid bills and bounced checks. I was so mad at Kelly that I could barely speak to her. The first check that she wrote for $100 on the day of my departure said it all. She had ripped me off big time, of that I had no doubt.

One of the worst parts of having no self-esteem is that on some level I believed that it was okay to steal from me. I never did confront Kelly. After two weeks of not speaking to her she moved out.

Steve and I had remained good friends so I went to him with my money problem. Santa Ynez was a still a small, tightly knit Valley, and if a horse person left town with a string of bad checks behind her I knew it wasn't a secret. Steve's father had started Todd Pipe and Supply Co. from nothing, and was now a self-made millionaire. Steve told me that he had once been in a similar situation to mine, and his father has insisted that he drive to each person he had bounced a check to, apologize, and set up a payment plan. I thought that a phone call or a letter would suffice but Steve insisted that it had to be face to face.

I swallowed my pride and went to the tack shop, feed store, and horse shoer, and explained my situation. They were all very kind and trusted me to pay my bills as soon as my horses came in. The feed store sent me home with a big bag of dog food. I was so relieved that they didn't all hate me.

Steve made me see that this was my mistake. He said that I should have never left Kelly, or anyone else for that matter, with signed blank checks. I gave her a license to steal. It was a case of country bumpkin meets the real world and I got walloped.

My horses came in as scheduled and I was once again busy breaking babies. I had enough horses this second year on my own that I didn't have to freelance at other farms. My deal with the Gardner Ranch included a groom to help me, so my barn was looking quite professional. It was fun working for myself, but I was still missing Scott and felt like the center of me was one big dull ache.

Alex and I were having a long distance relationship. He was either in New York, Engl, or Irel, and he called me almost every day. He sent flowers so often that the local flower shop teased me about my romance. What I didn't tell anyone was that Alex was married. His wife was "Lady" Maxwell and she lived on their estate in Ireland. Alex told me that there was no divorce in Ireland and that was the only reason that they were still married.

Alex came to visit me in the spring after the horses had shipped out. He brought along plenty of cocaine and we played hard. It was good to see him and he loved my little cottage and the Gardner Ranch. I took him to my favorite places, the nude beach and a hot spring in the hills near Gaviota. We would party all night and then take a bottle of champagne to the hot springs and watch the sun come up. We were telling each other that we were in love, but love on coke isn't real. We never had sex because Alex was impotent, probably from all the cocaine. He was more like a fun brother than a lover.

When my horses shipped out in the spring I wanted to find work in the Valley so that I could spend my summer at home. Summers were still very hard for me. I missed my old life with summers at Del Mar with Scott.

This year was to be different. Dick Sturgis, a wealthy businessman, had bought the most impressive farm in the Valley, Westerly Stud Farm. He put in a 7/8 mile track, refurbished the barns, and hired trainer John Fulton to run the farm. I was hired as a rider and was the only girl rider with five guys. The horses were all runners and would train at Westerly and then ship in to Santa Anita or Hollywood to run. Everyone was happy at Westerly. Horses, grooms, riders, and hot walkers were all treated with kindness and respect.

John Fulton spent half his time at the track and half at the farm. In his absence Chuck Maple, the assistant trainer, ran the farm. Chuck was from South Africa and had a way about him that offended almost everyone. He always appeared very busy, but actually did very little. The riders and the rest of the crew hated him, but I got along with him.

One day I had a horse on my set list that was scheduled to go to the starting gates. The horse was a two-year-old, not very well broke, and this would be his first time in the gates. He didn't want to go into the gates that morning and it took about twenty minutes just to walk him through. This is not terribly uncommon in young horses. Normally a horse like this would only be walked through the gates until he did it easily, then locked up and stand, and then jog out, gallop out, and finally break. It should be a long, slow, quiet, process to build confidence in the horse.

The next day John had returned from Santa Anita and was at the gates and asked Chuck what we were doing with this colt in the gates today and Chuck answered "Breaking." I am sure my face said it all, "Breaking, you idiot! The horse can barely walk through the fucking gates." John asked me how the colt was yesterday and I said it took twenty minutes just to walk him through, so John said just walk him through again. My silent sigh of relief must have been clearly visible on my face.

John was a good horseman and respected by all. He loved Westerly Stud Farm and was treated like a VIP in the Santa Ynez Valley, since he was a big name trainer from the track. It wasn't unusual to see him at the barn in the morning with a beautiful girl from the night before.

Somehow Kelly, my old roommate, and John were set up on a blind date. John was on his pony one morning at Westerly and asked me if I knew Kelly. John dated women who looked like models and Kelly wasn't even close. She was short, had big hips, huge thighs and oversized ears. It would have been easy to hide the ears but she always pulled her hair up in a ponytail and there they were. I only rarely sunk to being a catty bitch, but when I did, I was good at it. I told John that Kelly was very nice but don't look at her ears. He said, "What is wrong with her ears?" I replied, "Oh nothing, I shouldn't have said anything, have fun!" The next day on the track John told me that I had ruined his date. All he could do was focus on Kelly's huge ears, and he pretended to have a stomach ache and left early, before dinner. I was quite proud of myself that day.

I loved riding at Westerly. Since most of my horses were runners they were easy to ride. Our job as riders was to keep the horses fit, sound, and happy in between races. We were a very strong and balanced group of riders. I was best on silly fillies and did most of the work riding. The guys were all heavy which made me the lightest rider and most suitable to ride work. Working the horses was my most favorite thing in the world. John would decide the distance and the time that he wanted me to work in and I usually nailed it. I felt so free on a fast horse. When I was 100 percent focused on my horse; I was happy…nothing else mattered. I could go into another space and just feel the moment.

The other riders didn't treat me like a girl at all. I was one of the guys and part of their group. We had racetrack hours, training in the morning and afternoons off. This left plenty of time to train a few of my own horses and have some beach time. Sundays were off, so Saturday night was party night. By then we all considered ourselves to be experienced drinkers and partiers. I was always amazed at how my fellow riders could drink and party and still ride the next day. I usually only drank on Saturday nights because I didn't want to ride with a hangover.

One Friday night the gang talked me into drinking with them. We drank and did cocaine all night long and ended up in the kitchen of the bunkhouse at Westerly as the sun came up. The guys assured me that with a few cups of coffee I would be fine, but that was not the case. At 7:00 a.m. I was still drunk and not willing or able to ride. My only shot was to apologize to Chuck, who was in charge that morning. I told him I was sorry, partied all night, was still drunk, and that I couldn't ride. Much to my surprise he put his arm around me and laughed. I fully expected to be fired. He told me to go sleep it off and he got on my horses that morning. It felt so good to live through such a bad mistake. Race trackers are famous for partying hard and missing work, but it had never happened to me before.

Alex came to visit again and we mostly got high. He wanted me to come and stay with him in England for a month, but I couldn't take time off from Westerly. I was toying with the idea of quitting work and becoming Alex's mistress. This started as Alex's idea because if I was never available to play we would have no relationship.

I was very close to my two Dalmatians and two cats. They were my family and always came first. One day a man was driving a car without a muffler very fast around the Gardner Ranch. He was angry and searching for a girl who lived on the ranch who had just sold him the car which turned out to be a lemon. I heard my youngest dog, Emily, scream and I came running from the barn fearing the worst. I ran to where I had heard the scream and couldn't find Emily. Instead, I saw Billy Gardner talking to the driver of the car. Billy told me that Emily had been hit and had run back to my house. I remember making a fist and drawing back to hit the driver in the face. Billy grabbed my hand before I made contact and told me that he would take care of this, and

I should find my dog. I ran to my house and found Emmy with blood coming out of one eye and her body a mass of cuts and scrapes. Billy had called my vet, as well as his girlfriend, who was to drive us to the vet. I had Emmy in my arms and needed to stay calm for her sake. She went directly into surgery and had over one hundred stitches all over her body and a lacerated pupil. When I picked her up the next day a vet tech brought her out to me and I fainted. Emily was my breed dog, a perfect specimen of a Dalmatian with no faults, my beauty queen. What I picked up was Frankenstein's dog. She was shaved and covered with stitches and scrapes, but most disturbing was her eye. The vet had sewn her third eyelid shut and there was very little hope that the eye would be saved. I selfishly wondered how I could still love her and then hated myself for the thought.

I was very upset by the accident and Emily needed me by her side. There was no way I could ride because I couldn't stop crying and had to be with Emily. Alex offered to pay the vet bill and support me while I took care of Emily. I called Westerly and told them I would have to quit for now in order to care for my dog. They understood and I parted on good terms.

Emily's recovery was long and slow. She had a second surgery to remove her eye that had not healed. Eventually all of her stitches were taken out and she could go on slow walks around the ranch with me and Raven. Raven and I always looked out for her. Poor Emily would walk into a gate or a fence on her blind side and yelp and I would collapse in tears. I had to learn to watch her every second and guide her with my voice. She learned the commands 'whoa, honey' and 'be careful' and would wait for me or Raven to help her.

Alex had been spending more time in New York than England or Irel, and and we saw each other more often now. He paid for my rent, food, and vet bills, and I pretended I was a lady of luxury. I had always wondered what it would feel like to be a mistress. We still mostly partied together on cocaine and alcohol. Alex always drank Duers Scotch whiskey and had rocks of cocaine. Although I wasn't much of a drinker, I could drink like a fish when I did coke. The coke had a way of keeping me from being falling down drunk.

The negative side effects of cocaine were becoming more evident. I couldn't sleep after a night of drugs and would lay in bed for hours waiting for daylight. The next day I would feel like garbage, with no energy and only negative thoughts. My thoughts became increasingly dark, but I knew it was only the drug. Sometimes I would decide to quit doing coke and Alex would join me, but one of us always caved. It was becoming obvious that we could never quit together.

Walter and I were still close but I didn't want him to meet Alex because I knew that he would disapprove. Walter could size people up as easily as he could read a horse.

Walter was now in his late 70s and his health was failing. He had always been unhealthy and suffered from emphysema since he was a child. I visited him once in the hospital, and although he looked like death, his spirits were up and we shared jokes and funny stories. His sense of humor was wicked and he liked nothing better than a good hard laugh.

Walter's practical jokes knew no limits. If they made us laugh we had to carry on. One time Valerie decided that her twenty-two year old daughter, Natalie, would share the ranch house with Walter. This was never discussed with Walter and was all planned without his consent. Natalie was a bad roommate, ate all of Walter's food, made a mess of the house, and wouldn't chip in to pay the cleaning lady.

Natalie had a weight problem and fought to stay only chubby. Without the fight she would get huge. When Walter and I started our little prank she was only a little bit overweight. I was the perfect accomplice for Walter's schemes because I was so devoted to him, and I too had a wicked sense of humor. Walter asked me to buy him a very rich double Dutch chocolate cake from the only the finest bakery. I did as instructed and brought a huge beautiful cake to the ranch the next day, even though I knew that Walter didn't like chocolate.

Natalie couldn't resist chocolate and could eat an entire cake in one sitting. I bought at least three cakes a week and grocery bags of chocolate candy. Natalie went from pleasantly plump to very fat in just thirty days. She would be outside washing her car and Walter would tell me to get in the golf cart so we could go look at Natalie. We would casually drive by and note that her seams in her jeans were stretched and ripping but never crack a smile. Once we drove away we would die laughing.

Another one of our pranks was played on Walter's best friend John. Walter and I didn't have a lot of respect for my sister. She was staying with me on weekends and sometimes I could talk her into getting up early and going to the ranch with me. Once we arrived at the ranch I would ride all morning and Lizzie would sleep in the car. After she woke up around 11:00 she would do her nails for an hour while still sitting in the car.

Lizzie loved to bake and had baked an organic molasses cake at my house the night before. She poured in more than double the amount of molasses that the recipe called for and the cake was inedible. It was so bad that when I gave it to the dogs they walked away and wouldn't eat it. When the dogs wouldn't even eat the cake I decided to give it to Walter. He wasn't so easily fooled and one tiny bite nearly made him throw up. Never one to pass up an easy victim, Walter decided that we should give his old friend, John, a big piece of cake for lunch. John liked my sister Lizzie, and was far more polite than Walter and I could ever be. We all sat down for lunch at Walter's table, and Walter announced that Lizzie had made a cake especially for John. John was touched by the gesture and ate the entire huge piece of inedible cake. When he finished he said, "Now if I could just have a big glass of water."

Walter died soon after I visited him in the hospital. His funeral was attended by over two hundred people, mostly horseman. I cried at his funeral and knew that I would miss him forever. His friendship and the knowledge that he shared with me were the biggest gifts I had ever received from anyone.

Chapter 16

Centurion Farm

I was learning that it wasn't always fun being in business for myself. Breaking horses was easy, but talking to prospective clients was painful. I was still very shy and when trainers or owners made sexual advances I got furious. Nikie Holloway still sent me horses and tried to get me more clients. She organized meetings for me at Santa Anita with her people, but it always came down to sex for horses. Finally after several of her attempts to help me were unproductive, she told me that it was my fault. She said that if I couldn't be more 'friendly' to her trainer friends I would never get horses to break. I was still under the illusion that I should have plenty of horses to break because I did a damn good job.

The only horses I was getting in were the ones that no one else wanted. There was a farm near Temecula owned by Mr. Miel, of Miel Vacuum Cleaners, where he bred at least ten horses a year. The horses that were raised on his farm were as wild as Mustangs. Mr. Miel didn't like to spend money so the horses were only handled when they needed the vet or the horse shoer. I had heard that when the shoer came to trim their feet, the horses were hog tied and thrown down. My first introduction to Miel's horses had been at Walter's farm. They were all the same, terrified, and hated humans. At best, once I had them broke, they wouldn't hate me, but they never overcame their upbringing enough to be happy horses.

After Nikie's advice, which I could not follow, I was working on another option since I couldn't be 'friendly' to clients. Since Walter's death, Valerie had lost most of their outside clients horses and they needed a trainer/manager. I approached Ned, Valerie's husband and asked him to hire me. I knew it would be tricky because Valerie and I could no longer pretend to get along.

Valerie and I had a major falling out my last year working at her farm. The saddles at the ranch were falling apart and not safe to ride in. In fact, there was only one saddle that I could use and it needed a repair. I took the saddle to the tack shop that Valerie preferred, but they couldn't fix it for three days. Since this wouldn't do, I then went to a more expensive tack shop near Santa Anita and they agreed to fix the saddle that same day. I could pick it up in a few hours. I called Valerie to okay the repair and she refused. She said that Western Saddlery was too expensive and I should take the saddle back to Hobson's. I told her this is the only saddle I can ride in, and I am riding twenty horses a day. She didn't care about anything but saving a few dollars, so I had to take the saddle back to Hobson's and wait three days for the repair.

The next day at the ranch I was riding in a horrible saddle that didn't fit me or my horse. My first horse bucked me off, my foot got caught in the stirrup, and I was dragged on the track. I wasn't seriously hurt but I was seriously angry. That cheap fucking bitch of a woman had risked my safety so she could save a few dollars. I walked back from the track ready to call her and quit but Walter shut me down. Instead, we went to his house and had a quiet cup of tea while he explained that Valerie was absolutely impossible, but it would serve no purpose to argue with her.

My rule has always been that if you fuck with me, I will pay you back times ten before I consider the score even. The following Sunday I was at Clockers Corner at Santa Anita, and Valerie's husband, and Ned, was there. I didn't especially like Ned and he wasn't at all handsome. But when opportunity knocked, far be it for me to walk away. Ned only asked me how the horses were doing and I launched into an act that was worthy of recording. I became Miss slutty, flirty, Susan complete with giggles, throwing my head back and only just short of rubbing my body against Ned's. Valerie was sitting on her pony on the track in a rage that she could barely contain. She directed Ned to walk down to the wire and watch the next work. Of course I went along and almost held his hand walking down the full length of the grandstand. Since it was Sunday morning, there were plenty of people around to witness my show of 'affection.' Only a few knew what I was up to because they saw the hate in Valerie's eyes. This was a prank that would come back to haunt me.

Ned decided that he would hire me to manage his ranch and Valerie agreed, as long as he never went to his own ranch while I was employed there. When our old clients heard I had returned, the training barn was suddenly full, and there was a waiting list to get in. It felt so good to be respected as a horse breaker.

I lived in Walter's old house at the ranch, but it felt more like Valerie's house than my home. She had wedding pictures of one of her weddings on the wall of my bedroom. Valerie had been married five times and each of her five children had a different father. I was careful to keep my distance from her.

Ned and Valerie seemed to have plenty of money and bought expensive horses from France and South America. Although none of the imported horses ever ran well for Valerie, they continued to buy expensive horses.

I saw lavish displays of money at the farm. The youngest daughter, Alice, was only four years old and wore expensive jewelry. She was too young to understand the value, and lost an emerald ring when she washed her hands and let it get rinsed down the sink in the barn.

Valerie didn't like to spend money on tack or barn supplies. Instead of buying new polo wraps for the farm, she would send us her old ones from the track. The worn out bandages that we used had Velcro that would no longer function and should have been thrown away. Polo wraps are used on the track as support bandages, and when they begin to show even light wear, they should be thrown away. In good barns that consider the safety of horse and rider, wraps are taped or safety pinned at the top so that they can't come off on the track. There is nothing more deadly than a wrap that has come loose on the track

Em, a beautiful exercise girl and aspiring jockey, was Valerie's rider at Santa Anita. One morning she was working a horse when a polo bandage came off, tripped her mount, and she went down hard on the track. Em never walked again and will spend the rest of her life in a wheelchair.

I nearly fainted the morning that I heard about Em's accident. No one ever works a horse in polo wraps, because they are dangerous. Polo wraps are used only to jog or gallop, but never in a work because you simply can't risk a wrap coming off at thirty-five miles per hour. If a horse needs wraps in a work, Vetwrap is the safe choice although it is more expensive. Vetwrap is a 3M product that is stretchy, for support, and sticks to itself, but is a little pricey at $2.00 per roll/leg. Valerie chose to save a few dollars on wraps and crippled a rider for life.

I knew Valerie for who she was and the best I could do was to keep a safe distance. Had I not desperately needed a secure job I would have never worked for her again.

Breaking season was going well and I enjoyed being the farm manager/trainer and rider. We had over 100 horses at the farm including mares and foals. Alfredo had been the foreman for years under Walter and he and I worked well together. I asked him how he managed to get along with Valerie, and he told me that if Valerie said a chestnut horse was gray, he would just agree with her. Arguing with Valerie had always been pointless.

Valerie and Walter's sixteen year old daughter, Linda, was learning to gallop horses at the farm. She would drive forty-five miles before school to get to the farm, get on a few horses, and then drive forty-five miles back to Arcadia and go to high school. Linda was a good kid but struggled to make sense of her evil mother. Sometimes she would arrive at the farm in a rage over something her mother had done to her, and the next day would be oozing love for Valerie. She told me stories of how much fun she had with her Mother baking cookies and laughing with Ned and her little sister Alice. Then the next day she would tell me that her mother was a crazy fucking bitch. I was careful to never have an opinion.

One story she told me was disturbing but there was nothing I could do. Ned and Valerie had a beautiful young daughter, Alice, who was four-years-old. Ned bought her inappropriate gifts like the emerald ring that she lost in three days. Linda told me that whenever Ned bought Valerie jewelry or flowers he would also present Alice with an identical gift. Linda told me that one night at dinner Alice wanted to take a shower with Ned but they had not eaten dessert yet. Ned told her that she had to wait until after dessert. Alice threw a fit, and finally Ned caved, and he proceeded to have a shower with his four year old daughter. This sounded sick and perverted to me.

Linda would arrive at 7:00 a.m. every morning and was usually high. She smoked pot on her drive to the farm and would arrive wasted. Because her father, Walter, was such an amazing horseman, Linda thought she had inherited his talent. She didn't realize that raw talent isn't enough, and it would take years of hard work to be a good rider.

I would put Linda on three easy horses and rotate them every day because she couldn't teach them anything. When I rotated them out she couldn't do too much damage because she rode each one only once a week. Young horses need to learn to gallop in company, together head and head. Good riders can gallop so close to each other that their stirrups are touching. Linda couldn't seem to go head and head in any of the sets, ever. Instead, she would be ten lengths behind no matter what horse she was riding. This wasn't doing any of the horses any good and was driving me crazy. They would never learn to gallop in company if the company was always ten lengths behind. For months I waited for Linda to catch up on the track, every horse, every day. When I got too far ahead, Linda's mount would get upset and try to buck her off in order to catch up to me. Linda was always too stoned to even be aware that she was the cause of the problem.

Finally one day I ran out of patience and I didn't wait for Linda on our first set. Her horse tried to dump her and catch up to me. She made it back to the barn and said, "Thanks for waiting for me bitch!" I have never had patience with humans and had tried so hard to deal with this girl who was always stoned. I started out calm and told her that I had waited for her every horse, every set, every day, for two months. I told her that I had to rotate her mounts so that she didn't fuck anyone up too bad, and finished by screaming, "You are green, green, green!" Linda burst into tears but nothing ever changed.

Aside from Linda, breaking season was going well. We had so many horses to break that we turned our homebreds back out in the pastures in order to make room for the client's horses. I needed another full time rider and hired my old friend, Inger, from the track. We had the horses all galloping well so life was easy. Inger was one of the few people who got along with Valerie, and Alfredo warned me to be careful. I should have paid more attention to his warnings.

My work at the farm was exciting and fun and I was well paid. I still missed Scott and was very lonely. Alex had come out to visit me and I realized I didn't need him anymore. I didn't want to be doing many drugs and would fall right back into cocaine with Alex around. I wasn't quite ready to quit drugs and sometimes Alex would even mail me a gram of coke from New York. It was time for him to go.

The track at the farm was 7/8ths of a mile and bordered on three sides by dairy cows. We also had a flock of guinea hens that would wander around in the infield and then jump off the racetrack rail onto the track in front of galloping horses. Even on my best horses I always had to stay focused and give the horses enough confidence in me to get us safely around the track. The upside was that if a young horse could gallop past guinea hens and cows, Santa Anita would be easy for him.

On my Sunday off I would occasionally still go to Santa Anita and stand at Clockers Corner to watch horses gallop. One morning I was standing on the rail and felt like someone was watching me. I looked up and saw trainer Roy Martin staring at me with obvious interest. He had beautiful blue eyes and a friendly smile and I fell for him the instant our eyes met. Within a week he had moved into the ranch house with me. Roy was known to be a player, but I didn't even know what that meant. I was still very naïve in many ways, and I thought a player meant that he was very popular with women and could have whoever he wanted. Well, he chose me and that felt good.

Roy spent about half of his nights at the ranch and I didn't know where he slept on the other nights. I knew that I shouldn't ask too many questions. When you have no self-worth you feel lucky that a man even wants you. I always thought that if he really knew me he would be long gone.

Roy's best friend was a bloodstock agent from Argentina. Alberto wasn't nearly as good looking or charming as Roy. Roy and Alberto were always together and soon Alberto moved into my house. I wasn't the least bit interested in Alberto at the beginning. Roy began spending less time with me and more time away and I ended up with Alberto by default. Alberto told me that he and Roy had an ongoing contest to see who could sleep with the most women. They had a point system and if one of them stole a girl from the other they would be awarded double points. When Alberto told me this I understood that they were both young and popular and had plenty of women. I didn't get that they had no respect for women.

One night Roy and I had plans but Roy was a no-show, which was all too typical of him. I was beginning to see that he had used me for sex and a place to live. It was my turn to get even and that night I invited

Alberto into my bed. When Roy came home at 5:00 a.m. and found Alberto in my bed, I casually asked him to make us breakfast. Without skipping a beat, Roy made us breakfast and served it on a silver tray!

Alberto and I were spending more and more time together and I was starting to think that maybe he was okay. He sold some horses to Ned and Valerie and promised me a commission if I helped make the sale go. Ned called me to ask what I knew about Alberto and I answered that as far as I knew he was an honest bloodstock agent. After the deal was done and Alberto made a $40,000 profit I had to remind him that he owed me a commission, and then we argued about the dollar amount. He had forgotten that he had promised me $500 and tried to pay me only $200. I should have run from him then, but instead gave him the benefit of the doubt. Anyone with any self-worth would have been long gone.

Soon after Alberto's successful transaction my world was to turn upside down once again. It was spring in California and the last of our pregnant mares had foaled the night before. The foal was healthy but the mare had retained the placenta which can be very dangerous, although not unusual. The vet had given me a bottle of Oxytocin to treat mares with retained placentas, but I called him first. He was very busy that day and told me to give the mare a dose of Oxytocin. By afternoon the vet still had not arrived and the Oxytocin had not helped the mare who was an older mare. Comit Hill was lying down and thrashing in pain and bleeding when the vet finally arrived late in the afternoon. I was crying and covered with her blood when the vet told me that she had ruptured a uterine artery, and even if he had been there, she could not have been saved. He told me that he would put this in writing if I needed it. Unfortunately I told him that there should not be a problem and I didn't need a statement from him. I immediately called Valerie and told her that Comit Hill had ruptured a uterine artery and died just as the vet arrived. She thanked me for doing all that I could to help the mare. I was surprised that she took this terrible news so well.

Alfredo had left for the afternoon and when he came back the mare was dead. He told me that he had left because he knew she would die, and that I should be very careful. I told him that I had already spoken to Valerie and everything appeared to be okay. He repeated, "Be very careful."

Alfredo knew that Inger wanted my job and would do anything to get me out of the way. Three days after the mare died Ned called me at night and coldly told me that he heard about Comit Hill and that I should pack my bags and get out now. I was shocked to say the least, and told him that she had ruptured her uterine artery and bled out, I had immediately notified Valerie. He repeated that I should get out now.

If a mare retains the placenta and a lay person attempts to pull it out you risk tearing the uterus. Every lay person who knows even the basics about foaling out mares would never pull on a retained placenta. This is at the top of the 'something you would never do' list.

When the vet arrived the retained placenta was still attached to the mare so he knew I did nothing wrong. I called the vet and asked him to speak to Ned and he refused. Later, Alfredo told me that the vet admitted that he gave me a bottle of Oxytocin, but lied and said that he didn't tell me to administer the drug to the mare. The vet had covered his own ass and hung me out to dry.

Alfredo also told me that Inger had been working hard behind my back trying to get me fired. Valerie had been questioning Alfredo to verify Inger's stories. This is why Alfredo had been warning me.

I left the farm the next morning but not before I called every one of my clients and told them the true story, that I had been fired and hung out to dry. My people knew that I had done nothing short of a fantastic job breaking their horses that season and they were outraged. They were all track people and knew Valerie well. In a grand show of support, all thirty-five of the outside horses I was breaking were shipped out that week. It felt so good to have friendly people behind me and I so appreciated their kindness.

Inger was hired as manager/trainer and I heard that four horses died her first week on the job. She quickly realized that she was not qualified to be a trainer or manager and quit before her second week was over. She and Valerie both got breast cancer and nearly died a few years later.

Alberto and I took a couple of weeks to regroup at a friend's house in Pasadena. I was in shock that first week and still couldn't believe that Valerie was so evil that she would tell lies to get me fired. I don't know why this should have surprised me because I had witnessed many lies that she told her husband about the horses. She was not a kind trainer and if a horse had a problem, her solution was to fill them with drugs and carry on. When a horse with an obvious injury, like a bowed tendon, finally could not go on even with an obscene amount of drugs, she would send them back to the farm. I had often heard her tell Ned that a horse was just sent back to the farm to rest and must have hurt his tendon in the van while in transit.

I went to Hollywood Park one morning with Alberto and was walking around the barn area alone when I turned a corner and almost walked into Valerie. I asked her why, why had she made up a lie that I pulled a placenta out of a mare and killed her? She smiled a huge smile and said, "Sorry Hon." She emanated pure evil that morning.

I had gone from horse breaker of the year to exile in shame overnight. After foolishly spending most of the money I had earned on a new car I had little left.

Counting my blessings, I had Raven and Emily, Andrew my cat (Sherman had disappeared at the farm), a beautiful new turbo Saab and Alberto.

Chapter 17

Argentina

Alberto wanted me to move to Argentina with him and it sounded like the perfect escape to me. I packed my life into nine boxes to take with me along with Raven, Emily, and Andrew, and put my new car in storage.

I was off and ready for my next adventure. Alberto's family had a flat in Buenos Aires where we could live, only a few miles from their apartment. I nearly lost the dogs in transit when we stopped for a layover in Chile. I had been allowed to get them out of their crates and walk them while we changed planes. They were doing fine. We walked, had a drink and some food, and then I loaded them back into their kennels and went inside. As I was standing inside watching them being loaded, I noticed that they were not loaded into the same plane that our luggage was. I told Alberto that the dogs were on the wrong plane and he didn't react. I ran outside and stopped the workers and demanded that they put the Dalmatians on the plane going to Argentina. It would have been a terrible mistake since the dogs were on a plane that would land in Brazil.

Finally we all landed together in Buenos Aires. Alberto and I were standing in a long line with the dogs and Andrew when an official picked Alberto out of the line. I saw Alberto reach into his pocket and pull out some money and we were then directed to leave the line and walk through customs. Corruption was blatant in Argentina and Alberto had paid the man a bribe to pass through customs without even looking at health certificates for the dogs and Andrew.

Alberto's Mother and sister, Trudi, were waiting at the airport to pick us up and take us to our flat. Alberto had told me that the flat was beautiful, with a nice balcony overlooking the city. He planned to knock a wall out to make a huge master bedroom. When we arrived at the flat, Deana, Alberto's mother, turned the key and opened the door proudly. The flat looked like a lower middle class apartment in the United States in the 1950's. Although I said nothing I couldn't hide the disappointment on my face. Deana said, " Oh no, she doesn't like it." I assured her that it was fine, just not quite what I was expecting.

Alberto had lied and this is what shocked me. The balcony was two feet wide and was only a few feet from the building next door. You couldn't even see the sky without leaning out over the banister and looking up. There was no view. As for knocking a wall out, the only wall to take down would have opened the bathroom to the tiny living room. I had a sick feeling in my stomach that everything about Alberto was a lie.

I have never done well in cities, and Buenos Aires was no exception. Alberto and I went to Palermo Racetrack a few times in the mornings. It was winter in Buenos Aires, with a damp cold that went right through me, no matter how well I dressed. I was dressed like an American in a winter ski jacket, jeans and sneakers, and the Argentines thought I was a boy. On the track they thought I was a boy jockey and Alberto would explain that I was his girlfriend. He was embarrassed of me and complained about my short hair and my clothes.

I thought that if I could at least ride maybe I could handle the city. Alberto introduced me to the trainers that he knew at Palermo and one of them did finally agree to let me get on some horses. I arrived the next morning at 5:00 a.m. in the cold, and hung around the barn all morning only to be ignored. Alberto explained that this is how it is done in Argentina. He said that if I showed up every day for a week they might actually put me on a horse. I said, "Fuck that shit!" and never went back to the track.

My days in Argentina were long and dreadful. I would take the dogs to a park and sit on a bench all day reading books. Raven and Emily didn't know how to be city dogs and instead of playing in the park they would sit on the bench with me. After a long day of sitting we would go to dinner at Alberto's parents' flat. Dinners in Argentina are served late and very formal. A maid would serve courses and appear when Deana rang a little bell. Alberto, his two sisters, mother, and father would all dress for dinner, but I refused to wear anything other than my jeans and sweatshirts. They were all well versed in how to carry on a proper dinner conversation, but I was not the least bit interested. I actually preferred it when they forgot about me, and spoke Spanish rather than English, so that I wouldn't even have to pretend I was interested. Every night at dinner Deana would make a point of asking me what I had done that day. My answer was always the same, a very simple, "Fuck all." Like clockwork they would gasp and someone would drop their fork, and Deana would nervously ring the bell for the maid. For two months this was my only source of amusement.

One day I was planning a trip on the subway to buy shoes. Alberto had picked on me for weeks about my sneakers so I agreed to at least look for comfortable shoes. I had never been on a subway before, so Alberto took me to the station and told me where to get off. I sat on the subway and nervously watched for my stop, but I didn't see it. Miles later at the end of the track, I got off thinking I must have missed my stop. I didn't know that if I stayed on the subway it would eventually go back to where I got on. This was before cell phones and the pay phones took tokens instead of money, so I couldn't even call for help. I was miles from home with no money and spoke very little Spanish. Panic was setting in so I sat down in a park and tried to stay calm. A man in a uniform looked safe enough to talk to so I tried to explain my dilemma in broken Spanish. He worked for the electric company and told me to get in his truck and he would take me back to Buenos Aires. We drove for miles before anything looked familiar to me and finally he stopped at a park on the outskirts of the city. He reached over and put his hand on my thigh. I was terrified and I screamed, opened the truck door, and ran for my life.

I finally made it home after walking a few miles and I was still mad and scared. I told Alberto what had happened to me and he laughed. Later that night at dinner I did actually have a story to tell and to my amazement they all laughed. Deana told me that there weren't as many sex offenders in Argentina as the United States, but they are far worse. Alberto's sister, Trudi, told me that the subway stop Alberto had instructed me to get off at didn't exist.

After this incident I became very depressed. I took the dogs out for short walks, but I thought I had seen the man who put his hand on my thigh in the park so I no longer went there. My days were spent mostly in bed. I would close the curtains and lie in bed all day, thinking that there was no escape from this dreadful life in Buenos Aires.

One night Alberto's best friend from boarding school, Alejandro, came to our flat to visit and meet me. I was so depressed that I couldn't get out of bed. I closed the door of the bedroom, drowning in misery. Alberto was mortified and didn't understand how thoroughly depressed

I had become. He could only see that I was being rude to his best friend. By this time I didn't care if Alberto was mortified. He had lied about Argentina and told me that I would love it and I hated it. He lied about my age, telling everyone I was twenty nine when I was really thirty one. He was embarrassed of me and my clothes, and for the life of me I couldn't figure out why he would have invited me to live in this God awful place.

Buenos Aires was a city that I detested and found the people even ruder than in New York City. In New York cars don't slow down for pedestrians, but in Buenos Aires they actually speed up and blow their horns at pedestrians. I had jumped out of the way many times to avoid being run over. In Buenos Aires the drivers drive like they are driving bumper cars. I saw people run into each other on the road and not even stop. Instead of stopping, they would scream at each other. I once saw a bus slam into a parked car in front of a busy restaurant and he just kept driving.

I have no sense of direction and was often lost when walking around Buenos Aires. When I asked strangers for directions in my broken Spanish, nine out of ten of them would give me a dirty look and walk right past me.

Alberto's family was very tight but almost in a sick way. They didn't seem to have any boundaries. When I first arrived in Buenos Aires my luggage had been lost, and I only had a few clothes to wear. Deana insisted that I help myself to everyone's closet. She said that in her family everything belonged to everyone. Months later when I finally left Argentina, they wore my clothes that I had left behind for Alberto to bring back to the States. Alberto generously donated most of my clothes to a poor family without my consent.

Deana thought she was being kind to me when she tried to teach me that I should serve Alberto and know my place. One rainy afternoon Alberto, his sisters, father, mother, and I were watching videos. When lunch was ready the girls served their father and then began to serve Alberto. Deana stopped them and asked why Susan wasn't serving Alberto. I replied that I would not serve him because he had legs.

Alberto had two sisters, Trudi, the youngest, and Natasha, the princess, who was two years older. Trudi and Alberto were very close and an outsider would have guessed that they were a couple. Trudi was very sweet and kind and everyone seemed to like her. She kept a safe distance from me.

Natasha was the epitome of an Argentine princess and I found her unbearable. She had dreams of becoming a fashion designer and clothes were the most important thing in her life. The maids always despised Natasha because she was such a pain in the ass. Her day always started with breakfast in bed served by the maid. After she finished complaining about her breakfast (either it was served badly or not cooked to her liking), she would slowly get out of bed. She would then lounge around the house in her pajamas until at least noon. The first time I saw her in her pajamas at noon I asked her if she was sick.

One day I arrived at Alberto's parents flat for dinner and Natasha was very agitated. This was not unusual for her, but I had never seen her quite this distraught. She was pacing and smoking, waiting for me to ask what the problem was. Finally I asked her what was wrong. She told me that she had come home that afternoon and found the maid sitting in the living room on one of their good chairs. She said "Can you imagine, Susan, I walked in the door and there she was, sitting in that chair" as she pointed to a big comfortable overstuffed chair in the living room. In Natasha's world maids weren't good enough to sit in the best chair in the living room.

I did get along with Alberto's father, Jerry. He was a very handsome man and was employed by an American company in Buenos Aires. He was paid well enough to afford a flat in Buenos Aires and a farm in the south of Argentina, and he drove a company car. He was light hearted and seemed to see through the drama of his family. He didn't like the city and his dream was to retire on his farm in Baralochi and grow raspberries.

I found a park in the city that had a cement pond where people rented paddle boats. It was a quiet place where I could sit with the dogs and cry unnoticed. One day Alberto followed me there and caught me crying. He and I were barely speaking since my 'rudeness' with Alexandro. When he found me in tears, instead of consoling me, he yelled at me. He demanded to know why I didn't go back to California if I was so miserable. My answer was that I didn't have money to fly home and take my dogs and Andrew. He then shared that I had a round-trip ticket and could leave whenever I wanted to. Alberto had handled all of our travel plans and I didn't know I had a round-trip ticket. Had I known, I would have been long gone. I left three days later.

Alberto wanted to stay in Argentina for another three weeks and spend time with his family. He would bring Raven, Emily, and Andrew back to the States with him. I didn't even know where I would be staying so this was the best I could do for my animals.

I arrived in L.A., got my beautiful new car out of storage and drove to Del Mar. I now appreciated things like a nice road and my own car that I had taken for granted before. I felt my depression lift as I drove from L.A. back to my world.

It took me only an hour on the backside of the track at Del Mar to run into Freddy, a friend and rider I had met at Westerly. He was renting a house near the beach and invited me to stay with him for the rest of the summer. He knew that I was with Alberto and only offered me the room to help me out, no strings attached.

I felt so happy to be back in California where I had some control over my life. The first few days I hung out at my old favorite beaches enjoying the warm sun. Freddy was French and had no problem going to Blacks, the local nude beach with me. Although I missed my animals I was no longer depressed. I felt like an escaped prisoner. The hot summer sun warmed my soul.

Three weeks later when Del Mar was nearly over, Alberto arrived with Raven, Emily, and Andrew. Alberto had been taking risks in Buenos Aires with the dogs that I would never have taken and I was so relieved that they survived. They were both trained to heel off leash from their dog show days. To show off, Alberto had been walking them off leash in downtown Buenos Aires. When he first told me how good they were off leash I begged him not to risk their lives in busy city traffic. As I was to later learn, Alberto had no conception of safety for animals. His goal was to be the man, the Argentine man, who must be treated with respect at all times. It was his belief that a good woman would agree with him even when he was wrong. I couldn't do that.

Chapter 18

The Gardner Ranch

In the three weeks I had been in Del Mar I was busy finding horses to break and planned on returning to the Gardner Ranch. I had eight horses lined up to ship in for breaking in September. My cute little house was not available, but the house next door would soon be mine. Alberto wanted to move to Santa Ynez with me and I was willing to give it a try. Anyone with any self-worth would have already sent him packing.

We rented a U-Haul for my furniture that had been in storage in L.A. and made the two and a half hour drive to Santa Ynez. When we arrived at the Gardner Ranch I turned the dogs loose to play on their old turf. We were all thrilled to be back.

As Alberto and I we were unloading the U- Haul truck, old Peggy Gardner came by to welcome me home and asked me if I could help the vet pull blood from a weanling colt. Her ranch workers were gone for the day and the young colt was difficult to handle. I would never say no to Peggy and was happy to help. Alberto was annoyed and told me that I should have just told her I was busy. The vet was due any minute so I walked out to the paddock to catch the weanling. He was barely halter broke and hadn't been handled much, so I was following him around his corral quietly and waiting for Dr. Sands to help me catch him. Bill Sands was a good horseman, and I knew that together we could corner the colt, get a lead rope on him, and pull his blood. Just as Bill arrived, Alberto the 'Man' barged into the corral, cornered the colt by himself, and then roughly reached out to grab his halter. The frightened colt reared up and struck out at Alberto, hitting him in the face. Realizing that he didn't have the skill to catch this colt, Alberto went back to the house. I was ashamed of him, acting like an Argentine idiot in front of the vet. Bill and I caught the colt a few minutes later and pulled his blood without a problem.

Alberto was furious and somehow it was my fault that he had gotten hurt. He already had a huge black eye. He demanded that I give him the keys to my car and I refused so he left in the U-Haul van. Billy Gardner had seen us arguing and he saw Alberto with a black eye leaving in a U-Haul. He thought I had given him the black eye and was laughing his ass off as he teased me about hitting men.

I was confused. I had done nothing wrong, in fact I felt I had done everything right, but Alberto was mad at me. What I didn't fully understand then was Alberto's need to be the 'Man.' He expected me to know my place, a few paces behind him. Even though I had far more knowledge and experience than Alberto did with horses, he wanted me to defer to him. I couldn't do that.

My horses shipped in and I landed a local client with several horses. My immediate future was looking good. I did all of the breaking myself and had only one groom for twelve horses. There was plenty of work to be done.

Raven, Emily, and Andrew spent most of their days in the barn with me. Alberto was the only one at home. Our house was very close to the training barn, and whenever I went to the house, Alberto was doing nothing. He could do nothing all day, every day. He wasn't earning any money in Santa Ynez and wanted to spend more time in L.A. at the track, but didn't have a car. Although I didn't like sharing my car with him, I let him take it on weekends. This left me stranded at the ranch with no transportation. When Alberto would return, my dream car would be trashed. It was like I had loaned my car to a five-year-old, and it would come back with chocolate on the seats and steering wheel. If I left it for him to clean, the chocolate would grow mold.

One thing I did notice was that when Alberto was away for a weekend I was happy and had plenty of energy. When he returned, I felt zapped. I have always been high energy, but trying to get along with Alberto absolutely drained me. After several weekends of feeling happy alone, even without a car, I told Alberto that I wanted him to leave. I explained that I was doing all the work and all he did is make a mess of the house and my car, leaving me exhausted. I left the house to take the dogs for a long quiet walk, and when I returned, Alberto was walking from the bedroom to the kitchen with a big suitcase. His head was hanging and I could see that he didn't really want to go. I made a life altering decision and told him he could stay, but we needed to make some changes. He put his suitcase down in the kitchen and we kissed and made up. Three days later that suitcase was still in the kitchen. When I picked it up to put it away, I found that it was empty.

Alberto didn't like to get dirty and thought he was too good to do ranch work. Somehow, even though he had very little experience working with young Thoroughbred racehorses, in his macho mind he was a good hand. He was one of the worst horsemen I had ever met, and he was to stay that way. When someone is busy pretending to know everything, there is very little room to learn. I was doing all of the breaking, but I thought Alberto could as least help the groom, and get on some horses once I had them broke. He had won a small town rodeo in Argentina riding a bronco and considered himself to be a good rider.

My horses didn't like Alberto and bucked him off repeatedly. He had heavy, insensitive, hands, and when the horses tensed up with him because they didn't like his heavy hands, he would grab them tightly with his legs and stick his heels into their sides. This would set off a rodeo and he couldn't even stay on three jumps. These were all horses that I had broke, and they had never bucked. I couldn't have Alberto 'un-breaking' them, so after seeing how bad a rider he was I told him not to bother.

Alberto happily went back to sitting in the house all day. When I went down to the house for a quick lunch break, the house that was clean in the morning would already be a mess. Alberto wouldn't take his shoes off before entering and would track dirt and mud through the house. He always made a big production out of preparing his breakfast and the pots and pans would be stacked up in the sink. If he had already made his lunch, there would be food spilled and smeared on the counters and floor. It was like I had left a very bad five-year-old alone in the house. Deep inside me a little voice said, 'What about me?'

I was angry all the time now. My only breaks were when I gave Alberto my car and he was gone. We would fight, and when I lost control, Alberto would point at me and tell me I was crazy. I half believed him because I was acting crazy. When I lost my temper, I would throw things and hit Alberto. I was angry that he sat all day while I worked my ass off, and I was angry that he wasn't capable of helping out in the barn. He proved how incompetent he was over and over.

One day Alberto was helping the groom, Francisco, in the barn. It was lunch time, I had just gotten off my last horse and was starving. Francisco was a good horseman and I trusted him to give the horse a bath and cool him out while I ran down to the house for a quick lunch. I was back in the barn thirty minutes later and the horse I left with Alberto and Francisco was down in his stall and looked miserable. I got him up and saw that he had a hock that was badly swollen. I took his temperature and it was close to 105 degrees. Normal horse temperature is 99-101. This horse was fine thirty minutes earlier, I had just ridden him. I called the vet and quizzed Francisco, but he would only say, "Ask Alberto." When I asked Alberto, he told me that the horse didn't want to walk on to the wash rack so he had gotten behind him with a pitchfork to make him walk forward. Instead of walking forward, the horse had kicked at the pitchfork and punctured his hock joint. An infection in a joint on a horse is a nightmare and sometimes they don't even survive. Alberto, through his ignorance, had stupidly injured a horse and then not even treated the injury. This poor horse was very sick for months and I couldn't even tell the vet or the owner how he had gotten hurt.

Life went on like this for quite some time. I was mad that Alberto was lazy and preferred to sit all day. If I made him help in the barn, a disaster was sure to follow. I was tired and miserable.

Alberto decided to go to Argentina to find horses to sell and would be gone for three weeks. His sister, Natasha, the Argentine princess, had been writing to me from Buenos Aires and wanted to visit. She wrote about wanting to help me with the horses and work on the farm. Although this was hard to even imagine, somehow I believed her. I was terribly naïve still. She arrived as Alberto was leaving.

Natasha's visit was doomed from the start. I met her at LAX and although the other passengers looked tired after their long flight from Buenos Aires, Natasha's clothes and make up were perfect. She was the last one to make it to the baggage area where she had kept me waiting while she changed her clothes and did her hair and makeup. Could I have expected anything different from Princess Natasha? We waited and waited for her luggage and finally several over-sized, cheap suitcases arrived in the baggage claim area. I jokingly asked her if she was moving in for life. One of the cheap suitcases had been torn in transit and Natasha was outraged. She demanded to see a manager and had to make a written formal complaint about the damage to her cheap luggage. It didn't matter that I had already been waiting for over an hour for her.

On the way home we stopped in L.A. for gas and she got out of the car while I pumped the gas. I heard a commotion and sensed danger and I told Natasha to get back in the car. She didn't move and casually asked why just as three men ran within inches of us chasing another man, and they all were carrying clubs. I felt the adrenalin they were pumping and was amazed at my level of awareness. Oddly enough, Natasha didn't even blink.

Natasha slept in on her first day at the ranch and missed most of the morning training routine. She casually walked up to the barn in perfect clothes and matching shoes at 11:00 a.m. She had brought twenty-four pairs of shoes with her from Argentina. I gave her the benefit of the doubt and thought she must be very tired from the trip. The next three days were the same. She never appeared before 11:00 a.m. and her clothes were always perfect with matching shoes. Finally I asked her what her plans were. She had written that she wanted to help with the horses but couldn't get out of bed. She was offended that I questioned her integrity and promised to get up early and help the next morning.

Natasha was about as helpful as Alberto. I gave her some easy tasks to do, like mixing hoof dressing, and she made a mess of everything. It actually took me longer to do my work when she was 'helping' me. I had a quad with a little flatbed trailer that I used to clean my outside pens. When the trailer was full I would drive to the dump and unload it. One morning when Natasha had been more useless than her normal useless, I was driving the quad while she sat in the front of the trailer. I aimed for a huge mud puddle and splashed her with muddy water from head to toe. She didn't see me laughing and I let her think it had been an accident.

Natasha wanted to ride my pony horse, Gus. She claimed to be a good rider. I had a filly I was breaking who was difficult and needed to either go with a pony or go to the round pen before I took her to the track. The filly wanted to stop and rear instead of going forward so I was worried that she would fall on me. My routine of going to the round pen first to get her going, and then head to the track at a trot kept us both safe, but it took more time. It would be just as safe to get on her in her stall, hit her once and then head to the track trotting with the pony. Natasha knew that I wanted to take the filly out at 8:00 and I had both my filly and the pony tacked and ready to go. I was already annoyed when Natasha casually walked into the barn wearing perfect clothes with shoes to match a half hour later. I had told Natasha my plan and explained that all she had to do was stay with me. She knew that the filly was dangerous and there was no room for mistakes. I got on the filly, hit her once and said "Let's go" to Natasha, who was sitting on the pony. Natasha asked, "Go where?" and remained still on the pony. I calmly said, "Start jogging and stay with me on the track." Natasha said, "What is a jog?" I knew I was fucked. I told her just to stay where she was and I went to the track alone. The filly tried to rear a few times but I made it back safely. I put her and the pony away and then went to the house to deal with Natasha.

I had a dream the night before that I was in excruciating pain and couldn't move my neck. I realized now, that Natasha was the pain in my neck, and she must go away. I told her that she had put me in danger while playing princess, and it was time for her to leave. How dare she risk my safety when I had carefully explained how important her role on the pony was. She had assured me over and over that she knew how to ride, but she didn't even know what a trot was. She was borrowing her aunt Margarita's car so it was very possible for her to leave immediately. Instead of leaving, she got on the phone and called Alberto in Argentina and everyone she knew in the States, and told them I was crazy. Alberto called me and told me that I couldn't kick Natasha out and that this incident was entirely my fault for believing that she could ride the pony. I stood firm on my decision and Natasha left the next day. For the next three days Alberto's friends and family called me to ask how I was. Finally, someone told me that Natasha had called everyone that she knew in the U.S. and told them that I had suffered a breakdown and thrown her out of my house for no reason at all.

Alberto's three week trip to Argentina stretched into a three month long trip. In his absence I was happy, my car and house were clean, and the horses were not getting hurt. I had enough energy to make frequent trips to my favorite beach in the afternoons when all of my horse work was finished.

When Alberto finally returned, I really wasn't all that happy to see him. I had serious doubts about whether I should pick him up at the airport and made him wait three hours for me. My life had been very smooth with him gone. Again, I wondered if it wouldn't be better to get him out of my life. On paper, it was an easy decision. He contributed nothing and made life more difficult for me. Emotionally, I was still in that terrible self-loathing place where a man like Alberto fit perfectly. He treated me as badly as I treated myself. He could be very charming and soon wormed his way back into my heart.

Billy Gardner now managed the ranch and they were having financial difficulties. He gave me notice that my rent was to double, effective immediately. It was spring and my horses had all shipped out, so moving wasn't difficult. We rented a house in Santa Ynez for a few months. It was hard for me to live in town, even a small town, but Alberto loved it. The first thing he did was order cable TV and the TV was on all day. He continued to do nothing most days except when he was busy messing up the house.

Chapter 19

Santa Ynez

Natasha had not returned to Argentina and now lived in a rented apartment in Beverly Hills. She was in a nice neighborhood, with big trees lining the sidewalks and old houses that had been converted into apartments. Many of her neighbors were young Argentine women. The other side of her street was Culver City. She made sure that we all knew that she was on the Beverly Hills side.

She had forgiven me for throwing her out of the Gardner Ranch house and visited us often in Santa Ynez. Her weekend visits would start on Friday and she wouldn't leave until Monday morning. She had a way of treating me like a maid in my own house. I did not look forward to her visits.

Alberto had sold a horse and earned some money and I had done well breaking horses. For once we had some extra money in the bank. Natasha asked for a $1,000 loan to buy a car, and Alberto agreed without even discussing it with me. Later when I protested, he could only say, "She is my sister and she will pay us back." She bought an old Subaru that ran well but wasn't very pretty.

One weekend Natasha arrived for her long visit and she was crying. When I asked her what was wrong she sobbed that she wanted a Jaguar, not a Subaru. This was just the beginning of a very strange weekend. I had a few horses in training at a farm in Los Alamos and I left Natasha alone in the house all morning while I trained my horses. When I returned, I wanted to take a quick shower, and although Natasha had a nice guest bathroom, she had used my shower. My towel was wet and my hairbrush was left out on the counter. It looked like I had already used my shower. After I showered I went into the kitchen to make lunch and noticed that my vitamins that I always left next to the kitchen sink were gone. I looked everywhere knowing that I couldn't misplace them because they were always next to the sink in the kitchen. I didn't find them that day. I have never worn jewelry, but I had one gold chain that Scott had given me that I kept it in a dresser drawer. When I checked to see if it was there I wasn't surprised to find it missing. Alberto had been in L.A. and when he returned I told him what a strange day it had been. He told me I must have misplaced my gold chain and vitamins. Months later I found the vitamins hidden in the back of the freezer but never did find the chain that Scott had given me.

Summer is always the slow season for breaking horses. I was lucky to have a few lay-ups, but nothing in training. Alberto had sold a horse a couple of months before, but money was getting tight. Natasha had not paid back the $1,000 that she had borrowed and I thought that now would be a good time. She had found work in L.A. as a legal translator and was earning good money. Alberto really didn't want to ask her to pay back the loan, but I insisted. When she arrived the next weekend for her long visit, Alberto asked her when she could start to pay on the loan. Natasha flew into a rage and immediately drew up a payment plan of $100 per month for ten months. She was absolutely indignant that Alberto has asked her to pay back the money. After all, it was only for a Subaru, not the Jaguar that she needed. She practically threw her hand written payment plan at Alberto and then left our house. She made only one payment. She and Alberto never mentioned it again.

An old client of mine from Chino called and wanted to send me all of his horses. He had ten horses, mostly mares and foals, a weanling, a yearling and a two-year-old. I knew the man to be a good owner and fast pay, so I agreed to take his horses. It made more sense to rent a small farm than to pay a ranch owner most of my profit to board these horses. We found a nice little ranch on two acres in Santa Ynez. The neighborhood was very upscale, with huge houses and backyard horse properties. Our house was 3,500 square feet with a pool. This was way more house than we needed, but the rent was reasonable and we needed the pasture space. I loved the pool and swam every day that the water temperature was over 65 degrees.

The neighbors were all very friendly and several of them had empty horse corrals in their backyards. Many of the neighbors walked their dogs around the neighborhood and they all stopped to introduce themselves.

Alberto had become friends with a Brazilian trainer, A.C. Vila, who wanted to send us his lay-ups. It wasn't long before we had horses in our backyard and two other backyards on our street. There was a ton of work to care for these horses properly and I did it all, with very little help from Alberto.

Alberto invited Gus, an old school friend to visit from Argentina. Gus was from a very wealthy nouveau riche family who had made a fortune investing in amusement parks. Alberto explained to me that because they didn't come from 'old money,' Gus had been snubbed at boarding school. I liked Gus because he was down to earth and always happy. One morning Alberto and Gus went to town and came back with a beautiful new Mitsubishi mountain bike. Gus said it was for me and I was as happy as a little girl would be with her first bike. No one had ever given me a bike and it would be so useful, since I had horses at three different properties on our street. Alberto interrupted Gus to inform me that the bike wasn't for me, that he had bought himself a bike. I was crushed and couldn't hide my disappointment. Gus said, "Oh look at her face" and tried to hug me but I shrugged him off and walked away. I silently chastised myself for being stupid enough to believe that anyone would be kind enough to give me a bike.

We had agreed to be responsible for the landscaping at our rented house in return for reduced rent. This too, became my responsibility. The front yard was large and I mowed it with a push mower. Alberto said that he would be willing to mow if we had a riding mower. I didn't have time to argue and it was easier to just mow it myself. The neighbors often commented on how hard I worked and asked me what Alberto was doing. I never answered them because I was too embarrassed by the truth, that Alberto did as little as possible, always.

Alberto's dream was to be a horse breeder. His idols were the famous Thoroughbred breeders and trainers in Argentina. Most Thoroughbred breeders can quote bloodlines from memory and the good breeders also have an eye for a horse. Alberto had a fantastic memory and could quote bloodlines all day, but he had no eye.

Every January the Barretts sales company hosted a Thoroughbred mixed sale, and Alberto wanted me to go and look at a list of mares. He had been selling mares with good bloodlines as broodmare prospects to Argentina.

My friend Lisa from Oakview Ranch was selling a two-year-old at the sale, and she invited me stay with her in North Hollywood, at her brother's house. We had too much fun with her brother that night and got very drunk. We giggled and laughed long into the night.

The next morning I had to be at the sale early to look at the list of horses that Alberto had given me. I was at the sale early, but I was so hung over that I had to duck into the ladies room several times to throw up. Most of the mares on Alberto's list had serious confirmation faults and were easy to discard. I called him and told him of each mare's faults. He thought I was being too critical and wanted me to look at them all again.

Finally I looked at the last horse on the list, a gray mare with a beautiful pedigree. She was very fat and someone (another horse) had eaten her tail so she was unusual looking. But, if you could see through the fat and disregard the tail, she looked like an athlete. I liked her, and the only thing I didn't check were her feet. She was wearing wide web aluminum shoes that signified a serious foot problem. I was so hung over from drinking all night with Lisa and her brother that I couldn't bend over to pick up a foot without throwing up. I called Alberto and told him that this mare was worth buying and he told me to bid up to $3,000 for her. She was worth more than $3,000 in Argentina as a broodmare so we wouldn't lose anything at that price.

The mare's name was First Spring and I was the only bidder at $1,200. I had a sick feeling that I had missed something when no one bid against me. After I signed the paperwork, I went back to the barn area to have another look at our new mare. It was then that I saw the shoes for the first time. I felt like such a fuck up because I knew that had I not been hung over, I would never have missed those shoes.

Alberto loved to catch me in a mistake so I didn't tell him that I had missed the wide web aluminum shoes. I took Spring home and unloaded her at our house. Alberto couldn't see through the fat and missing tail and thought I had failed miserably. He didn't even notice the shoes. He was very condescending as he gave me a hug and thanked me for trying. I pointed out that underneath the fat was a body of an athlete but he couldn't see it. He was happy that I had only paid $1,200 for her and told me that from now on he would go to the sales instead of me.

Although Spring was bought as a broodmare prospect when I turned her out in our backyard, on hard ground, with the other mares she didn't act like a broodmare. She played and ran circles around the other mares all day. The ground in our paddocks was bad, very hard, and mostly clay. A horse with sore feet would have been suffering, not playing. I had my vet look at her feet and he said that he didn't even want to take my money to x-ray her, that the shoes were all the proof he needed to know that she probably had a serious hoof disease, Navicular. I watched Spring play harder and harder over the next couple of weeks and I chose to disregard the vet's opinion and put her in training. Alberto was sure that I would be wasting my time, but I insisted on following my intuition.

I had rented stalls from Millwood Richards at Silent Oaks Farm and was ready to bring horses in to break. One more horse wouldn't be that much additional work. Spring loved training and was fun to ride. She lost the fat and turned into a beautiful athlete. I galloped her for three months and then started working her. Alberto wasn't the least bit interested until Spring worked her first half mile in 48 seconds flat. 48 seconds is a good time on a mile track. Silent Oaks had only a half mile track with tight turns. I had worked her myself, with a tight hold and still she went in 48 flat.

Spring shipped into Santa Anita and broke her maiden for $32,000, and then won her next start for $20,000 and got claimed. We made a lot of money on her, but I cried all the way home from Santa Anita when she got claimed. I loved her and didn't want to lose her.

Alberto had sold a horse in New York the year before, and as a commission, he took a yearling filly, Far Frau. Sally, my old friend from Oklahoma agreed to keep her for a year at her ranch in Minnesota until she was old enough to break. When Far Frau was two years old, Sally trailered her to New Mexico for us and I had to pick her up. We had bought an old truck and a new two horse trailer. I was looking forward to a road trip. Alberto was on yet another trip to Argentina and had been gone for three months. Sally wasn't familiar with the ranch where she would be dropping Far Frau off, and we agreed it would be best to pick her up immediately, instead of leaving her with strangers.

This was to be my first long road trip hauling a horse and I didn't want to go alone, so I invited Faith, an English woman I had met at Silent Oaks Farm. Faith had met Millwood Richards in England while at a horse breaking demonstration for the Queen, and she had traveled to Silent Oaks Farm to learn his breaking method. Once she arrived at the farm she told me she realized that instead of making the world a better place for horses as he claimed to be doing, Millwood was making the world a better place for himself. She was horrified that the horses in stalls in the training barn all had filthy water and set about cleaning each automatic waterer. Faith was eccentric but had a wonderful heart. She wanted to see New Mexico so we were off. It was the middle of summer and I didn't have horses in training, but had twelve horses at home that my groom, Francisco, would be caring for. I planned on driving nonstop and being home in three days.

Our trip went well to New Mexico and we picked up Far Frau on schedule. On the way back I was getting tired and asked Faith to drive. Before she left she told me she was a good driver, but when I needed her to drive she admitted she couldn't drive a stick shift. There was nothing I could do but take this in stride and I instructed her to keep talking to me so that I stayed awake. I had a feeling that I should get home fast.

We arrived safely at home in two and a half days, way ahead of schedule. When I pulled into my driveway my intuition that I needed to get home fast was confirmed. It was really hot and had been over 100 degrees every day since we had left. The horses had tipped over their empty water troughs and were fighting because they were desperately thirsty. I ran to the hose and got water to them as quickly as I could. My poor horses were unbearably thirsty, in extreme heat, and fighting to drink. I was so angry that I screamed at the sky. My horses had never been thirsty while in my care. I was crying, ranting, and screaming, while running around getting water to everyone. If Francisco had been there, I am sure I would have killed him. He showed up a few hours later smelling like alcohol and I fired him on the spot. His wife called me for days trying to talk me into hiring him back.

I finally told her that her husband was very lucky to even be alive, since I wanted to murder him for the suffering he had inflicted on my horses.

Far Frau was easy to break and I had high hopes for her as a racehorse. She loved to train, had a nice athletic body, and perfect legs. She wasn't sweet like First Spring, but very serious for a young horse. Alberto planned on selling her to Argentina as soon as she was broke. I wanted to keep Far Frau and run her and we went round and round about this. Alberto thought that I had fallen in love with this young filly and wasn't thinking like a professional. Nothing could have been further from the truth. I admired her athletic ability, but she wasn't personable. My confidence was growing since I had picked a winner against all odds with Spring, and I wouldn't take no for an answer. Alberto brought several prospective buyers to the farm to look at Far Frau and I ruined any chance of selling her. Besides my negative rants about the 'piece of shit filly', I galloped her slow and missed every lead change on purpose. I would get off and say, "Damn filly is too sore to change leads."

Since we couldn't sell her, we sent her to the track when she was ready. Twenty-one days after she arrived at Santa Anita, she ran third in her first start. I was thrilled that my intuition was validated once again, this girl could run.

Her next two starts were bad. After the last bad start, the trainer told me she couldn't run, just didn't have any ability. I was crushed and couldn't believe that I was wrong. I walked back to the barn after the race following my filly and we both had our heads down. I sat in her stall and watched the hot walker cooling her out. When she had walked about ten minutes I saw gobs of thick yellow snot coming out of her nose. I casually asked the groom how long the snotty nose had been going on and he told me since after her first race. I asked him what they were doing for her and he showed me with a rub rag how that they had been wiping her nose. That was all they were doing, wiping her snotty nose! This poor girl had been running sick and still she tried. I picked her up the next day and brought her home for my vet to treat. He scoped her and found one of the worst throat and lung infections he had ever seen. We treated her with antibiotics and a topical throat flush for thirty days before we had the infection under control.

When Far Frau was healthy again I started her back in training at the farm and then shipped her in to a different trainer at Santa Anita. She won four races and over $65,000. I was validated once again by a racehorse.

Alberto never acknowledged that I might have a good eye and a good feel for racing prospects. My success was a threat to him. If he picked out a horse to buy and I disagreed, he turned it into a personal attack against him. He was still stuck on his idea that I should know my place. It didn't matter that my racing prospects won races and his didn't even make it to the races.

My breaking business was going very well with the help of trainer Jude Feld. Jude had an owner who bred or bought at least fifteen yearlings every year and they wanted me to break them. I was still renting stalls from Silent Oaks Farm and had a good groom, Chewy. Chewy really cared about the horses and worked his butt off to make them happy. His only fault was his memory and he would often forget important things. One day I was exasperated that he had forgotten a filly on the hot walker and she had walked for three hours instead of thirty minutes. I was really mad at myself because I had walked by her empty stall several times before I noticed that she had been out for far too long. I asked Chewy what his problem was; how could he just forget about the poor horse. His reply was so sad that I will remember it always. He told me that when he was young in Mexico his family didn't have enough food to feed him and his brain had been affected. Poor Chewy had a heart of gold. I learned what compassion felt like on that day.

I was grossing over $20,000 per month on my breaking business and my net profit was healthy. Alberto spent more and more time in Argentina. The trips were always for business and always stretched from three weeks to three months. His business wasn't going well. He rarely sold a horse and he resented that I earned more money than he did.

We moved down the street in Santa Ynez to a better horse property, but it also required more maintenance. We had grass pastures that needed to be irrigated, an arena that needed to be dragged, paddocks to clean, and a yard to mow. The landlord, Denny, had showed Alberto how to use the tractors and riding lawn mowers. Denny didn't realize that as usual, I would be doing all the work. After visiting a few times,

Denny said that he should have taken the time to show me how everything worked, not Alberto.

Alberto had always wanted a riding lawn mower and now we had two of them. He mowed once and looked quite happy with his bottle of beer, but once was enough for him. After that, the yard became another one of my responsibilities.

It was a continual source of amazement for me to witness how an Argentine man thinks. Alberto was only an inch taller than me so everything about me was a threat to him. It was deeply instilled in him that a woman should serve her man. I was beginning to see him as an excuse of a man who was lazy and egocentric.

Alberto could not take even the most basic common sense direction from me. One day after a rain, Alberto was riding a nice yearling colt that I had just broke. The arena was sand and mostly good footing even after a rain, but there was one big puddle that wasn't safe. I had stumbled twice on other horses in the puddle already, so I told Alberto not to ride through the puddle. As soon as I said that, he steered his horse right into the middle of the puddle. The young horse stumbled, and immediately went lame. The horse had twisted his ankle and his poor little face contorted in pain. Alberto thought the young colt should be tougher and was going to continue trotting him even though he was dead lame, but I would not allow it. It took me screaming at him to 'get the fuck off that poor horse' to make him stop.

I had a round pen and an arena at home now so I could do my first thirty days of breaking from home. When they were ready to track, we would ship them to Silent Oaks Farm. We also had at least six lay-ups most of the time from Alberto's trainer friend, Vila. Our farm was full and busy.

Vila was Brazilian and he and Alberto shared similar attitudes about women. He wanted things done his way. He and I disagreed on almost everything. One point he was adamant about was that he wanted his horses to all go barefoot while they were laid up at our farm. Most of the horses that have been running have sore, bruised feet and unhealthy soles and walls. When I pulled their shoes they went dead lame within a day. Some of them would get abscesses in their feet and need to be soaked in hot water and Epsom salt and then poulticed to draw the abscess out. A hoof abscess is extremely painful and can even be mistaken for a fractured bone in the hoof.

One of Vila's horses, Alson, had particularly bad feet. I had pulled his shoes and he had already abscessed three times. I filled him with bute for the pain, and then soaked and poulticed him each time. Alson was an older gelding and very sweet and kind. One day it was lunch time and I was hot, thirsty, and starving, when Alberto came down to the barn to ask me what I was making for lunch. Even though Alberto had done nothing all morning he expected me to make him lunch. We went through this every day, and every day I told him I had no intention of making his lunch. On this day as I was walking out of the barn, I noticed Alson was standing on three legs and holding up a sore hoof. He had been fine earlier in the morning but obviously was in distress now with yet another abscess. I told Alberto that it was his turn to soak and poultice Alson, since it was his idiot client that refused to allow the horse to wear shoes. Alberto took one look at Alson holding his leg up in extreme pain and walked out of the barn. He told me it was lunchtime and Alson must wait. I can't bear to see an animal in pain, especially a sweet kind horse like Alson, so I took care of him. When I finished soaking and poulticing Alson, I went up to the house, called the horse shoer and ordered shoes for all of Vila's horses. I had my vet and shoer to back me up because Vila didn't understand that his horses just couldn't go barefoot. They were all in danger of foundering and that would end their careers as racehorses. I knew Vila and Alberto would be furious, but I also knew that if I didn't act, it would be my fault when they all foundered. I couldn't let a pair of idiots cloud my judgment.

Vila bought a two year colt from Alberto in Argentina and was complaining that the horse wasn't broke and didn't know how to turn right or left. I found this hard to believe since the gauchos in Argentina literally break horses to death. They are so rough that at least two out of every five horses die while they are being broke. The horses who survive are always well behaved and know how to turn and stop. Vila sent the colt to me and I checked his mouth before I rode him. This poor colt had huge open cuts in his mouth because his teeth hadn't been worked on. Horses need their teeth floated (filed down) to eliminate sharp edges that will cut their mouths. My vet did his teeth, I gave him some time to heal and he ended up being very well broke.

His problem was only that his mouth hurt and Vila should have been the one to find the problem. In typical South American style Vila blamed everyone including me. I think he despised me because I found the problem in minutes that he hadn't found in weeks.

Alberto and I were fighting all the time now. Every fight would end with him yelling, "You don't know your place" and I would scream, "I am equal." I was always tired because I was working so hard and I had little patience for Alberto. I ran the farm, the house, the books, and even was responsible for car and truck maintenance. Most of the money I earned went right back into the farm and our own horses.

We were living Alberto's dream of breeding horses and it was very expensive to raise horses in California. We rented some big green pastures on the farm that bordered our property and did a good job raising our youngsters. The only thing they lacked was speed. I would sit on the fence and watch the babies run and play, but only one or two of them looked like they might be runners. The others looked more like beautiful young riding horses to me. Alberto disagreed and was sure that he had bred outstanding racehorses.

For the eight months that I had horses to break, we managed to pay all of our bills and stay on top of everything. In the summer when Alberto needed to pick up the slack and earn money, we went broke, and somehow that was always my fault. When breaking season started again in the fall, it would take at least two months just to get caught up on our bills. I never felt financially secure with Alberto. If he needed money his first thought was always who could he borrow money from. His next thought would be 'what could he sell of mine to get money?'

He almost talked me into selling Gus, my pony horse and favorite riding horse. He desperately needed money to cover a debt in Argentina and I agreed to sell Gus and give him the money. I showed Gus to a hunter/jumper trainer and was offered $5,000 to be paid the following day. I couldn't sleep that night because I loved Gus, he was a wonderful pony horse and I needed him. The next day I backed out of the deal. For once I looked out for myself, but Alberto was furious. He said that if I loved him and was a supportive wife, I would have sold my pony for him. I knew that I loved Gus but wasn't so sure that I loved Alberto. It had become painfully obvious that Alberto would always have money problems and that selling Gus would only be a temporary fix.

Our fights escalated to violence more often than not. Alberto would never hit a woman, but I had no problem with attacking him. I would get so mad at him that I couldn't control myself and I would hit him hard, usually in the face with my fist. Once after a particularly bad fight, Alberto told me that he couldn't live like this anymore and that if I continued to hit him he would leave. Since I had treated Gary the same way, with violence, it really did look like I had a problem. Alberto suggested that the next time that I felt like hitting him I should just turn and walk away. I agreed to try this instead of hitting him.

My first test came about a week later. Natasha, the princess, had arrived for another long weekend and had brought her roommate Alexandra with her. It was a beautiful Saturday afternoon and I had been riding all morning and was tired and hungry, but excited because Sunday was my day off. A day off wasn't really a day off for me. I would give my groom the day off and turn the horses all out in paddocks to roll and play. I always looked forward to my Saturday afternoons by the pool and an easy day on Sunday.

When I arrived home, the first thing I saw was my new coffee/cappuccino machine taken apart in pieces that were scattered around the kitchen. The machine was expensive and I had bought it as a rare gift for myself, because I was working so hard and I wanted cappuccino in the mornings.

Natasha and Alexandra were sitting by the pool and barely said hello to me, but asked me what was for lunch. They had made a mess of the house and the pool area with clothes and garbage from Burger King thrown on the ground. Trying hard to stay calm I found Alberto and told him that we had a problem. I knew that I shouldn't have to explain that I was tired and hungry since I had just galloped twenty green horses. I told Alberto that I couldn't deal with two Argentine princesses right now who had made a mess of the pool area and my house. He refused to step in and told me to handle it myself. I told him that if I did, he wouldn't like it.

I went back out to the pool and told the girls that they had overstayed their welcome and must leave now. I think I could have left it at that if Natasha hadn't told me I was crazy. That is all it took, and I went off. I told her that I was sick of her treating me like a maid in my own house, making a mess of the pool, leaving her clothes all over the house, and how dare she take my new coffee machine apart. I yelled, "Get the fuck out! Out! Out!" The princesses were ducking for cover and were gone within a few minutes.

Natasha only stopped long enough to tell Alberto how crazy I was and what I had done to them. Once they were gone Alberto asked me why I had thrown the girls out. I reminded him that I had asked him to handle it and he refused. Now he was telling me that I had gone about it all wrong. I calmly turned around and walked away from Alberto so that I wouldn't hit him. A voice in my head was saying, "I am walking away, I am walking away." Then Alberto said, "Natasha is right, you are crazy." It was then that the voice in my head said, "And now I am turning around and I am going to beat the shit out of him." Alberto saw my right fist clenched so I hit him hard with my left and then scratched the shit out of his face with both hands.

We survived this fight like we had all of the others. I felt that my actions were completely sane. The princesses had treated me like the maid, I asked for backup, Alberto told me to handle it myself, I warned Alberto that he wouldn't be pleased with the outcome, and then he complains? I should have hit him harder.

Alberto and I had been together for three tumultuous years. Only a woman with no self-worth would have stayed and then married him like I did. I treated myself as badly as Alberto treated me. There was such an enormous amount of work to do and most of it involved live animals. I would work until I literally fell down in a state of exhaustion, and then get up and continue to work. Animals need to be fed and cared for no matter what. A person with self-esteem would have demanded that her mate either pitch in or get out.

Chapter 20

My Wedding

Alberto went to Argentina yet again and had been gone for months when he finally managed to sell a horse. He had earned a huge commission and wanted me to join him in Buenos Aries and marry him. I agreed to marry him, not out of love, but because one of my biggest fears was that someday I would be an unloved old woman who dies in her house with sixty-five cats. I think Alberto was motivated by his need for a green card.

We got married in a courthouse in down town Buenos Aires with Alberto's friends and family in attendance. I didn't have friends or family and the location made for an easy excuse to explain why I was alone. Since I had stopped sending my family money, they didn't have much use for me and I had not even told them that I was getting married.

Natasha, the want-to-be fashion designer, spent days taking me to dress shops in Buenos Aires in search of the perfect dress for the reception. I was very fit from riding and ranch work, and had huge shoulders, a strong back, and big biceps. With my short hair I looked like a freak in a feminine ruffled strapless party dress. Even so, Natasha insisted that I try dozens of them on. I finally lost all confidence in her as a fashion consultant and bought a nice pair of black gaucho pants, black blazer, and a white blouse. The look was elegant and understated, and I was comfortable. Natasha wore a borrowed strapless gown that was too big for her and held up by visible safety pins pinned to the back of the dress. She spent the night with her arms clamped to her sides to keep the dress from slipping off.

For the wedding ceremony I borrowed a gray skirt and striped blouse from Deana. Sitting in the courthouse listening to the ceremony in Spanish, the voice in my head was saying, "Run! Run!" I answered myself with the question "But where?" With no sense of direction, I would likely end up hopelessly lost in Argentina. I remained seated and said, "I do." Since that day I have wished a thousand times that I had listened to my intuition and run for my life.

The reception was held at Alberto's old boarding school, and Natasha and Deana had done all the planning for the event. I told them that I would attend but would not help organize. These were my terms since I didn't see the need for a party. They had one problem that they sought my advice to solve. The two of them had been locked into a fierce argument for days before the wedding. They were fighting in Spanish so I had no idea what the problem was. Finally, when they had worn themselves out and still not come to an agreement, they came to me. Deana wanted to serve the hor d'oeuvres on plastic trays and Natasha, ever the princess, was mortified, and demanded that they buy or borrow silver trays. It was beyond my comprehension that a person could argue about something so trivial for three days and I answered, "Who gives a fuck!" Deana suddenly saw the humor in her dilemma and said, "You are absolutely right Susan, who gives a fuck!" Natasha ran out of the room in tears.

The wedding and the reception went off without a hitch and the next day we opened our wedding presents. Some of them actually made me

laugh. We received wooden duck decoys from three people and everyone else gave us silver trays. I sent out the required thank you notes even though I didn't like any of the gifts. Alberto and his family talked for months about how little we received. The family and friends were known for being generous, so I thought that they probably didn't like me. Maybe it was Alberto they didn't like because they didn't know me.

I had to return home a few days later because I had horses shipping in. Alberto stayed in Argentina another month. We planned to have a honeymoon sometime in the future.

Nothing changed after we were married. Alberto continued to do as little as possible but occasionally sold a horse. Jude Feld continued to send me fifteen to twenty horses every year to break, and Vila sent more lay-ups.

I was usually too tired to even think about whether I was happy or not. I was thrilled that my business was going so well. Jude was the best person to work for and only praised me. I did such a good job breaking the babies that riders at the track looked forward to riding my horses. When the horses shipped out, I would write out detailed reports about each horse and Jude loved that I paid attention to detail. My reports were unconventional to say the least. A typical report on a horse would detail how far he is galloping, how long he has galloped, and health information. My reports would cover all the basic information and then go on to tell Jude what kind of rider each horse would be happy with. I would tell Jude to give this horse to your favorite rider, this one is very sensitive so don't hit him, this one wants a girl rider, and so on. Jude and I worked very well together.

I continued to rent stalls from Millwood Richards, and although it wasn't a perfect situation, we managed to make it work. When I had worked for Richards a few years before, a horse got out of his stall in the middle of night and broke a leg. He was found a few yards from the barn the next morning, with his leg dangling from the knee. It looked like the knee was only attached by skin. The horse needed to euthanized, but since he was insured, the vet had to wait until the insurance company gave the authorization. The poor horse was loaded with drugs but still in extreme pain as he waited for two hours to be put down. At the time I was sick with the horror of the situation, but didn't suspect foul play.

My first year renting stalls from Millwood, another horse got out of his stall at night, broke his leg and had to be euthanized. This horse was also insured and the vet had to wait again for the authorization to put the horse down. Now I was becoming suspicious, mostly because it is not possible for a horse to open his own stall door at Richards' farm. The doors in the main barn where both of these horses had been stabled, slide closed and there is a short chain with a snap that hooks on the outside of a door. The snap is not accessible to a horse locked in a stall. I found the fact that both horses were insured was interesting, but I couldn't prove anything, so I had to let it go. Only a monster could hurt a horse like the one I had seen with his knee dangling by skin only.

I often drove to my barn at Silent Oaks Farm at night or in the evening just to check on everyone. I never found a problem, because Chewy was so good, but I still liked to check anyway. One night, just before dark, I was checking on my horses and saw Millwood's car parked near the side entrance of the main barn. Millwood rarely walked through the barn, and never parked where I saw his car.

The next morning one of Millwood's riders told me that a horse had gotten out of his stall in the main barn the night before and had broken his leg. The vet was standing by and they were waiting for the insurance company to authorize euthanasia. Now I had no doubt that Richards was killing horses for insurance money. I was beyond horrified. I threw up behind my barn, sick that I couldn't have helped the horse the night before when I saw Richards' car parked at the barn. It was important to hide my thoughts and feelings because no one had seen me at my barn the night before, and no one knew the extent of my knowledge of the previous dead horses. When I finished training my horses I went home and called an equine insurance company in Los Angeles and told them what I knew. I explained that I was in the horse business and had to remain anonymous. The only other person I told was Alberto who thought it would be best if I just minded my own business. Animals in danger or distress are my business and always will be, so I couldn't remain silent.

The next day an insurance investigator was sent to the farm. Paul instructed all of the riders and the grooms to say nothing when questioned. There was little doubt that they would lose their jobs if they spoke. As far as I know, nothing was ever proved, but no more insured horses mysteriously got out of their stalls at night and broke their legs. I was sick knowing that I had failed to help the last dead horse, and will always wonder what I would have seen if I walked into the main barn the night that I had seen Millwood Richards' car parked at the barn.

Chapter 21

My Honeymoon

Alberto and I had never had a honeymoon and he was planning a trip to Argentina in the spring when my horses shipped out. He invented an elaborate story of how he wanted me to meet his old girlfriend, Katrice. She was his first love, a beautiful model, and the most wonderful person, who according to Alberto, I absolutely had to meet.

Katrice was now married to Larson, who was an actor and hosted a TV show for children. Larson and Katrice lived in Sweden and were touring the world. The plan was for the four of us to meet in Argentina and then travel to Brazil and Chile together. This plan was presented to me in the form of our honeymoon. It didn't make sense to me, but I am always up for an adventure and Brazil and Chile sounded exciting.

We met in Buenos Aires and our 'honeymoon' was a disaster from the start. Katrice and I had nothing in common and I found Larson to be unbearable. He always had to be center stage and would sing silly songs, and perform skits, demanding everyone's attention. Alberto and Katrice seemed to enjoy him, and laughed at his skits and songs, but I couldn't fake it.

Our first night together we went out to dinner at a restaurant famous for its roast beef in Buenos Aires. Argentina has the best beef in the world according to the Argentines. Since I am a vegetarian, a restaurant famous for serving beef was not a good choice for me, on my honeymoon. Had it at least been a short dinner I could have faked my way through it. Alberto, Larson, and Katrice considered themselves to be elite, and dined as such. First there was wine and hor d'oeuvres, then more wine and a main course, then more wine and dessert, and finally coffee or just more wine. A meal could last three hours and the bill was always $300-500, with me only ordering a salad. I wasn't drinking anymore and had never liked wine. Once again, I was the odd one out, the girl who couldn't fit in, even on her own honeymoon.

After dinner Alberto, Larson, and Katrice wanted to go out drinking and I begged off. They stayed out until four a.m. and were very drunk when they came back. I am a morning person, but they slept until noon. We were scheduled to spend two weeks together and had I known how bad it would get, I would have flown home immediately.

We stayed in Buenos Aires for three days and they were all the same. Three hour expensive lunches; Larson entertaining us all day, followed by a three hour dinner and then they drank the night away. The last night in B.A, Alberto came in at four in the morning falling down drunk. He was mumbling something about what a piece of shit he was. Ever the supportive wife, I told him he was wonderful, how could he call himself a piece of shit? Finally, through his drunken babble, he was able to tell me why he was a piece of shit. That night, on our honeymoon, he had sex with a prostitute and had not worn a condom. I so did not want to hear that and I completely tuned it out, pretended that he had not even said it. He was so drunk that I wanted to think it wasn't true. I never brought the subject up again.

Our next stop was Baralochi, in the south of Argentina at Alberto's family raspberry farm. We stayed a few days with the family and Larson continued to entertain everyone. I wasn't feeling very well and whenever Larson started to sing I had to leave the room. Alberto thought this was extremely rude, even after I explained that I felt sick and his singing made me feel worse.

One afternoon the four of us we were playing croquet with Deana and Alberto's youngest sister, Trudi. Argentine rules are a little different than U.S. croquet rules. There is an option to hit an opponent's ball out of range instead of taking your own shot. I used this option to hit Larson's ball as far away as I could. While he was gone looking for his ball in the brush, Katrice gave Alberto a long, lingering hug right in front of me. Alberto hugged her back and the embrace was more like a lover's embrace, than old friends hugging. Trudi caught my eye and saw the pain and disbelief I was feeling. I wanted to leave, throw down my croquet mallet and go home to the States, and to this day I wish I had. Larson finally returned to the game with his ball never knowing that his wife had hugged my husband like a lover.

We made two day trips to Brazil and Chile. The countries were beautiful but I still didn't feel well, and wasn't having a good time. When we returned to Baralochi, I was very sick and had no energy. I spent the next few days in bed but only got worse instead of better. Alberto thought I was faking an illness so that I wouldn't have to spend any more time with Larson and Katrice. Deana insisted that I go to a doctor, and I was feeling so awful that I agreed. I was diagnosed with an STD. I had only had sex with Alberto and he had admitted to having unprotected sex with a prostitute. Instead of being angry at Alberto I felt embarrassed. To me, this disease was proof that I was scum. I didn't want anyone to know why I was sick and felt that it was my fault. This was some really twisted thinking on my part, but it served Alberto well.

We arrived home in California and never spoke about the trip, Larson and Katrice, or my sickness, ever again. Only a person with absolutely no self-esteem could have endured that trip. Although it was my 'honeymoon,' I was treated like a pain in the ass, and I knew that they would have been happier if I had not been there. For sure, I would have been happier if I had not been there.

Chapter 22

Home again

When we got home I jumped back into my normal routine of being too busy to think. There was a certain sort of emotional safety in exhaustion. I continued to be responsible for everything, animals, business, house, and car and truck maintenance. When I couldn't tolerate Alberto sitting and doing as little as possible, I would demand that he help me and disaster usually followed.

Alberto had weird ideas about raising young horses. He didn't think that they got enough exercise on their own, and he would chase them around the pastures. This didn't seem safe to me, but Alberto insisted that he knew what he was doing and this is how it was done in Argentina. One day he was chasing yearlings with a whip and in their excitement one colt stepped on another colt while they were galloping. The injured colt had a cut that went completely through a tendon on his hind leg. The vet came and took hours to stitch him up. It took months to completely heal. A man with an ego smaller than a short Argentine's, might have been able to see that it was his fault that this colt had been hurt, and that horses shouldn't be chased with whips. Alberto could never accept responsibility even for the most obvious fuck ups.

Another one of Alberto's favorite tricks was to tie a horse up on a long rope and let him eat grass. He would insist that this was absolutely safe, even though most horses will get tangled in the long rope, panic, and get hurt. Alberto hurt several horses like this.

I would leave the farm to run an errand and come back to chaos and blood. If I wasn't already crazy, I was definitely headed in that direction.

Another breaking season was going well at Silent Oaks Farm. Chewy and I were a good team and all of the horses were healthy, well broke, and scheduled to ship out soon.

One day I was in a stall soaking a bruised hoof in hot water and Epsom salts, which required me to stand and hold the horse for twenty minutes. I was minding my own business, quietly soaking this horse when one of Millwood's riders stopped by to chat. He was from England and had been here to learn Millwood's horse breaking method. Even though Millwood had treated him like shit, he was still very loyal. Millwood had devised a plan to get free help on the ranch by recruiting students. They lived and worked on the farm, but did not get paid. Millwood had given this boy, Kevin, a tack room with no heat to sleep in, and he had been cold all winter. Kevin stopped by under the pretense of bidding me good bye since he was returning to England the next day. He asked me what my opinion on Millwood Richards' breaking method was. I regret now that I shared my honest opinion. I told him that I knew that Millwood's 'method' was a sham. I had seen horses being prepped for horse breaking demonstrations, although Richards' begins his demonstrations by announcing that this horse has never been in the round pen. Not only have the horses been in the round pen previously, but they have even been ridden. I had first-hand knowledge of this, so it was more than an opinion. Kevin ran straight to Millwood Richards and reported what I had said.

The next day Millwood, his wife Kay, and his trainer Paul, called me into the office to blast me for sharing my opinion. At first I tried to explain that Kevin had come to me while I was soaking a hoof, it wasn't like I was running around the farm telling everyone that Millwood was a fake. They were very angry and told me that I threatened their livelihood with my opinion, and that I didn't have the right to express my opinions on their farm. I have always tried to be open minded and I could see their point, so I apologized. If it had ended there our business relationship could have been salvaged. Instead, the three of them continued to yell at me, even after I apologized.

The next day I told Paul that I would ship all of my horses out within a week and be gone. He seemed surprised, and told me that he didn't want me to leave, and shipping out wasn't necessary. I was so hurt that Paul had taken part in the attack on me that I just couldn't stay. Paul and I had been friends for years and had never had a cross word. I told him that sitting in a wheelchair is no excuse to act like a piece of shit, and that a friend would have warned me of the impending attack, not joined my attackers. I was absolutely livid.

That night I was putting blankets on the horses at home and talking to Alberto about my situation at the farm. He agreed that I should ship out and that Paul was a shit. Alberto was leaving the next day for Argentina and I had asked him not to leave. As I blanketed the last horse, I was bending down with my right arm extended to fasten a hind leg strap, when the horse spooked and ran over me. She hit me hard in the shoulder and knocked me to the ground. I was in so much pain that I couldn't move. Alberto saw that my elbow was scraped up, and he thought I was unable to stand because I scraped my elbow. He actually said, "Oh poor little girl scraped her elbow and she doesn't want me to go to Argentina." I was indignant. I have always been really tough, and won't admit to pain unless it is so severe that I can't deny it. In yet another act of complete self-loathing, I got up and pretended I was unhurt. My shoulder had instantly swollen and I couldn't move my arm, but I thought, fuck it, I will not be accused of faking an injury. I took a triple dose of Motrin and went to bed. The next morning I tried to drive to the farm in the truck, but couldn't shift the gears with my arm that wouldn't move. I turned around and switched to the car that was also standard, but easier to shift. Alberto finally realized that I was injured and he postponed his trip to Argentina.

With perfect timing, Jude called me and was ready to have the horses shipped in to him at the track. I couldn't ride and didn't want to be at Silent Oaks Farm another minute, so this was good news. My shoulder was diagnosed as separated with torn ligaments and I needed some down time to heal.

Chapter 23

Trainer's test

In the last couple of years breaking horses and taking in lay-ups I had discovered that I knew as much, or more, about horses than most trainers. I was getting tired of only breaking horses and contemplating taking my trainers test, but not sure that I was brave enough to pull it off. There was a big hurdle to cross and Jude helped me once again. I was still painfully shy and the mere thought of being in a room with the State Vet, two Stewards, and a trainer, all firing questions at me, was terrifying. I told Jude that I knew I couldn't do it, but he told me I was wrong. He told me that I would be so sure of myself that it would be a breeze. Jude told me to memorize the racing rules in the condition book and to read The Lame Horse by Rooney. For the next two months, I memorized both books and called Jude countless times with questions and doubts. Jude never wavered from his, "You can do this." Jude always had this thing about helping women and I had seen him help several women on the track. He had more faith in me than I did in myself. Alberto was busy tearing me down and Jude was on damage control.

Finally the day before my test I drove down to Santa Anita and stayed at my favorite hotel, the Santa Anita Inn, so that I could have one last night to study before taking my test in the morning. I had decided that I could sit in a room with four people asking me questions as long as I knew the answers, frontwards, backwards and sideways. I called Jude in a panic, because the only detail I had missed was that I didn't know what to wear. I knew this seemed like a silly question, but it was important to me. I trusted that Jude would understand and not laugh at me. He told me khaki pants, a nice blouse, and a sweater would be perfect. He didn't laugh at me.

When I had called Santa Anita two months earlier to schedule my test, I was told that I needed to work with a trainer first. I informed the secretary that I had been running my own farm, breaking babies, and taking lay-ups for over five years, and I was ready to take my test now. She gave the phone to Dr. Bell, the State Vet, and he agreed that I could sit for the trainers test, but I could tell that he didn't think I would pass.

When I walked into Dr. Bell's office at Santa Anita I felt a wave of panic sweep over me. It felt like when I had to try out for band in high school. We held tryouts to decide who would be first, second, and third clarinets, in front of the entire band. I was only a freshman and should have been a third clarinet, but my friend, Carol, who was a sophomore, was a second clarinet, and I desperately wanted to sit by her. We had been given two weeks to practice a difficult piece, and would be required to sight read another piece. I practiced for hours and could play without even looking at the score. On tryout day, I started playing very softly because I was so shy and scared. When I realized that most of the kids in the band weren't even listening to me play, I got bolder and I Played. I played loud and clear and so well that everyone stopped goofing around and talking, and listened to me. When I finished the piece you could hear a pin drop. They were all wondering, where did that come from? I won the solo seat in the first clarinet section, which was unheard of for a freshman.

I wanted to dazzle the world again but I felt frozen. Dr. Bell asked me the first question and my mind went blank. I was petrified, terrified and mortified, and Dr. Bell (bless his soul) saw that. He instructed me to take a deep breath and as much time as I needed. He went on to the next question and I pictured the young girl who was afraid to play her clarinet, but still won the solo seat, and then the answers came to me. I answered every question that was fired at me and I stayed cool and calm.

The trainer in the room was Janine Sahadi, and she tried to disagree with some of my answers but Dr. Bell sided with me every time. He asked me to explain what an osselet was, and as luck would have it I had studied osselets in depth that very week, because a young colt of mine had just been diagnosed with osselets. I think Dr. Bell would have been satisfied if I had answered that it was an ankle problem. Instead, I launched into a dissertation on osselets, pathology, causes, treatments, and how to avoid. When I looked around the room I saw that I had dazzled once again. When I had covered everything you ever wanted to know about osselets, I was told to wait outside while they conferred. Within one minute, Dr. Bell invited me back inside, shook my h, and and told me I was incredible.

It felt so good to have passed my trainers test. Most people fail at least the first time and some fail many times. I knew that failure wasn't an option for me, in part because I could only talk myself into taking the test once. Suddenly I was validated with a Trainer's License from the state of California, and I thought Alberto and Vila would realize that I did have valid opinions backed up by knowledge.

Unfortunately, nothing changed at the farm. If anything, I became more of a threat to the combined South American egos of Alberto and Vila. When Alberto and I fought instead of hitting him, now I would jump in my car and leave. I would never have a plan and be lucky if my wallet was in the car, and then just pick a direction and drive. Knowing that my animals were at a very real risk with Alberto in charge, I could never stay away longer than a few hours. Sometimes I wanted to just keep driving and never go back, but I couldn't leave my animals.

Vila wanted me to put blisters on all of his lay-up horses and I refused. Blistering is very common on the race track, but cruel and inhumane and I couldn't hurt a horse. A chemical agent is painted on a horse's legs in order to cause a burn (hence the term blister), which in theory, will increase circulation and speed healing to a sore joint or shin. At Silent Oaks Farm I saw blistered horses in extreme pain because their legs were on fire. If the horse wasn't wearing a collar to keep his mouth away from his legs, he would further damage himself by tearing his own flesh off. Secondary infections are not uncommon as the hide and skin peel off the leg. There was absolutely no way I would do that to a horse. Vila could insist until the sky fell down and I wouldn't budge.

When Vila realized how set my mind was he came to the farm to blister the horses himself. In order to get a really good blister he would paint DMSO on their legs first, so the blister would go very deep. I couldn't even hold the horse for him. I wanted nothing to do with torturing horses. The horses trusted me, how could I hold them, and allow someone to torture them. He put the blistering agent on two horses and really rubbed it in, and then he and Alberto had a barbeque. I knew that Vila would stay long enough for the blister to start to burn before I could wash it off, but I had to act as if I didn't know why he was lingering. I went on a trail ride, desperate for Vila to leave so I could help the horses.

The minute Vila was gone I ran to the barn, washed off the legs with soap and water, and then and gave the horses bute. While I was doing this Alberto was at the house and Vila called him to warn him that if you give bute to a blistered horse they will founder. Alberto ran to the barn and arrived breathless (since he never ran) and screamed at me not to bute the horses because they would founder. I saw Alberto clearly as the fool that he was, as I explained to him that bute is an NSAID and could never cause a horse to founder. Bute is the drug of choice to treat founder. Bute would lessen the effects of the blister and that was my intention.

Chapter 24

San Luis Rey Downs

I had the summer to decide where I was going to break my horses next breaking season. Silent Oaks Farm had the best track in the Valley, but it wasn't very good, only ½ mile with tight turns and the surface was marginal at best. I couldn't even imagine going back there after being attacked by Paul and the Richards.

I had heard a lot of good things about San Luis Rey Downs Training Center in Bonsall. SLRD had a mile track, starting gates and crew, nice barns, and stall rent was cheap. The only down side was that I would have to leave my beloved Santa Ynez Valley. I had always made it a practice not to grow roots so that I would be free to chase opportunities. I didn't want to be a person who couldn't follow her dreams. My dream now that I had my Trainer's License was to train horses to run and not just break horses. To accomplish my goal I needed a mile track. Santa Anita and Hollywood Park were not options for me because I knew I couldn't live in the city. Bonsall was a small town and there was still plenty of open space. Del Mar and my old favorite beaches were only thirty minutes away.

Jude had twenty horses for me to break and his owner wanted to save money by breaking them at his ranch in Bradbury, near Santa Anita. Jude and his family would be at Del Mar, and I would live in the guest house and break the horses. They paid me very well and when the horses were ready, we would ship them all to SLRD.

I took my Dalmatian, Raven, with me and left Alberto in charge at home. This was risky and I only hoped that he didn't kill or hurt too many animals. I called him twice a day to check in. One day I called him at noon and he told me that he had a young horse tied up on a long rope in the back yard, and he was very content eating grass. I calmly asked him to please not do that because the horse would surely get tangled and hurt. Alberto was busy telling me that I didn't know what I was talking about, when I heard a huge commotion in the background. Alberto dropped the phone, but I could hear a horse thrashing. The horse had gotten tangled and was in a state of panic, with the long rope cutting into his legs as he kicked.

I couldn't be in two places at once and felt like I had sacrificed my own horses to break Jude's, and earn money. The truth of the matter was, that if I didn't earn money, my own horses wouldn't eat, so I had no choice. I almost felt guilty that I was enjoying my time away. Although I had twenty horses to break, I also had some free time and even went to the movies a few times.

On Saturdays when I was finished riding, I would drive two hours back to Santa Ynez and spend my day off at home. We were preparing to move and ship everyone to SLRD in two months. My days off were more tiring than my work days. I would take a quick walk around the farm to check all the horses and find everything Alberto had missed. I didn't want to fight anymore so I began to side step Alberto's ego. Instead of saying a yearling filly had an eye injury that was at least two days old, only an idiot could have missed it, I would say, "Oh, the yearling filly has an eye injury that must have just happened, so let's get some ointment in her eye today." Part of me choked on the lie but I couldn't waste energy fighting with a fool.

Vila had a plan to buy twenty yearlings in Kentucky and send them to me at SLRD to break. These along with Jude's twenty, would give me a full barn. I penciled out all of the expenses to buy equipment, hire grooms, riders, and hot walkers, pay stall rent, pay workmen's comp, and it looked profitable on paper, so I agreed. My only stipulation was that Alberto would get out of bed every morning, go to the track, and work as my assistant. There wasn't money to pay a real assistant and I thought Alberto would be better than nothing. I planned on riding as many of the horses as I could myself. Someone had to be in the barn all morning while I was on the track.

I went to Bonsall with Raven a few days before Jude's horses shipped in and stayed at a hotel. The barns were in okay condition but painting the trim would make my barn look good, so I started painting. I had planned on having a beautiful barn with lots of hanging baskets full of flowers but Alberto ruined that plan. I bought the baskets and filled them with potting soil and cuttings of geraniums one Sunday on my day off. I spent hours working on them because I wanted twenty baskets, one in front of each stall. When I was finished, I instructed Alberto to only water them on Wednesday. The best way to kill cuttings is to over water them because they get root rot and die. When I returned the following weekend my baskets were soaked in water and all the cuttings were dead. All of my work had been for nothing and I would have no flowers for the barn. I asked Alberto why he couldn't have done as I requested and only watered on Wednesday. He told me that our groom wanted to water them every day. I was so hurt that I cried. Once again, I had been ignored, as if I didn't matter.

I hired a crew and Jude's horses shipped in. The horses all looked fantastic and were well behaved. The riders at SLRD nicknamed my barn 'the riding school' because we were so proper. Life was good even without my flowers.

Two weeks later Vila's twenty horses shipped in from Kentucky and I was still waiting for Alberto. These horses had all been through the yearling sale and the long van ride from Kentucky, so they were exhausted. Most of them got off the van and immediately went to sleep in their new stalls. They were too tired to even be interested in their new surroundings. I had never seen a group of young horses so quiet and tired, and assuming that they must be sick, I immediately started checking temperatures. Three of the horses arrived with fevers and I expected the rest to follow. By the next day twelve of the horses were sick. I knew that it wasn't unusual for horses to get sick after a sale and a long haul, but it was important to stay on top of it. I had a new vet at SLRD and we checked every horse, every morning, together. We put the horses with fevers on antibiotics and stall rest, and the others we monitored closely and only hand walked, to give them time to recover from the trip. Eventually, all but two of the horses were sick and on meds. Alberto still wasn't here to help.

I was getting all of Jude's horses to the track early every morning and then working on the sick horses. Since I needed to know that each horse really got his meds I was the only one allowed to medicate. Sometimes grooms get sloppy and the horse spits out his meds, or someone forgets to medicate and then lies about it. The only way to insure that important things, like medicating sick horses, were done properly was to do it myself. I would mix the antibiotic pills up in an oral syringe, add some sugar and dose everyone first thing in the morning, and then again in the afternoon.

The worst thing you can do to a young, sick horse is give him a bath. It is common knowledge that sick horses should never be bathed. The virus we had in our barn could easily turn into pneumonia, and then the horses would die, or suffer lung damage, and be useless as racehorses.

Vila made a trip down to see his horses a week after they arrived and found most of them sick and dirty. I had reported that they were sick and updated him every day. Alberto had finally moved down to Bonsall and was at the barn to deal with Vila. I saw them order a groom to take a sick horse to the wash rack for a bath. He and Vila were both obviously disappointed that I had dirty horses in my stalls and they jumped to the conclusion that I was too busy to do a proper job. I stopped the groom as he entered the wash rack with the sick colt and told him to take the horse back to his stall. Although I was furious, I knew it was important to stay calm in front of my new crew, because a woman can't act like a girl on the racetrack. I calmly apologized to Vila that his horses were dirty and explained that he would kill them if they were bathed and I could not allow that to happen. He and Alberto looked at me in disbelief. It was obvious that they thought I would allow Vila to run my barn. I tried to hide my scorn for them.

Two days later Vila sent his own vet down to check the horses. Dr. Prida was from South America but he didn't have the attitude that Alberto and Vila shared. We examined the horses together with Vila and Alberto in tow. Vila once again ordered one of my grooms to bathe a sick horse. The poor groom just looked at me in confusion. I repeated that we don't bathe sick horses here and Dr. Prida told Vila that I was right. Prida agreed with the meds that I administering, agreed to stall rest and no baths, and told me in front of Vila that I was doing a good job. Vila was speechless for once.

With rest and antibiotics all of the horses eventually recovered and I could begin breaking them. Jude's horses went to the track early and I would work with Vila's when we were finished tracking. We had four riders besides me and all of them were good except for Suzette.

Alberto and I had been looking for a small ranch to lease near SLRD for months. While we were still in Santa Ynez I found a classified ad in the *Horse Trader* for a ranch for rent in Temecula. We made the long four hour drive from Santa Ynez to meet the ranch owners, Gus and Suzette. They were in financial trouble and losing their ranch. Had they told us the entire story on the phone, we would never have made the drive all the way to Temecula. The farm was nice, but they wanted to park a trailer on the ranch for them to live in, share the kitchen and bathroom in the small house with us, and they wanted to keep five of their own horses on the ranch. Rent was high and paying too much rent and sharing the house and paddocks didn't make any sense. I was ready to leave as soon as I heard the terms, but Suzette insisted on us all sitting down and talking about it.

Suzette is one of those people who can talk non-stop for hours and Alberto could sit and listen for hours. I managed to sit for one hour and listed to the non-stop chatter, and then I asked to use the bathroom and said that we really must be on our way. When I was in the bathroom Alberto hired Suzette to ride at SLRD. When I entered the room she was saying, "Oh thank you Alberto, this will really help us." We left and on the long drive home I asked Alberto what he could have been thinking of. He said that she was English, probably a very good rider, and we would need riders soon anyway. I told him that you don't just hire a rider; you watch them ride and make sure they are competent, especially since all of our horses were green babies.

I was hoping that Suzette would find something else to do in the next two months and forget about me. Unfortunately Alberto had given her my phone number and she called every week to ask when I was shipping in to SLRD. Again my lack of self-esteem was evident when I couldn't tell her "Sorry, but I actually won't be needing you." I didn't feel that I had the right to decide who would be in my life, even when they drove me nuts.

Suzette was a disaster as a rider. She was at least forty years old, and her body was no longer lithe. She was stiff and scared. When the grooms legged her up on colt she had no spring, and the grooms had to lift her like dead weight. She couldn't swing her right leg over the horse, so she would kick the horse in the butt, because she couldn't pick her leg up high enough to clear it. One morning I was on the other side of the barn and I heard the cry of, "Loose horse", and saw Suzette's mount gallop away. I always gave Suzette the easiest horses to ride because anything difficult would kill her. The horse she was trying to get on was a sweetheart, who had never bucked. A few minutes later I heard, "Loose horse" again and her horse galloped away again. I walked over to the other side of the barn and Suzette was pissing and moaning about how these damn horses weren't broke right. When the horse was caught I watched Suzette get legged up and saw her kick the poor horse in the butt. The difference, this time, was that the horse was prepared for the awkward kick in the butt, and didn't bolt and run away. I told her that if she couldn't get on without kicking her horse in the butt she would have to leave. I added that I had not had time to teach them to stand still while being kicked in the butt, so she should blame me, not the poor horse.

My patience had already worn thin with Suzette. She talked non-stop and most of it was negative chatter about how cheap my horses were. According to her, they were all cheap pieces of shit. One morning on the track, we were galloping together and she was going on and on and on about how the horse she was riding was garbage, and a waste of her time. I told her to pull up and we both stopped on the training track. I launched into her and told her that she had done nothing but talk shit since she arrived and that I couldn't stand her another minute, or subject my horses to her negativity. I told her to get off her horse, turn him loose, and then just go away and never come back. She started crying and promised to keep her mouth shut, and begged for another chance. I finally agreed that she could stay, if, she shut the fuck up.

A few days later she was on the track with an easy filly. The filly spooked and turned back quickly and suddenly was galloping the wrong direction, into traffic. Instead of quickly turning the filly around, Suzette was frozen with fear and did nothing. I saw her face, she was absolutely panic stricken. The  outrider on the track caught her horse and got her turned around. When we got back to the barn I told her she shouldn't be riding because she was terrified. She argued that I was wrong, but I had seen the terror on her face. My intuition was screaming at me to get her out of my barn, so I had to let her go. Alberto insisted that I be polite and keep her, but I couldn't risk a workman's comp claim, and knowing her, a civil suit would follow. I saw her a few weeks after I fired her, wearing a medical halo after she broke her neck riding for a trainer at Hollywood Park. She wouldn't speak to me.

Suzette was replaced by Mary Sue, who is one of the best riders I have ever met. Her husband and Justin also rode for me, and he was a good hand too, but the horses loved Mary Sue. She rode them like I did, soft and kind, and was never disrespectful. Jude's horses were all galloping super by now, and I was still getting Vila's broke.

I wanted to break all twenty horses by myself to ensure that they were broke properly. I would start my round pen/arena work as soon as we were finished tracking. The round pen was a long walk from my barn and up a hill. In order to save time, the grooms would bring the horses to me one at a time, and I would stay up there until I was finished. It was hot and I was usually tired, but if I could stay focused on the horses and not my discomforts, I could get through them and remain positive.

It was Alberto's job to ensure that a horse was sent to me every twenty minutes. Not a difficult job, but he couldn't do it. I would be finished with a horse and wait fifteen or twenty minutes for the next horse. Finally, I would walk down to the barn and explain for the umpteenth time that I need a horse every twenty minutes. I would be so damn mad, that here I am once again doing all the work and Alberto can't even handle getting the horses up to the round pen. Not a single day went smoothly when Alberto was involved. The hardest part was that I couldn't show my anger in front of the crew. I didn't want them to think I was a crazy angry bitch. I would walk down the hill, into the barn, and calmly ask why I had been kept waiting for twenty minutes when I still had twelve horses to work with? Alberto was incapable of saying he was sorry and usually had some stupid excuse like it was Fernando's horse I was waiting for, but it was also Fernando's turn to make a run to the kitchen, so that was why I was waiting. The only thing that Alberto was capable of organizing was the runs to the kitchen. He had a schedule of who would make the kitchen run and take orders from all of the grooms and hot walkers for breakfast, lunch, and snacks. He thought this was important and he was proud of his system. I hadn't expected much in the way of help from Alberto and he didn't disappoint me.

We still had twelve horses boarded in Santa Ynez and I had arranged for friends to check on them. One day after three weeks of boarding, I got a call from my friend, Arlene, who told me that the horses didn't look good, and I should get up there quickly. When I arrived in Santa Ynez the next day I was shocked at the condition of my horses. The weather had been harsh, with cold windy rain storms. I always fed double and put blankets on in a storm, so the horses stayed warm and didn't lose weight. This farm didn't do anything extra for them. Even my pregnant mares were very thin.

I was horrified at their condition and moved all of the horses immediately to a farm in Los Alamos. The new farm assured me that they would make sure that the horses ate round-the-clock and were never hungry. The next two Sundays I drove to the new farm and didn't find the horses with hay in front of them either time and they had not gained any weight. Clearly, they had to be moved again.

I called my vet, Dr. Sands, in tears and asked for his advice. My mares were in their last trimester and skinny, their unborn babies were surely suffering too. Dr. Bill told me to bring all of the horses to his farm where he would board them and feed them as much as they could eat. All of the horses put on weight quickly with proper care, but one foal was stillborn and a mare died after she foaled. I was devastated at the loss of the mare and foal and felt responsible for their deaths. Had I been able to check on them every single Sunday this would not have happened. The fact that it was a four and a half hour drive to Santa Ynez, and I was exhausted from riding and managing a forty stall barn, didn't matter. A baby and a mare were dead because I fucked up was my bottom line.

Chapter 25

Bonsall

Alberto and I had rented a house near the track on a month to month lease because we were still looking for a farm to lease. The house was nice but was in a housing development and didn't have a fenced yard for the dogs. My darling Emily Jane had succumbed to cancer, but I still had Raven. I had adopted another Dalmatian, Star, who had been used as a breed dog, but didn't produce enough milk to feed her puppies. Her owner, who supposedly loved her, needed to get rid of her. I have always hated the term, 'get rid of,' in reference to an animal, so when I heard that this breeder was 'getting rid' of a Dalmatian, I took her. Star was six-years-old, beautiful, sweet, and once she got over her sorrow of being dumped, was totally devoted to me. I nicknamed her Star Dog I because when I called her to come from a distance, she ran as fast as a rocket ship to get to me. Dalmatians were my favorite breed and I loved having a pair of them.

One day Alberto and I were on our way to Santa Anita to watch a horse run and on the 210 freeway we saw the cars in front of us slamming on their brakes and swerving to avoid hitting a small black and white dog. She had nearly brought traffic on this major highway to a standstill. A cop was on the side of the road trying to catch her with a long pole with a noose on the end. Every time he went near the dog, she ran into traffic to avoid the pole. I told Alberto to stop the car, but he refused because we would be late for the race. I yelled "Pull over now or I will jump out" and then he stopped. Alberto stayed in the car while I got out and asked the cop if he needed help. It was obvious that he did, because he was chasing the poor, frightened, little dog into traffic. I was shocked when he said yes, but I wouldn't have let a no stop me. I walked away from the road and said, "Come here little dog" and she ran to me. She didn't have a collar on, but I was squatting down petting her to prove that she was not dangerous. I thought the cop would see that he was stupid to be afraid of this little dog and put the noose away. Instead, he still put his noose on her, tightened it, and flipped the poor little dog upside down. He had her pinned with the end of the stick on her throat and choking her with the noose. She screamed only once, because she didn't have any air, and then she locked eyes with me. I saw the look of terror and pleading in her eyes and I had to help her. I am sure we both hated cops together at that moment. She didn't understand why she was being tortured and neither did I. I forced myself to remain calm for the dog's sake, and asked the cop what he planned to do with the dog now. He told me he had to wait for Animal Control, but since the dog was vicious, and had no identification, she would be euthanized. I asked him if I could have her and he said yes, but I should be very careful. I told him to turn her loose and I opened my car door and said, "Let's go little dog" as she jumped in.

When we arrived at Santa Anita, we tied the dog up at Vila's barn for an hour while we watched our race and then took her home. Since she wasn't a Dalmatian, I had no intention of keeping her, but Alberto wanted her. I named her Greta because she was a tough, hard headed, street dog. She looked like a Dalmatian Queensland mix and we butted heads often. I had finally realized that I had taken my love for Dalmatians too far, when I couldn't accept another breed into my life. When I snubbed Greta I felt racist against mixed breed dogs. Since this is not who I wanted to be, I had to accept Greta into my life. She became one of my all-time favorite dogs, and died in my arms of a heart attack fourteen years later. By then, I had softened her name to Greta Gumdrop, and her friends (she had many) called her Gummy.

Chapter 26

Ramona

We were still paying board on twelve horses at Dr. Sands' farm in Santa Ynez and I was driving the nine hour round trip to see everyone once a week. I knew that I could trust Dr. Bill, but I was so wrought with guilt over the dead mare and foal that I had to see everyone at least once a week.

Finally we found a nice twenty acre farm in Romona for lease. The owner was a retired Thoroughbred trainer and he had designed the farm himself. The pastures were only dirt or sand, but they were huge, and most of them had three-sided shelters. The barn was beautiful with twelve oversize stalls. The house was small, but cozy with a wood stove. The farm was big enough for all of our horses and we could take in outside horses as well.

We shipped everyone down from Santa Ynez and they loved their big pastures. The orphan foal, whose mother had died, was doing well and hung with the other mares and foals. Bill had fed and cared for them for three months until everyone was fat and happy again. I was still apologizing to all of my horses for the hunger they had suffered. It had been a nightmare and I didn't know if I could ever get over it.

Ramona was a forty-five minute drive to SLRD, down a windy mountain road. I left early every morning driving the Saab, and for a week wondered why it didn't grab the windy road like it should. There were accidents on the mountain almost every day. I didn't feel safe driving in the darkness of early morning with a car that was sliding around the curves. I finally took a minute to really look at my car and found the front tires were completely bald, with metal clearly visible. I laughingly told Alberto that I was about to become a victim of the mountain road, because I was tempting fate with bald tires. I asked him to please find time to go to a tire store and buy new tires for the Saab. He looked at my bald tires and told me they were fine. This was the first time that I saw clearly that Alberto didn't love me, and probably didn't even like me. As hard as I tried not to see it, this was blatant. I couldn't pretend it wasn't real.

I had not done drugs in several years, since we lived at the Gardner Ranch. I had tried to stay away from cocaine, but always went back to it until I had an epiphany one day. I was standing under one of my favorite old oak trees near the track at Gardner Ranch, feeling like a useless loser because I had snorted cocaine with my drinking buddies the night before. A powerful thought ran through me that if I really wanted to quit coke, I had to believe with my heart and soul, and then it would be as easy as being a vegetarian. I had been a vegetarian since I was seventeen, and it never took willpower because it was one of my core beliefs. There was something magical about that moment under the lovely oak tree, and I never got near cocaine again.

My life was very hard in Ramona but I was not tempted to do drugs again. Instead, I felt myself falling into a bottomless pit of depression. This depression was more subtle than ever before, and I felt like I was slowly slipping away from reality and into my own private hell. I fought these feelings as hard as I could because I had so much work to do. The animals all needed to be fed and cared for, no matter what I felt like.

In the spring, Jude's and Vila's horses all shipped in to Santa Anita and we were left with only a few of our own to train. Far Frau was back in training after a long lay-up. Vila had been the last person to train her and he said that her ankles needed a rest. I know now, that he had injected her ankles with steroids numerous times, until even that didn't help. She was finished as a racehorse. The first time I rode her on the track at SLRD I could feel that she wasn't the same filly I knew. Her step was flat and rough, she wasn't lame but she wasn't right. I wanted to cry and take her back to the farm, but instead, I decided to try her and see if I could get her back to the races. She got better with training and when she was ready to run I entered her in a race at Santa Anita. She was a grass horse and had won an allowance race, but the only races for her at Santa Anita on the grass were really tough.

Far Frau was my first starter and even though she was running over her head, in a tough race, I was hopeful. The day before the race I bought the Racing Form and was reading as I ate lunch at home. Alberto grabbed the Form from me and laughed as he said, "You don't know how to read a racing form, give it to me." I was getting to the point where more often than not I accepted his put downs. Part of me knew that I was in dangerous emotional territory, but I was no longer strong enough to fight it off. After eight years of fighting Alberto, I was now accepting his emotional abuse.

Far Frau ran bad and came back sore. Alberto blamed me for Far Frau's bad race, and on the way home from Santa Anita told me that maybe I should consider selling flowers instead of training racehorses. I was already upset that the race had not gone well, and Alberto's comment was like a kick in the face.

The day after the race my vet examined Far Frau and said that in order to run again we would need to inject her ankles. Alberto and I discussed our options at length, and finally agreed to retire her. She had earned $67,000, had an excellent pedigree, and would make a good broodmare. For months after the race, Alberto told me every chance he got, that if Vila was training Far Frau, she would still be running. I would remind him that we had agreed together not to inject her ankles and go on, but he didn't hear me.

We had two beautiful young horses by the stallion Almamoon, and the oldest, Cricket, was three-years-old and ready to run. She had trained really well for me at SLRD and I thought she would run well. I had heard that Almamoons trained well, but were heartless in a race. I so hoped that the rumors were false. He was a new stallion and his first crop was just now running, and they were all running bad. Alberto was 'Mr. Pedigree' and he had bought a Pretense mare in foal to Almamoon, with an Almamoon foal by her side, over two years ago.

Cricket ran terrible in her first race and my new friends at SLRD were quick to point out that she was an Almamoon filly, and was bred to disappoint rather than win. Alberto blamed me for another bad race and advised me to quit training. He said that I had given it a good try and probably should just sell flowers. Part of me hated him for saying that, but I started to believe it could be true. Maybe I wasn't cut out to be a trainer and my dream was stupid.

I was exhausted emotionally and physically from being responsible for everything. Alberto had caused some bad accidents at the farm and I could see clearly that his ineptitude was even greater than I had given him credit for.

One day we were walking around the farm together and as we walked by a paddock with a stud horse, one of Vila's lay-ups, the horse opened his gate and got out. Right in front of us, he flipped the latch on his gate, and escaped. Alberto had not closed the gate properly with the chain that was welded onto the gate. The farm was designed well and a loose horse couldn't get into much trouble. However this horse ran to another one of Vila's stud horses, and the two of them were fighting over the fence. Alberto and I were close enough to end the fight quickly before anyone got hurt, but the gate opened. Alberto had not closed this gate properly either, so now we had two stud horses fighting. We managed to separate them and neither horse was hurt. Alberto could never admit that he had made a mistake and he didn't see that this was his fault, for not closing the gates properly.

Another time I had left the farm for a few hours because I was desperately in need of some time on the beach. I was very depressed that the horses had run badly, and the beach always made me feel better. I was gone only four hours, and when I returned, I saw a yearling colt hanging his head at a strange angle. Alberto was in the house doing nothing, and I asked him what happened to the yearling colt who was hanging his head. Alberto said that he had tried to jump the fence to get to the mares, and broken his neck. Our pastures weren't cross fenced so extra care had to be taken when deciding who to put in each pasture. I had put geldings next to colts, with the mares far away. Alberto loved to move horses around, and he had put the mares next to the yearling colts while I was gone for the afternoon. He had watched the colt try to jump the fence to get to the mares, and when he saw that he was seriously injured, he put him in a small paddock by himself. I assumed that this had just happened minutes ago and the vet was on his way, but I was wrong. Alberto had not even called the vet and the colt had already been in pain for three hours. Alberto had not given him any drugs. I called the vet, who arrived in minutes, and euthanized the colt because his neck was badly broken. Again, Alberto couldn't take responsibility for this catastrophe that he had created.

One morning in Ramona, the dogs, Star, Raven, and Greta, all started barking at 4:00 a.m. Alberto insisted on letting the dogs out even though I said it was not a good idea, they needed to be kept safe, inside the house. Alberto argued that it was their job to protect the farm and he let them out. Seconds later I heard a blood curdling scream from a dog, and Star and Raven ran back to the house and jumped into bed trembling. Alberto went outside and found Greta in the driveway, unable to move. She had a big, deep scratch across her pelvis, and her hind legs were paralyzed. I was to learn that this is typical of a mountain lion attack.

We didn't have a small animal vet in Ramona so I called Dr. Paul, my vet at SLRD, and asked him to recommend an emergency small animal vet. Paul instructed me to put Greta in the car and head to Parkway Pet Clinic in Escondido, where his friend, Dr. Henderson, would meet me in thirty minutes. He gave me directions as I put Greta in the car and drove down the mountain as fast as I could.

Greta and I arrived at the clinic and Dr. Henderson took one look at her and said she had been attacked by a mountain lion, and probably had a fractured pelvis. He immediately gave her I.V. pain meds and put her on sub cue fluids while he set up his x-ray equipment. Since it was still very early, not even five a.m. yet, the Dr. didn't have a vet tech to help him. I was his only help so he asked me to move the sub cue fluid needle to another spot. Administering sub cue fluids in dogs is not difficult and I knew how to do it. Greta had been unconscious, but when I moved the needle, she woke up and bit me. Her teeth went right through my fingernail and I was suddenly in extreme pain with my finger pouring blood. The pain and the emotions that I had suppressed took over and I fainted. I was only down for seconds when I willed myself to stand and help my dog. When I got up, Greta reached over and kissed me. She was in far more pain than I could even imagine, but yet, she worried about me. I fell in love with her that second, and through my tears, I was able to assist the doctor.

Once Greta was stabilized we took x-rays and her pelvis was badly fractured. Dr. Henderson wanted me to take her to Davis for surgery and estimated that the bill would be around $3,000. I didn't have $3,000 to spend, so I tearfully told him to euthanize her. Dr. Henderson is a wonderful, old fashioned, country vet, and he said that he could try to do the surgery at his clinic for about $500. I happily agreed to the surgery and left to go to the track. I called Alberto to update him and to make sure that he fed the horses. I always fed in the dark before I went to SLRD because I couldn't trust Alberto to feed them.

When I finished at SLRD I went back to the clinic to check on Greta, who had just gotten out of surgery, and now had a pin in her hip. Dr. Henderson had vet techs that looked like homeless people, but they were all very sensitive and super kind. They weren't as professional as real vet techs, but they were soft and loving, and added to the old country vet clinic atmosphere of Dr. Henderson's clinic. A tech was putting Greta in a cage as she was just waking up from surgery. I could only see her head because the tech's body was in front of her body. I said gently, "I am here sweet girl" and the vet tech excitedly told me that she wagged her tail. I couldn't see it, and asked him if he was sure, and when she heard my voice a second time, she wagged her tail again. The vet tech was as excited as I was. He told me she would be fine, that he was sure of it.

Dr. Henderson wanted to keep Greta for a few days because she had an IV catheter for pain meds and antibiotics. I came back the next day to visit Greta and everything had changed. She had become very unfriendly and growled at everyone who walked near her. Dr. Henderson changed his mind about keeping her and told me to take her home now. I made a stretcher for her and we carried her out to my car.

When I got home, I carried her into the house on her stretcher and set up a cozy quiet spot for her in the large bedroom closet, so that I could hear her at night. Poor Greta was in extreme pain even with I.V. pain meds. Over the next few weeks, I often wondered if I had made the wrong decision. I was sure that no animal should endure this amount of pain.

I still had horses at SLRD and had to leave early every morning to train them. Greta was completely helpless and needed around-the-clock care. She couldn't move at all without screaming in pain. I gave her water with a big oral syringe and tried to get her to eat. She couldn't get up to go to the bathroom outside, and would try so hard to hold it that she would tremble. I had layers of towels under her and the stretcher was covered with plastic so that when she urinated, I could easily change the towels and she could stay dry and clean. Still, I would have to sit next to her and tell her to go potty, that it was okay, I would clean her up. Finally she would relax and urinate, and no matter how gently I changed the towels, she would scream. I can't stand to see any animal in pain and this little dog, who had tried to fight a mountain lion, was breaking my heart. I could feel her pain and sat next to her and cried for hours.

Every night I would be exhausted, but I have always been able to program my brain in sleep to wake up if an animal needed me. Greta would whimper once before she screamed and I would jump out of bed to see what she needed. Alberto would ask what was wrong and in my sleepy state I would answer, "Greta wants." I didn't know what Greta wanted, but I knew she needed me. Sometimes she would need the towels changed in her bed, or water from the syringe, and then I would kiss her and go back to sleep. Other times she needed more pain meds or me to sit with her.

I was gone at least four hours every morning and Alberto had to care for Greta while I was training. I didn't want to stick her with any more needles, so I was giving her water every hour with the oral syringe and expected Alberto to do the same while I was at the track. Every day I would come home from the track, get out of the car and go straight to Greta. She was always thirsty and I gave her as much as she could drink out of the syringe. I would ask Alberto when she last had water, and every single day he would say that he had forgotten to give it to her. She was losing hair in clumps and becoming dehydrated, and Alberto couldn't remember to give her water.

After three weeks of horrible suffering, one day I came home from the track to find Greta sitting up. She had not been able to move since her accident and I was beyond thrilled to see her sitting. When I walked into the room and saw her sitting, I screamed in delight and clapped my hands, jumping up and down like a little girl. Greta knew that she was the cause of my delight and had a very pleased look on her face. Alberto rushed in to see what the commotion was about and I said, "Look, look, Greta can sit!!" Alberto didn't see the significance in this and told me to stop acting stupid. Alberto had a way of crushing my very soul.

Greta continued to heal and eventually could walk and even run again. Every time she passed a milestone, like the first time she took the steps instead of the long way to the barn, I would scream and clap in delight. I found myself retreating into my own world where it didn't matter much what Alberto thought of me.

The last time Alberto was able to send me reeling was after a bad race at Santa Anita. It had become obvious that our horses couldn't run, and somehow it became all my fault. Alberto had bred them, they had been raised well, but they had no speed. Most of the stallions that Alberto chose to breed to eventually became geldings because they had failed as stallions, but still it was my fault.

We had just run badly again, and all the way home from Santa Anita, Alberto blamed me. According to Alberto, we couldn't afford for me to train any longer. It had been a fun experiment, but time to grow up and admit that I couldn't train. According to him selling flowers was probably my only option. I started believing that Alberto could be right, maybe my dream to train was stupid and I had wasted all of these years with racehorses. The very thought put me in a state of deep depression. When we got home I told Alberto to feed the dogs and I went to bed.

I was so miserable that I stayed in bed for three days and was surprised that Alberto was kind to me. I thought that maybe he really did care about me and I just hadn't noticed before. The ugly truth was that he had finally broken me and I was in a weak state of submission. Finally, now that I was beaten down, he was stronger than me and could be the 'man.'

While I was in bed I read a book that described depression as anger turned inward. I thought back to when Alberto had killed the yearling colt and how I had reacted. Even after he killed a horse, he argued when I insisted that the colts had to be moved away from the mares immediately. Instead of telling Alberto the truth, that only a complete idiot would have put yearling colts in a pasture bordering mares, I had quietly gone into the house and taken a shower. While the water was running and the door was closed, I had cried my heart out, and then began hitting my head on the tiled shower wall. I banged my head so hard that my forehead started to bleed. I knew this was strange behavior, but I couldn't stop. Somehow the physical pain combined with the emotional pain I was feeling purged me.

When I finally got out of bed after three days, I sat down in the dining room and had a cup of coffee with Alberto. I had not been out of bed for fifteen minutes when he made a typical Alberto remark to make me feel like shit. I had lived with his emotional abuse for almost eight years and suddenly I saw it clearly. I stood up, picked up my antique oak dining room chair that I loved, and tried to break it over Alberto's back. He ducked behind the table, and in my rage, I picked up the heavy oak table and threw it at him. He was yelling at me to stop, and telling me I was crazy. I knew that this was the most sane I had been in quite some time, as I directed my rage at Alberto.

Things went downhill fast after that. I had been breaking our yearlings and instead of giving each one a chance on the track I wanted to cull. I believed that horses that had no athletic ability should become riding horses instead of racehorses. Alberto disagreed of course, and thought that each horse deserved a chance on the track. This made no sense to me since it costs thousands of dollars to get a horse to the races and countless hours of my time. To make it worse, when they proved that they couldn't run, it would always be my fault.

We had one sweet cute little filly I had named Widget. When the other young horses ran and played, Widget preferred to stand in the middle of the pasture and watch them. Finally, when her friends were tired and slowing down, Widget would join them and play for a few minutes as they were winding down. She had no speed, but was smart. When I broke her she was as kind and quiet as a riding horse, but showed no desire to run. I wanted to find her a good home as a riding horse, but Alberto wouldn't hear of it.

We had a half mile track that went around the pastures in Ramona and I insisted that Alberto come outside and watch Widget gallop. She preferred to gallop slowly, and I wanted him to see that she did not have the makings of a racehorse. Alberto thought that if he got on the pony and went with us, she might feel more ambitious.

We both went to the track and were only jogging when we hit a soft spot on the track that Alberto had created. Months earlier when it was raining, there was one section of the track that flooded. Alberto insisted on digging a hole and putting a drainage pipe under the track. We had a groom who had done the actual digging. The track drained better now, but there was a dangerous ten foot wide soft spot, that I could only jog on, because galloping would have been fatal.

We were only jogging slowly and Widget was so safe that I didn't even wear a helmet. When we came to the soft spot on the track, Widget stumbled and fell on her face, and then somersaulted over the top of me. It felt like slow motion as my face and neck were being crushed between the horse and the dirt of the track. I screamed from the pain and fear. I was well aware that I was being crushed and had not worn a helmet. Finally Widget was able to stand up and got off of me. I was hurt, but relieved that she hadn't killed me. I couldn't move at first and a man in a passing car stopped to see if we needed help. He had seen the two loose horses with saddles, and me still down on the track, unable to move. Alberto told him I was fine and we didn't need his help. I wondered how he could be so sure.

My face was black and blue for weeks after the fall. I felt like finally the outside of me matched the inside.

There was a lot of heavy work to do at the farm and often I had no help. When I was sore from overwork, I would take Motrin and had gotten to the point where the Motrin didn't help anymore. My worst pain was coming from an old injury to my sacroiliac. I had gotten so sore that I couldn't ride, so I found a chiropractor in Ramona. He wanted to see me three times a week for treatments and I was improving. He didn't understand why I couldn't rest and let my body heal. I had explained that I had twenty-three horses to take care of and no help. He asked me if I lived alone and I told him no, that I was married. I wasn't about to share my pathetic story with anyone, especially a stranger, but when I sadly said that I was married, he understood. He looked me in the eye with a look of compassion that I mistook for pity. I was so embarrassed that I had let my guard down. I chastised myself for being weak.

Alberto eventually came to the realization that his breeding program was a failure. He wanted to sell or give away all of the mares, and although I had bonded with them I couldn't disagree. We found homes for the cheap mares, and sent the better mares to Kentucky. Alberto knew a farm owner in Kentucky who could get the mares bred to good stallions with foal sharing agreements. On a foal share the stud fees are waived and the profits of selling or racing the foal are shared.

Alberto had been gambling with Vila at the track and usually he lost. They had a scheme going where they would hold a horse for a few races and then instruct the jockey to let him run and cash a bet. One day they got lucky and Alberto won $80,000 on a bet.

Although we were still living in the rented house in Ramona, Alberto bought a satellite dish for $3,000 and had it installed in the back yard. He must have been one of the last people to buy the huge, twelve foot diameter, old style dish.

He bought himself a Nautilus weight training machine for over $1,000 and left it in the box in the garage for months. Alberto invited his father on a trip to Europe and at first I mistakenly assumed that I was going too. Alberto soon made it very clear that I wasn't invited. He felt very generous when he bought me a new vacuum cleaner at Costco.

Alberto was very busy spending his money and he went to an auction and bought four sheep. He said it had always been his dream to own sheep. We didn't have a corral fenced for sheep, and they went right under the horse fences, so they were loose all day. At night they had to sleep in a stall to be safe from coyotes. Alberto was spending more and more time in L.A. with Vila so the care of the sheep fell to me, what a surprise. One night I was so tired from taking care of the twenty-plus horses that I couldn't get the sheep to go in their stall. I chased them for thirty minutes and finally gave up. One of them was killed by a coyote that night and Alberto was furious.

I had never wanted sheep and knew nothing about them, but it was obvious that Alberto had paid top dollar for sick sheep. They all had snotty noses and two of them had tumors hanging off of their necks.

When I fed the horses I would load my feed cart with grain and hay, and push it through deep sand to get to each paddock. This was hard for me even before the sheep. Since the sheep were loose, they would see me with the feed cart, and come charging at me. I would try to chase them away but they would go right through me and knock me and the cart over. My buckets of grain with meds and supplements mixed in, would be spilled into the sand, and I would have to start all over. My poor body was almost worn out and I was always so tired, that fighting with the sheep was just too much.

I finally told Alberto that he had to either get rid of the sheep or put them in a paddock, because I was too sore and exhausted to deal with them. He promised to do it soon, but Alberto's soon, could be months away. One day the sheep knocked me down, and I finished feeding the horses, got in my car, and drove away. I called Alberto from a hotel in Bonsall and told him that I wouldn't return until the sheep were properly fenced. I hated to be away from my animals, but Alberto and his sheep were driving me crazy. Finally three days later, Alberto told me the sheep were fenced in and I went home.

Alberto had a friend, Kit, who visited us often with his wife, Alice, and their two young sons. They would stay for two or three days, and although I liked them, I did not look forward to their visits. From the moment they arrived their children became my responsibility. I was lucky if they only trashed the house. I had caught them putting corn into the engine of the lawn mower, and dumping my horse meds on the ground. The boys were only three and four-years-old and too young to be turned loose. When they went home, our house would require hours of cleaning and Alberto refused to help me. Alberto thought he was helping me if he noticed that I was falling down tired, and would insist that I go to bed and finish vacuuming the next day. I finally told Alberto that if his friends were to continue to visit us, he would have to clean up after them, or tell the parents to be responsible. He told me that I was being rude and stupid and refused to speak to Kit and Alice. The next time they arrived for a visit, I explained to Alice that I didn't have time to be a hostess, or clean my trashed house, after she turned her kids loose for a weekend. I asked her if she could take an active role in policing them. She said she understood, but what she understood was that I hated kids, and they were no longer welcome. Once again I was the impossible bitch and they never returned.

Alberto was now spending most of his time with Vila in L.A. If I needed to speak to him I would call Vila's house and ask to speak to Alberto. I had only met Vila's wife once and we weren't friends. Alberto told me that I was rude on the phone because I didn't exchange pleasantries with Vila's wife. Alberto, Vila and his wife, had all decided that I had no class because I lacked telephone etiquette.

Alberto and I had been together for eight years. We were married the first three and living together the last five years. After three years of marriage, I could see that it wasn't for me. I would choke on the word husband. In our worst arguments Alberto would tell me that I didn't know my place and I would scream that I was equal.

Christmas was always hard for me because I didn't have a family. Scott was the only one who ever understood how painful Christmas was for me. In Argentina, Christmas Eve is the special family night when all of the presents are opened and the holiday dinner is served. Alberto spent every Christmas in Argentina with his family. He told me that it was only natural that he loved them more than me because he had known them longer.

One year, a few days before Christmas, Alberto's aunt Margarita came to visit for a weekend. I always liked Margarita because she was a free spirit and not afraid to be unique. Alberto was in Argentina and had called the house and talked to Margarita because I was still at the barn. He was all excited that he had been on a ski trip to Chile with some old school friends, and had paid $500 for a new sweater.

When I came home, Margarita told me I had just missed Alberto's call, and that he had bought a $500 sweater while on a ski trip. She then asked me why my refrigerator and cupboards were empty.

My clients at the barn were usually really good pay, but if they paid late I couldn't buy food. I had accounts at the feed stores so the animals would never go hungry, but I might. I was too proud to tell Margarita the truth, that I didn't have money for food, but when she looked in my eyes, she saw the truth. Alberto, the man, who should have been the provider, was wearing a $500 sweater while his wife ate peanut butter.

On this same Christmas I was home alone on Christmas Eve eating peanut butter and waiting for a call from Alberto. I knew that he was with his family, and I was hoping that they were at least thinking of me. All day I kept my cordless phone near me, waiting for the call that never came. I cried myself to sleep that night. I had never felt so alone, and utterly forgotten.

Alberto called the next day and I told him I wanted a divorce. I told him I didn't have food because I hadn't been paid, but he was wearing a $500 sweater. He had spent Christmas Eve with his family without even a thought or a phone call for me, and then I hung up the phone. Deana called me back a few minutes later and said that it was all her fault, she had told Alberto to wait and call me on Christmas day because the rates were lower. It would have taken less than a minute of phone time to call me, and tell me that I was loved and missed. I felt like an idiot. I gave and gave and gave, and got absolutely nothing in return.

I got paid the next day and went to a little bookstore in Santa Ynez and spent $20 on a do-it-yourself divorce book. I filled out all of the paperwork, forged Alberto's signature and filed for divorce. When the final divorce declaration arrived six months later, I intercepted the mail, forged Alberto's signature again, and was legally (sort of) divorced.

I had a few horses at SLRD and would train them every morning. Galloping on the track was the highlight of my day. I was free when I galloped, and the reality of my miserable existence was not my focus.

Alberto wanted to take my pony, Gus, to Santa Anita because Vila needed a pony on the track. Vila was our main source of lay-up horses for the farm, so I felt obligated to at least consider loaning him Gus. When I questioned him and found that Alberto was to be the pony boy and ride Gus every morning, I had to say no. Gus and Alberto didn't get along, in fact Gus hated Alberto. I explained to Vila that Gus was a good horse and he hated Alberto, so sorry, I can't send him to Santa Anita for Alberto to ride. Vila said he understood. I think he only understood that he sent me horses and I wouldn't reciprocate.

When we had first arrived at SLRD we desperately needed Gus to take the young horses to the track. Since I was in Bradbury breaking Jude's babies, Alberto had been responsible for getting Gus fit enough to work at SLRD. I rode him every Sunday when I was home but that wasn't enough to get him fit, and I wanted Alberto to at least lunge him during the week. It never happened, and Gus went from a long rest straight to hard work, when he shipped into SLRD. Alberto rode out with each set, and between sets would tie Gus up on the corner of the barn. One corner of the barn had sun and the other was shade. It was easier for Alberto to tie Gus up in the shade, and on cold mornings he needed a blanket. After every set I would take the tack off my horse and notice that Gus was hot, and tied up once again, in the cold shade, without a blanket. I would ask Alberto to please remember to put a blanket on the poor beast and then do it myself. Within a week Gus predictably got sick and needed antibiotics and two weeks off to recover. In typical Alberto style, he insisted that he could ride a sick pony, and the crew came close to seeing me explode as I said absolutely not.

One morning we were on the training track at SLRD and Alberto was very hung over from a party the night before. Gus, who had never bucked in his life, bucked Alberto off on the track, in front of everyone. Alberto was furious when I laughed at him, and he demanded that I give him my whip. When I refused, he ordered Mary Sue to give him her whip. She started to give it to him and I shouted that if she gave him a whip to beat Gus, she was fired. I knew that Gus was as fed up with Alberto as I was, and nobody whips my pony.

One day I took a horse into Vila for her last work before her first race at Santa Anita. I was walking her in the afternoon just to get her out of her stall for a bit, when I heard a dog scream. It was a horrible scream, and I was picturing a dog getting hit by a car, except that the scream went on and on. It took me a minute or two to put my horse back in her stall, and then I ran towards the scream. I found a Dalmatian chained to the end of Vila's barn, screaming because his owner was looking at him. The owner was one of Vila's grooms, and I had seen the dog that morning in the barn. He was locked in a stall, standing on his hind legs to try to see out of the stall, but he wasn't tall enough to see over the door, and could only look up at the ceiling. Whenever anyone walked by his stall he would growl and snarl, so he was called the devil dog.

That night I couldn't sleep. The scream I had heard haunted me. Never in my life had I seen an animal so terrified of a human. I had to do something for that poor dog.

The next morning I asked the groom what was up with his dog. Why had he screamed the day before and why was he so ferocious in the stall? He explained that someone, not him, had hit the dog in the head when he was chained up, with a two by four, and cut his head open, so he didn't like to be tied up. He said that he needed to find a home for the dog.

I knew that I had to rescue the Dalmatian immediately, or I would never sleep again. The grooms warned me not to go into the dog's stall, but I walked into the stall and sat down on the dirt in the middle. I started talking softly and only looked at the ground, not at the dog. I sat there, looking down and speaking softly for five minutes and then the dog peed on himself and walked over to me. He was young and handsome, but his thin body lacked muscle tone. I heard Vila ask the grooms who was in the stall with the crazy dog, and then I heard him say, "She is crazy too." The dog finally sat next to me in the stall and I asked him if he wanted to be my dog. He looked at me with sad, scared eyes, and peed on himself again. I stayed in the stall with him for an hour talking gently to him and eventually he let me pet him, under his chin. When I left, he looked at me with painful longing, and I promised to come back soon and help him.

The dog was still intact and needed to be neutered. I didn't want to take him home with testicles because he would be more inclined to fight with the other dogs. I asked Vila's vet, Dr. Maribella, if she could suggest a small animal vet near the track who could neuter him immediately. She generously offered to take him to a small animal clinic owned by a friend, close to the track. I explained to her that he appeared to have been horribly abused and would need to be kept muzzled because he was a fear biter. I had to leave but would put a muzzle in front of his stall door, and meet her back at the barn when the dog was out of surgery.

Maribella didn't heed my warning and muzzle the dog, but she got him in her truck and drove to her friend's clinic. When she arrived at the clinic she left the dog in her truck and went inside. When she came back out, the dog wouldn't let her open the door of her truck. She told me that for twenty minutes she and the other vet tried to get him out of the truck, but he would go ballistic every time they opened a door. Finally they decided to open both truck doors at the same time, thinking that either he would do nothing, or only bite one of them.

The surprise attack worked and they were able to get him out of the truck and into the clinic.

I picked the dog up a few hours later at the barn. He was still sedated and had his muzzle on. Maribella explained to me that he was a fear biter and I should be very careful and keep him muzzled.

I took the dog home to the farm and named him Chance, because he needed one. I wasn't sure that I could do anything with him, but I knew that I had to try.

We had a big dog of Vila's staying with us for a few months and he didn't like Chance at all. His name was Dobey, and he weighed at least eighty pounds and would attack Chance for looking at his food bowl from across the room. Chance was smart and played by Dobey's rules, and I was always there to protect him. Raven was old now and not very interested in the new Dalmatian. Gummy and Star just thought he was weird.

It didn't take Chance long to relax and start to trust me. He acted like a city dog on the ranch at first. Instead of ducking under fences like the other dogs, he would sit at a gate and wait for me to open it for him. We had a big hill behind the house and Chance would run up and down the hill for hours. Soon he was muscular and strong. One day I was squatting down to pet him and moved my feet a little to get comfortable, and Chance screamed and ran backwards. He thought I was going to kick him in the belly. I had learned that his previous owner, Vila's groom, was addicted to crystal meth, and had beaten the dog senseless more than once, and had burned him with cigarettes. This made me love him even more, and I promised him that he would never be hurt again.

One day Alberto was playing with Gummy and the vacuum cleaner, and it was upsetting Chance. Gummy would attack the vacuum cleaner and Alberto thought it was funny. Chance didn't understand that it was a game, and he saw Alberto attacking his new friend Gummy, with an evil vacuum cleaner. I told Alberto to stop playing before we had a problem. Alberto never listened to me and wasn't going to start now, so he continued the game and Chance bit him. He bit him hard in the ass, and tore his jeans from the seat to the pant leg bottom. Alberto was furious and chased Chance into the bedroom, but I got between them and told him that no one touches this dog but me. Chance and I went outside together, and I realized we were bonded for life. We both knew what it felt like to be treated like garbage. Chance was my bodyguard for the next twelve years and never let me down.

We lived in Ramona for almost two years and I was miserable. In the summer, the temperature would go over 100 degrees by 10 a.m. The mares were gone, but we still had yearlings and lay-ups. Sometimes I could afford a groom to help with the horses, but usually I worked alone. Alberto was spending most of his time with Vila in L.A., or in Argentina with his family. I felt lonely and abandoned.

I didn't have any horses at SLRD so I was at the farm all day, every day, with the dogs and horses. I didn't have any friends in Ramona and had been too busy to make friends at SLRD. When my horse work was finished, or when it was too hot to be outside, I would drive into town and walk around Kmart looking for blue light specials. I hated my life.

Chapter 27

Free at last

I can see now that it was all part of the plan, when Vila called for his lay-ups and stopped sending me his broken-down horses. We got very low on horses and decided to leave the farm and move closer to SLRD.

We rented a house in an avocado grove close to SLRD and moved in with Gummy, Star, and Chance and some cats. Raven had been euthanized in Ramona when she was sixteen and her body gave out. Alberto had never been much help packing and moving, but he was even more useless than usual for this move. He loaded the U-Haul in a rough uncaring manner, denting the washer and dryer and just throwing things in. This should have been a clue for me.

Once the U-Haul was unloaded Alberto did nothing else. He explained that he had helped load and unload and now he was finished. Everything we owned was in boxes and I pointed out that I, too, had loaded and unloaded, and now it was time to unpack. Alberto refused to lift a finger to help.

I had a few horses at SLRD and would leave early to train and then come home and unpack. One day I had been unpacking books and putting them on some nice built-in shelves when the shelf broke. The books all fell on the floor and I was too tired to try and fix the shelf, so I left everything and went to bed. The next day when I came back from the track Alberto was sitting on the couch reading a book. I knew that the book had come from the pile of books that was still on the floor. I asked him how he could sit and read and not even think of fixing the broken shelf and picking the books up off the floor. He told me that he felt like reading and I should leave him alone. I saw Alberto clearly at that moment as a self-centered piece of shit who didn't care about me at all. I told him to get out. He didn't argue and packed a bag and left.

A few days later when he still had not returned I had a feeling that this was different than our other fights. He finally came home to talk and told me that he was leaving for good. I had kicked him out so he was gone. We talked and talked and for some sick reason I asked him to stay. After eight years of being emotionally abused I wasn't ready to let go. Alberto had rented a hotel room in Del Mar, the same hotel where Vila was staying, and had no intention of returning to me.

Alberto left and I cried uncontrollably for hours. My little Gummy dog sat by my side and I held her in my arms and cried my heart out. Everything made sense now and it was all so ugly. Alberto, the Thoroughbred breeder, had failed, so he no longer needed me to take care of the horses he bred. Vila had stopped sending lay-ups so that we would leave the farm and Alberto would be free. Alberto had dented the washer and dryer so carelessly because it was no longer his. He refused to help unpack because he was leaving.

I had been the victim of Alberto's scam and it had lasted for eight years. Even knowing this, I wanted him back. I had a million reasons to leave him, but he left me. The fact that he had been planning this for months in secret was something I couldn't fully comprehend. The hard, ugly truth was unimaginable.

I cried for days and days and my Gummy dog sat with me to console me. She completely took over and bossed Star and Chance around and even made the cats behave. I cried like I did when Scott died and was so depressed that I wanted to die. My thoughts were weird, and would switch from wanting to be dead to wanting to kill Alberto.

I still had to unpack all of the moving boxes. At first I put all of Alberto's things gently in a bedroom near the garage. Within a week I was no longer gentle and was throwing Alberto's things into the room. When I threw some crystal wedding presents into his room and they broke, I smiled and said, "Woops" out loud to myself. I didn't want anything of his in my house.

Alberto had bought a very powerful, thirty-aught-six rifle when we were in Ramona and it was in the bedroom with everything else of his. One day when my emotional pain was unbearable, I went into that room and got the rifle out. I didn't think it was loaded, but I wanted to see exactly how I could use it to kill myself. I put it on the ground and put my forehead on the barrel and reached down with a toe to pull the trigger. Just then, Gummy walked into the room, took a strong stance and gave me a look like 'don't you dare.' I broke down in sobs and hugged her promising never to leave her.

It was that day that my thoughts turned to murdering Alberto. I finally saw him as the scumbag that he was. He had taken advantage of me for eight years, spent my money, allowed me to work like a man until my body gave out, and then left me with nothing. I was now officially nothing in my own mind.

I dragged all of his shit out of the bedroom and piled it in the driveway. I called him and told him to pick up his shit before 6:00 or I would have a bonfire. I left and went to the beach to try to calm down. When I returned he had picked up his stuff and was gone.

I was consumed with rage and plans to murder Alberto. Suddenly I understood the women I had read about in the news who had killed their husbands. I had always thought that they were crazy, but I could see now that they weren't crazy, they were fucking pissed.

When I am really upset and angry I talk to myself and that was happening to me all the time now. I went into the grocery store in Bonsall and noticed that people were staring at me. I had been muttering, "Fucking piece of shit, I hate the mother fucker." When I realized why they were looking at me I ran out of the store.

My daydreams of murdering Alberto were vivid. I could imagine shooting him in the head and the sight of his blood and brains splattered on the ground would make me smile. I would feel a big smile on my face through my tears and I knew I was losing my grip on sanity as I became overwhelmed with a fierce hatred.

One day I decided to proceed with my plan to murder Alberto and I went to a shooting range in Oceanside. I had called ahead and knew that they sold guns. When I walked in, I told them I knew nothing about guns and wanted them to tell me what gun to buy. They never asked what the gun was for so I didn't have to lie. The clerk showed me five guns and told me to pick them up and decide which one felt best in my hand. I picked up the first gun. As I held the gun, I knew that I would have the power to make my dreams a reality with this gun. The feeling of power, combined with the hate and rage I was feeling, scared me. I dropped the gun and ran outside.

I decided that I wasn't willing to spend the rest of my life in jail for murder. Alberto had taken eight years of my life and I couldn't give him the rest of it.

I still wanted to be dead but Gummy wouldn't let me. Whenever the thought of suicide became too strong to bear Gummy would find me and I would hug her and cry into her soft coat. One day when Alberto and I had first broken up he came to the house to talk. I was on my bed with Gummy and Alberto sat down on the bed. Whenever we talked I ended up in tears and Gummy knew that. She got on top of me and draped herself over my stomach to protect me. She looked at Alberto as if to say, "Don't fuck with my Mom." We met on the beach at Del Mar once to talk and Gummy wouldn't even look at him, but stayed very close to me.

I knew that I could never leave Gummy and my other animals, and I knew that I couldn't continue to live as I had been. Something inside me had to change so that I never ended up with a man like Alberto again.

I began searching for a therapist to help me and started calling numbers in the yellow pages. I didn't have much money, but I didn't know what else to do. I must have called a dozen numbers and none of the therapists felt like a good match for me. Finally one day I was in the little health food store in Fallbrook and a business card on their bulletin board caught my eye. The card advertised life transformation and I sorely needed a transformation. Even before I called the number on the card I knew it would be the person I was searching for. When I called, Karen answered and her kind voice filled me with hope. She could see me the next day, money wasn't a problem, and she did counseling at her house in Bonsall.

My first appointment with Karen was the next day. She had made room to see me immediately. As I walked into her house the first thing that I said to her, even before I sat down, was that my parents were alcoholics but that it hadn't affected me. Karen just smiled and invited me to sit down. We talked for two hours that day and I told her about my plans to kill myself and/or murder Alberto. Instead of judging me, Karen said she understood that I was very angry and invited me to tell her why.

For the next five years I saw Karen once or sometimes twice a week and I told her why I was so angry. I told her all of the horrible things that Alberto had done to me. She would always agree that yes, Alberto was an asshole, but why was I with him? What had made me stay? With Karen's help I began to realize that there was a definite pattern here. I had been treated like shit by my parents, Gary, and Alberto, and I also treated myself badly. I made it clear that I wanted to break out of this pattern because I would end up dead if I continued without change. I knew how close I had come to losing my sanity and I was ready to move away from the pain.

It was summer and I had no horses to break, so no income, and nothing in the bank. With Alberto gone I couldn't even pay rent on the new house. Alberto had agreed to pay me $1,000 per month for ten months to help pay off my credit cards. We had run up a huge debt, and all of the credit cards were in my name. I had seen Alberto not pay his family and friends back in the past. I knew I couldn't count on him to pay me.

I put a sign up at SLRD for roommates and Patrick called me. He was a big handsome black trainer and said that he wanted to rent a room. He moved in the same day and was willing to pay half of the rent. This still left $550 per month for me to cover and I advertised in the local paper for another roommate. Catherine answered my ad and moved in and we each paid a third of the rent.

I was still very sad, but was getting a handle on it. An old horseman at SLRD was helpful in my recovery. One day at SLRD when my emotional wounds were still fresh and raw, I was telling John all of the horrible things Alberto had done. John was a simple, kind old man and he listened until I was finished. Alberto had formed a corporation a few years before and we put our few assets in the corporation. Our new truck, the horse trailer, and all of the horses were legally owned by the corporation. The only thing that remained in my name was my Saab, which was now eight years old and had close to 200,000 miles on it. When Alberto left he took everything and told me that he would leave me my car. Alberto promised to sell the horses and share the net profit, but all I got was a letter stating that sorry, there was no net profit. So, I was telling John all this and I finished my story with 'he can't do this to me.' John, with the wisdom of an old horseman, only replied, "It looks to me like he already did."

At SLRD every trainer had to be covered by workman's comp and I had recently paid $2,500 for my policy, which was also in Alberto's Corporation's name. One month later I got a call from the insurance company to tell me that Alberto had cancelled my policy and they had refunded him $300. I now had no Workman's comp and didn't have another $2,500 for a new policy. Patrick generously offered to add me to his policy at no cost and I was able to remain at SLRD.

Another horseman at SLRD stepped up and helped me get back on my feet. His name was Jack and he was a super trainer, a lot like Walter. He also had a wicked sense of humor that I appreciated. We went out for drinks at a nice Mexican restaurant in town and I told him my sad story. I admitted to him that I wanted to murder Alberto. He had known Alberto for years, and with his keen insight had seen right through him. He congratulated me for being free and then told me that I should be thinking of getting even rather than staying so damn mad. Humor, even evil humor, was exactly what I needed. Jack and I began plotting my revenge.

I had told Jack about the gun that I had almost bought. He was glad that I hadn't followed through with my murderous plan and he had a better idea. He saw Alberto at the races in Del Mar the next day and told him that he had been shooting with me at the shooting range in Oceanside. He told him that when I shot at the human target I only aimed for testicles and never missed. He said I could shoot a gnat off an apple at 100 yards. That night we met for drinks again and he told me that Alberto had turned white after he heard Jack's story. Revenge was fun.

The next part of the plan was to ruin Alberto's bloodstock business. I recruited Ronald, another bloodstock agent who despised Alberto, to help us. Since most American owners and trainers are skeptical of Argentine horses and agents this plan was easy to carry out. Ronald and Jack would tell me who they had seen Alberto offering horses to at the track and I would follow up. All I had to say to a prospective buyer was, "Be careful of the Argentine agent" and any deal was dead. It was that simple. Sometimes I even approached his client's right in front of him in the Club House at Del Mar.

Alberto finally figured out that Ronald was leaking information to me and challenged him to a fight in the paddock in Del Mar. They fought in the paddock during the races and were both thrown out. Everyone who knew me assumed that Alberto and Ronald were fighting over me, and that was embarrassing since I didn't like either one of them. For weeks after the fight in typical racetrack style, my friends on the backside teased the heck out of me. Had they only known the truth they probably would have been proud of me, but I was good at keeping secrets.

Jude had lost his big client who sent me twenty horses every year and I was scrambling to find horses to break. Trainer Tony Locke, who always had a positive outlook on life, told me not to worry because there were plenty of horses to break. He had more than he could ride and gave me two clients off the track. I went to some small local farms and broke a dozen horses. Tony was the difference between me starving and me surviving those first few months.

My idea to share the rented house with roommates started off good with Patrick and Catherine. Patrick and I were really attracted to each other, and I finally experienced good sex at the age of thirty-nine. We both knew it was only sex, with no strings. After two months Patrick couldn't pay his rent. He promised to get caught up the following month but didn't. Instead of paying rent he explained that he was a little short so had gambled and lost all of his money. We were in the kitchen discussing this money problem and I told him he would have to leave. I couldn't pay 2/3rds of the rent and I wanted him to move out immediately so that I could rent his room out. He started to cry and told me he was sorry, and then he took his belt off and told me to hit him. This was some weird sick shit and I was scared. I told him to please just leave and he did.

Catherine had also gotten weird. One day she was sitting on the couch with a book and a pen and closed the book for a minute to talk to me. Gummy was sitting right next to me. When Catherine finished speaking to me she forgot that she had put her pen in her book. She screamed at Gummy, "Where the fuck is my pen?" Poor Gummy just looked at me as if to say 'what is her problem?' Catherine wasn't a country person and wanted to live in an apartment in town. She moved out and we were happy to see her go.

I ran my roommate ad again in the local paper and Mark moved in. He seemed like a nice normal guy and had a job. He lived in the house for about a month with no problems.

Our third roommate was a woman who was very strange. Her name was Katie, and she came from a wealthy family who had pretty much cut her off. Her rent checks came directly from her family but they wanted nothing to do with her. They only paid her rent because when they had completely cut her off, she ended up homeless, living in a park. She was on disability because she had Hepatitis C. She was friendly enough at the beginning and had three nice Greyhounds. When I got to know her a little, I saw how unbalanced she was. Her drug of choice was Vicodin, and she always wanted to go to SLRD with me to score drugs. It felt like my mother lived with me because I would come home from the track and she would be high on drugs, sitting outside smoking a cigarette. I was good at keeping my distance from her and the rent checks always arrived on time so I thought I could handle her as a roommate.

One night Mark got drunk and spent the entire night on his phone. It sounded like he called everyone in his phone book and had the same conversation over and over. He was yelling and crying that they should have just let him die, why can't everyone just let him die. Drunks have always frightened me and I didn't sleep all night. I kept the dogs awake so they could help me if I needed them.

The next day I put a lock on my bedroom door and told Mark that he would have to move out. He argued and told me that by law he had thirty days. I left and went to the track to talk to my new friend, Donny. Donny was a nice guy without a whole lot of ambition but he was a good rider. I told him about my latest dilemma and he asked me if I wanted to borrow his gun. There was just no way that I was going to suffer through thirty days of living with Mark now that I knew he was a drunk, so I borrowed the gun. I went home and told Mark again that I wanted him to leave now. When he refused, I pulled out my gun, pointed it at his balls, and told him to leave now before I shot his fucking balls off. The gun wasn't loaded and I was having trouble keeping a straight face, but Mark turned white and ran out of the room.

As he ran past Katie she told him that I was a crazy bitch and he better leave fast. He was gone within thirty minutes. Katie and I found dozens of empty wine bottles hidden in his room.

Katie was strange, especially when she was on Vicodin. She was very unattractive, big with bleached blond hair and the raspy voice of a smoker. She told me she had come from Lake Tahoe where she had a pet sitting business and showed me a business card to prove it. One day I came home from the track and Katie, in a very serious tone, told me we had to talk. We sat down in the kitchen and she told me that my cat, Andrew, had been fighting with a neighbor's cat, and when she picked him up to save him, he scratched the shit out of her. I could see that he had clawed her legs and arms. I asked her why on earth she would have picked up an angry cat and she told me she was helping me. I had not asked her for help and told her that although I was sorry that she got hurt I couldn't be held responsible for her bad choices. Katie was furious and told me that I owed her $600 for medical bills and this didn't include the cat fever that she would surely contract from Andrew. I laughed at her and told her she should move out. She refused to leave and began to retaliate. When I came home from the track the next day, she was gone but had left the air conditioner that I never used on high with all of the windows and doors open. The refrigerator and freezer door were both left wide open.

I was just beginning to realize that I had some control over my own life, especially in my home. I didn't want to wait and see what Katie's next move would be, so I took the offensive and went to the county courthouse and got a restraining order against her. She was served the next day and I never saw her again.

The next roommate was a friendly guy who had a job and enjoyed the dogs. His name was Chris and he was even neat around the house. We shared the washer and dryer and I had told him that if I left clothes in the dryer and he needed it, to just throw them on my bed. Instead, he would neatly fold my clothes for me. One day I needed the dryer and his clothes were in it, so I felt I should reciprocate and fold his clothes for him. In his load of laundry I found women's granny style underpants in a huge size that would fit him. I had never been the least bit attracted to Chris and his underpants were none of my business, but

I just thought this was too weird. I couldn't talk to him without envisioning his granny underwear.

Chapter 28

Lake Hodges

My business at SLRD was slow and I needed a more stable income. My vet, Dr. Paul, had always looked out for me, and told me that Cedar Hills Farm in Rancho Santa Fe was looking for an assistant manager. He was tight with the manager, Nancy, and could get me in if I wanted it. I knew the farm was beautiful, and a steady paycheck would be nice, but the thought of working at a farm didn't thrill me. I thought about it for a few days and decided that the security of a paycheck was what I needed. I had Gummy, Star, Chance, a few cats, and my pony Gus to think of, and they all liked to eat.

I met Nancy at the farm and didn't like her, but was careful to hide my feelings. She was overweight and wore tight jeans, pulled up high with a polo shirt tucked in. Suffice to say that she left very little to the imagination. Aside from being uncomfortable, I wondered how she could show the world her huge lady parts, and not be embarrassed. She had a strict dress code at the farm and we were all ordered to wear jeans or pants, never shorts, with shirts tucked in. I knew this would be a problem for me since I get very hot in the summer and must wear shorts. I have never liked being told what to wear.

When Nancy hired me as assistant manager she wouldn't budge on the 7:00 to 4:00 workday, but promised me occasional afternoons off, with pay. I had wanted to either start earlier or work through lunch, to get home sooner, and have time to spend with my dogs.

My rented house with Chris was a forty- five minute drive from Cedar Hills and my days were very long. The dogs weren't happy with me gone all day and it hit Gummy especially hard. She dragged all of our dog beds out of the house into the driveway and would sit there and wait for me to come home. When she ran out of patience, she destroyed each bed.

I found a cute little house at Lake Hodges, only twelve minutes from Cedar Hills and rented it. Lake Hodges is a unique area with dozens of old fishing cottages that surround a beautiful lake. It is only a few miles from the city of Escondido, but feels like miles from any town. Now I could come home for lunch and my animals were much happier. I spent twenty-four minutes driving back and forth, and that left thirty-six minutes to spend with the dogs. After work we would take long quiet walks around the lake.

My job at Cedar Hills was the only horse job I have ever had that I didn't like from day one. The days were so long, and for the first time in my life I was one of those people who hated Mondays and loved the end of the week. I worked five and a half days a week and counted the hours until Saturday afternoon. The occasional afternoons off that Nancy had promised were a lie.

Nancy was my biggest headache at the farm. She had been assistant manager for years under the previous manager Sheryl, who had built the business and helped to design the farm. Sheryl had been fired with no notice, and I always thought Nancy must have had something to do with it. The reason given for Sheryl's termination had been that she was conducting her bloodstock business on farm time. Since she was selling horses for the farm owner on farm time this didn't make sense. I knew that Nancy was very jealous of anyone who would dare to make a commission on farm horses. She warned me not to cut her out of any deals.

Nancy may have been a good office worker, but she was a useless horse woman. She couldn't see a lame horse if it fell on her. The training track was a tiny little 1/4 mile track with very tight turns. It would have been a good track just to break the horses and get them galloping and then ship them out. Nancy didn't understand that galloping fast on tight turns made the horses sore. She would stand on the deck outside of her office when I was on the track, and yell at me to go faster. Eventually most of the horses did go lame and I would have to tell her that the horse was lame and on which leg. Nancy would always disagree about which leg the horse was lame on. Dr. Paul was the farm vet and he would always ask me first what the problem was. I would say, "Left hind" and Nancy would loudly disagree and tell me that no, it is the right hind. It would take Dr. Paul about two seconds to agree with me every time. I had to wonder why she didn't just stay quiet since she didn't know anything.

Nancy was very insecure and very much had to be seen as the 'Boss lady.' She rarely left the office and sat at her desk all day. Aside from all of my horse responsibilities, it was my job to vacuum the office and take the trash out. Nancy would make a big deal out of lifting her fat legs for me to vacuum under her desk, and then refuse to hand me her trash can, but make me reach for it. Sometimes she would be painting her nails and ask me to dial a number on her desk phone for her. I despised the woman once I got to know her, but I always smiled and hid my feelings.

Nancy knew very little about breaking and training racehorses and was threatened by anyone who might know more than she did. Cedar Hills had lay-up horses from good barns at the track, and we always had plenty of horses starting back. Sometimes a lay-up would have been turned out in a pasture for a year and they came back in wild. It would have been easy to make these horses safe with a little bit of tranquilizer. Nancy was against using tranquilizer and she got many riders hurt.

We had a big strong gray colt starting back from a year-long lay-up and he was very difficult. He wanted to rear and it was hard to keep him moving forward, even in the round pen. Without drugs to help me, I planned on spending several days or even a week or two in the round pen, before taking this horse out on the track. Nancy wanted everything to go according to her schedule. She thought that three days was long enough to spend on any horse in the round pen, and then they should be on the track. She wasn't capable of looking at a horse who couldn't behave in the round pen, and understanding that he wasn't ready to go to the track.

I was good at tuning her out most of the time, but one day after she asked me to dial a number for her because her nails were freshly painted, I was angry. I was riding the gray horse in the round pen without drugs and he was being a jerk. A blind horseman could have seen that he wasn't ready to go to the track if he couldn't even behave in the round pen. Nancy was watching me ride and said, "What's wrong, are you scared of this one, are you going to stay in here all month." I rarely use the C word even in my thoughts, but I was thinking, 'you stupid fucking C.' She wouldn't shut up so in anger I said, "Open the door." A groom opened the round pen door and I rode the horse out to the track. We made it around the track once. I wanted to call it a day and bring him back in, since I only just barely had control. Nancy saw me start to pull up and told me to go around again. The colt stopped, refused to go forward, and started rearing on the track. He lost his balance and fell, landing hard on my knee. The horse ran off and the grooms caught him and brought him back to me. Nancy insisted that I get back on and take him another lap, for my own good. I was hurt and so angry at the stupid fat woman, that I did get back on and ride one more lap.

By the next day my knee was so sore I could barely walk and couldn't ride. The workman's comp Doctor Nancy sent me to, told me to get tough, that I was only bruised, and sent me to physical therapy. Physical therapy lasted only a few days because my knee got much worse. I demanded to go to a better Doctor and was diagnosed with a tear to my MCL and cartilage tear. I was given a knee brace and ordered to rest and not ride.

A person with self-esteem would have told Nancy to be quiet, instead of riding a dangerous horse like I did. I now had a choice of going on workman's comp or working light duty. There was a stigma attached to workman's comp with horse people and I couldn't get through it, so I chose to work light duty. Again, my lack of self-worth kicked in. Instead of taking care of me, I chose to work at a farm I didn't like under a manager I despised.

The knee brace I wore was big and bulky and wouldn't fit under jeans and was too uncomfortable over my jeans. I broke the dress code and wore shorts with the brace. Since I had chosen to work when I could be home resting, I thought Nancy could bend a little. I should have known that she was too fat to bend. I wore only long shorts, almost to my knees, and hoped that Nancy could let it go.

For two days Nancy didn't say a word about the shorts. On the third day I was in the round pen doing groundwork with a very aggressive, hard to handle colt in my shorts and knee brace, and my knee hurt. I was sure that groundwork in the round pen wouldn't be classified as light duty, but I was determined to do a good job on this colt. Nancy was watching and instead of seeing that I was doing a damn good job she said, "You look like shit." I said, "Excuse me?" and she repeated, "You look like shit and you are breaking the dress code. I can't have you wearing shorts." I asked her if we could talk about this when I finished with my horse and she said, "Yes, but I won't change my mind."

I put the horse away and went into her office and she again told me that I looked like shit. I was wearing a button down blouse and Bermuda style jean shorts. Even after hearing Nancy tell me that I looked like shit three times, I couldn't believe it. My only reply was, "But these shorts are Calvin Kleins."

I told her that my knee hurt, the brace was uncomfortable, and I had to wear shorts. She stood by her foolish dress code so I quit on the spot and went on workman's comp. My decision to quit felt so good. Finally, I knew what it felt like to take care of me, to value my own wellbeing. Eventually I had a total of four knee surgeries before I was sound again.

When I first moved into my new little house with the dogs and cats we all loved it. Like a little girl I would walk into each room and say to myself, 'this is My office, this is My bedroom, this is My kitchen.' I had cried buckets of tears in our last house and I knew I could never be happy there. This house felt like a fresh start, full of hope.

The new rent was high and I could barely survive financially. Two months after I moved in, I paid rent and all of my bills, and I had 78 cents left in the bank. This was cutting it too close for me and I wasn't comfortable. I didn't see an alternative to looking for another roommate, so I ran my roommate ad again.

Susan answered my ad and could pay the $500 that I was asking for rent. She had a job and was very friendly, but about 200 pounds overweight. I didn't realize at first that her weight problem was a lifestyle choice that would annoy me. The truth was that anything that bothered me, I either ignored or toughed my way through it.

Susan was so heavy that she broke all of my chairs and the hand railing on our porch. If she dropped something, usually food, on the floor she couldn't bend over to clean it up. I saw her drop a cupcake and instead of picking it up she called Gummy.

On weekends she would invite an overweight friend over, and the two of them would buy huge party platters at the grocery store and feast all day. The first time I saw three party platters in the kitchen I thought she was having a party and inviting lots of people. When she wasn't feasting on a weekend she would stay in her room and watch TV all day Saturday and Sunday. It was like having a beached whale in the house.

One day I came home at lunch time and saw a stain six feet in diameter on our white Berber carpet. The stain looked like coffee and I could easily imagine Susan spilling an entire pot of coffee and walking away from the spill. I worked for days on the stain and repeatedly asked Susan what it was, but she could only blame the dogs. Even Gummy couldn't make coffee and then spill an entire pot of it, so I knew she was lying.

In spite of our differences, Susan was still one of the best roommates I had ever had, and I tried to get along with her. Saturday afternoons were my favorite time of the week because I had a day and a half of no Cedar Hills and Nancy in front of me. I was getting ready to take the dogs to the beach one Saturday and I felt, more than heard, something outside hitting the ground hard. I was in my bedroom close to the deck, and I swear my floor moved like an earthquake. When I walked outside to see what was going on, I saw that Susan had fallen down four cement stairs that led to the driveway, and was in a crumpled heap on the ground. Her weight had made the earth move. My first thought was that I had looked forward to a Saturday afternoon with my dogs all week and no one could take that from us. My next thought was a little more human, that I should at least make sure Susan was dead before I left for the beach. I planned on calling 911 when I returned. Susan was motionless and I couldn't tell if she was breathing, so I asked her if she was dead. I didn't expect a reply and was heading towards my car with the dogs when she said, "No." Now I had no choice, the beach day was called off, and I would have to help Susan get to the hospital.

I was still finding a middle ground between being totally selfless and totally selfish. Karen was helping me to realize that I saw everything in black and white, there was no middle ground for me. I still saw Karen every Wednesday and our sessions were often the highlight of my week. She was always kind and it felt very safe to talk to her. Karen is the first person I had ever really talked to in my life and I was thirty-nine when I met her.

Gummy had put herself in control of the other dogs and me, and decided that I needed a man in my life. On the beach she would find a single man, act really cute with spins and leaps, and lead him back to me. I didn't agree with any of her choices for me, but I did appreciate her efforts.

At Lake Hodges Gummy had met a man who rode his horse by our house almost every day. He had two horses and rode one and led the other. Gummy decided that he was the man for us and would follow him and his horses. He had to bring Gummy back to me every day and finally introduced himself as Roger; he lived less than a mile away. Roger invited me to ride his extra horse. Gummy, Star, and Chance were thrilled to be out with horses again. We rode together often and eventually started dating. Roger seemed very sane and not abusive in any way, which was a welcome change for me.

We had been dating just a couple of months when Roger went to a weekend party at a friend's ranch. He told me that the party was an annual event where everyone camped out, got drunk, and then helped the ranch owner brand his cattle. I didn't think that Roger was experienced in handling cows, and a group of inexperienced drunks working with cows sounded like a disaster in the making to me. I told him that drunks and cows shouldn't mix but he didn't listen to me.

The next day I got a call from one of Roger's friends telling me that he had been kicked by a cow and was in the hospital. He had fractured his femur and needed surgery. I never stopped to think about how I felt, but went straight to the hospital. Roger was in extreme pain and yelling at nurses for more drugs. I don't handle hospitals well at all. I left as soon as I could.

If I had paused for a moment to consider how I felt about a drunk guy getting kicked by a cow he was trying to brand, and I would have concluded that he was an idiot, had not heeded my warning about getting drunk and playing with cows. Now he could deal with the results by himself, without any help from me.

Roger was discharged from the hospital a few days later and I went into dutiful girlfriend mode automatically. My plate was already full between the job I hated, and spending time with my own animal family, but I didn't give a thought for myself. The religions that teach that this is what 'good people' do are wrong. I have learned the hard way, that when you give 100 percent of yourself away there is nothing left.

Even though I had just played that game with Alberto, I did it again with Roger. He was in a lot of pain and couldn't do anything himself. I have always hated sick people and couldn't be a nurse if my life depended on it. I forced myself to spend as much time with him as I could, popped in to say good morning, stopped by at lunch time, and spent evenings with him.

Roger's horse that I had been riding was a sweet gentle mare named Penny. While Roger was incapacitated Penny got sick with colic and Roger couldn't afford to call the vet. I had treated many horses for colic in the past and knew that I could help Penny. It rained for a week and poor Penny was in too much pain to stand, and so she just layed down in the deep mud of her corral and shivered. I put a blanket on her, and with Dr. Paul's help selling me drugs at cost, I worked hard on the old girl for five days. At one point I was ready to give up because her eyes and lips turned yellow, indicating liver failure. Dr. Paul told me to keep treating her, and finally she rallied and I backed off the drugs.

Once Penny was up again and eating and drinking, I noticed that she would only drink sparkling fresh water. I was dumping the water trough every other day and filling it with fresh water. Although the water I dumped out wasn't bad, Penny wouldn't drink it. Roger didn't keep the water trough as clean as I did and Penny had a history of colic. My discovery of the cause of her colic was significant and easy to remedy. I told Roger that Penny needed absolutely fresh water or she would colic again and probably die. I suggested that he dump the trough and rinse it every day to keep her drinking. He wasn't very interested in my opinion. I had just saved Penny's life, spent only $60 on drugs, figured out the cause of her colic, and he wasn't very interested. It was beginning to feel a lot like dealing with Alberto and I backed away. Poor, sweet Penny died the within a year of colic.

After a couple of weeks Roger was getting around on crutches so I only spent evenings with him. Every night he would lie on his couch and watch TV and I would sit on the hard floor next to him. It was winter and floor was drafty, hard and cold. I was cold, uncomfortable, and tired but still I volunteered to spend time with him.

Finally with Karen's help I saw that I was making the decision once again to treat myself like shit. When I talked to Karen she always asked me, "How does that make you feel?" More often than not my answer would be, "Like shit."

The last straw with Roger was a grocery shopping trip. He still couldn't drive so I was helping him by driving him to the store. I needed a few things too so it wasn't a big sacrifice. I was pushing the cart and Roger was following me slowly on his crutches. It was Saturday afternoon and I was desperate for some 'me' time but here I was playing the dutiful girlfriend. I was trying to make the best of a bad situation by being light and cheerful. Since I hadn't taken time to eat lunch yet I was starving I and opened a bag of bread in the cart that I intended to buy. As I ate a slice of whole wheat bread in the store Roger came unglued. He told me that I couldn't do that; I should never open a bag of bread in a store and start eating. My reply was to eat another slice. We nearly came to blows in the store and I finally told him to shut up or walk home. We broke up soon after that fight in the grocery store.

I was so disappointed in myself because I had once again jumped back into an unhealthy relationship. I asked Karen how I could escape this shit once and for all and her answer was 'to become aware.' We went back over my relationship with Roger and she pointed out all the red flags that I had ignored. Karen warned me that change can take a while, and the best thing I could do was to pay attention to how I felt. Although this is a simple concept it was brand new to me. I never paid attention to how I felt. I was stuck in survival mode, and how I felt was insignificant to me. I could see that changing my life wasn't going to be easy, but failure wasn't an option. Karen was quick to point out that I was already making progress. I had suffered through eight years with Alberto and only a few months with Roger. That is progress.

Chapter 29

Florida

I was feeling ready for an adventure and was offered a job in Florida. Tim and Jim were twin brothers from the Philippines who owned a ranch near Ocala, and needed a trainer/manager. They wanted to try their hand at pinhooking, buying yearling Thoroughbreds, breaking and training them for about eight months and then selling them as two-year-olds. They offered me a generous salary and a huge four thousand square foot house to live in. I met Jim in Los Angeles and we discussed details. The house would be mine except for the master bedroom, which the brothers would use when visiting the farm. Tim lived in the Philippines and I would meet him in the fall when he arrived for the yearling sales in Ocala. It all sounded fantastic to me and I planned on driving to Florida with my dogs and cats the following month.

After I broke up with Roger I started dating a black race track veterinarian, Lance. I had a secret crush on him for years but had never met him. Whenever I saw him on the back-side of Santa Anita, I would adjust my walking route to walk by him, but he always had his back to me. I was too shy to speak so we had never met. Lance was gorgeous, with a lean athletic body, and I had always been attracted to veterinarians. A friend introduced us properly and he invited me out to dinner. He lived in L.A. and drove two hours to Lake Hodges for our first date.

Lance had crazy erratic energy, and I hate to admit that I found that attractive. He was always up, bouncing off the walls, and usually in a good mood. We were spending a lot of time together, either at his house or at mine, and I fell in love with him. In my mind he was the logical replacement for Scott. He would call me on the phone and talk for hours and I was so enthralled with him that the sound of his voice could captivate me for hours. I didn't really listen to his words because he was often speaking gibberish. With my lack of self-esteem I was thrilled that a busy veterinarian would spend hours on the phone with me. I could easily ignore the fact that much of it was gibberish.

When I visited Lance in L.A. I noticed that he never had his vet truck and always drove an old beat up BMW. He told me that he kept his truck parked at the track and I believed him. At first I assumed that he was taking time off to spend with me and I was flattered that a race track vet would do that. Track vets never take days off. Lance loved to say, "You are special honey" and that was music to my ears.

One weekend I was planning on spending Saturday night and Sunday with Lance in L.A., but I also wanted to attend the Del Mar horse show late Saturday night. I called Lance to cancel because I would be arriving at his house very late, after the horse show, but he insisted that he didn't mind the late hour. I went to the show and again called Lance to tell him that I wouldn't arrive until 12:00 and made sure that he still wanted me to come up to L.A. He told me that he would be waiting for me. I always took the dogs with me and Lance seemed to like them. They weren't crazy about him, but that was a red flag I chose to ignore.

I drove two hours and arrived at Lance's house around midnight. When I walked into his bedroom I felt a strange sense of foreboding overtake me. The hair on the back of my neck raised and I felt like I was in danger. I said hello to Lance and in a strange loud monotone voice he said, "Get those mother fucking dogs out of here." I wanted desperately to think that he was either talking in his sleep or joking, but he repeated his command to get the dogs out, again in the loud monotone. I asked him if he remembered that he had invited me and the dogs and we had spoken on the phone just two hours before. He could only repeat in the loud scary voice, "Get those mother fucking dogs out."

Chance, who had been so horribly abused by a crystal meth addict, was visibly shaken by Lance's weird behavior and started to throw up. Suddenly I was furious. Lance wasn't my dream man, but a sick piece of shit and probably a drug addict. I got my dogs together and we left.

I still had two hours to drive home and I was so sad and tired that I couldn't stay awake. I tried everything, the radio, talking to myself, opened the windows and the sunroof, and still I felt myself dozing off. Finally, just as I falling asleep while driving, I felt water being thrown in my face. I had the sunroof open but it wasn't raining and I had no idea where that water came from. My jacket and face were wet so I knew it was real.

We arrived home safely and went to bed after I apologized to the dogs for keeping them up all night and nearly crashing the car. Chance was still upset, but he was happy to be home and away from Lance.

I didn't plan on ever speaking to Lance again, but the next morning he called me and asked why I wasn't with him at his house. He told me that he didn't remember anything from the previous night and must have been talking in his sleep. I wasn't buying his shit and I told him that I thought he was doing drugs, dangerous, and out of his mind. It was obvious that he didn't even have a vet truck or a practice. He was a lie. I had turned him into my dream man.

For three weeks he called me every day to apologize and eventually his charm won out and I started seeing him again. He swore that he wasn't doing drugs and just had a lot of energy. I think I must have been the only one in the world who believed that lie.

I knew that Lance wasn't doing cocaine because he didn't disappear every thirty minutes to do a line, and still always seemed high. Whatever he was on was a drug that was unfamiliar to me. I had finally gotten to the point that I needed to know the truth about Lance and drugs. He talked fast and non-stop, sweated a lot, and looked very muscular, although he never worked out.

I decided to play narc even though I have always hated narcs. One day I called Lance and told him that I had just had a terrible day and wanted to do drugs. I asked him if I could come up to his house and do drugs with him. He said, "Sure, come on up." When I arrived two hours later, Lance was sitting on his couch and had a mirror with two huge lines and a straw waiting for me. When I asked him what it was and he told me it was crystal meth. It was too late to back down and for the only time in my life I had a reason to do drugs. I remember wondering if real narcs ever put themselves in this position. Lance and I both did the lines. I was up all night speeding my ass off and Lance went to bed. My answer was now crystal clear, Lance did so much crystal meth that it seemed to have no effect on him.

I so didn't want to know that Lance was a drug addict and had lost his veterinary practice already. I was getting ready for my trip to Florida and thought that the distance away from Lance would be good for me.

I was feeling crushed, taken advantage of, and stupid. One weekend Lance had driven down to visit me, and when his car died we found a local mechanic to fix it. When I took him to pick up his car he couldn't find his wallet and had to borrow money from me to pay for the repair. He put on a big show of being embarrassed and thankful and promised to pay me back the following day. What a fool I was!

I had taken Lance to meet Karen and she had not been at all impressed. He wasted our time by continually trying to talk over Karen. He was like a child who didn't know that people take turns speaking. Karen asked him nicely five times to be quiet and then she yelled at him to, "Behave or sit in the car."

I had a friend, Janice who was a therapist and we had ridden our horses together the day after Lance yelled at me, with his scary monotone voice. I am always happy when I ride but I couldn't even fake it that day. When Janice asked me what was wrong I told her my strange story about Lance. She was dating a therapist and later in the day she called me to tell me that she and her boyfriend both thought that Lance could be dangerous and that I should stay away from him.

My trip to Florida was well timed. Lance was very helpful with my move. I rented a storage area for my furniture and only planned on taking the dogs and cats with me in the car. I spent my last night in California at Lance's house and was leaving for Florida early the next morning.

It had gotten very hot and I was concerned about traveling with the cats and dogs all crammed into my car in the heat. The dogs were all good travelers but I wasn't sure about the cats.

Andrew had disappeared at Lake Hodges, and I only had two cats now. Jet, was an old black barn cat and Lacey, was a beautiful gray cat who I had found as an orphan kitten at Silent Oaks Farm. I loved them both and wanted to do what was best for them. Lance suggested that I leave the cats with him for a few weeks until the weather cooled down and then they could fly to Florida. He agreed that cross country in the car during a heat wave wasn't a good idea for cats.

I started my trip on schedule the next morning and left the cats with Lance. I have always loved road trips and was looking forward to this one. To be safe I had taken my car to a mechanic for an oil change and tune up. I was driving a Saab 9000 and it always ran well. When I got to Texas the car started misfiring. If I drove over forty-five miles per hour it would backfire. I stopped in the next town and had a mechanic look at my car, and he found a major problem that required a $1,000 part that would require ordering and waiting a day for delivery. My other option was to drive to the nearest Saab dealer 200 miles away where the part was in stock. I chose to drive forty-five miles per hour to the Saab dealer. The dealer found that the problem had been caused by my own mechanic not screwing in a spark plug properly when he tuned up my car. Luckily I had enough money to pay for the repair and was on the road again a few hours later.

It seemed to take forever to drive through Texas and it was hot. I had all of the windows and the sunroof open to make sure the dogs got plenty of air. Chance never ate when he was upset and had not eaten since we left home. I didn't get concerned until he also stopped drinking. I found a drug store and bought a thermometer to check his temperature. He had a high fever of almost 105 degrees. I forced myself to stay calm and found a vet clinic in the same shopping center as the drug store and took him in.

When I walked Chance into the clinic he was acting like a normal dog, which was abnormal for Chance. He always bounced off the walls and was barely under control. I told the vet that he was very sick with a 105 degree fever and he told me I must be mistaken. When he checked Chance's temperature it had gone up and was now 105.2. The vet administered IV fluids and started Chance on antibiotics. He wanted me to leave Chance with him for a day, but I explained that we were on the road. As soon as the fluid bag was empty and the vet took the catheter out, Chance jumped off the table and was ready to go back to our car. We continued our long journey and Chance recovered quickly.

We arrived in Florida a few days before the yearling sale. The house and farm were beautiful. Tim had leased a barn from his neighbor, Carl Roley, and we had access to very nice one mile sand track. Carl was a well-known pinhooker who sold over 100 two-year-olds each year. The track was owned by Carl, who leased rights to the surrounding farm owners.

I couldn't help but notice that no one in Florida seemed very happy to meet me. I understood that the locals wanted my job and were insulted that a woman from California was hired, but I wasn't prepared to be disliked on sight. When Carl's crew saw me with nothing to do for a few days before the sale, they suggested that I ask the weekend farm manager at my farm if he needed help. Ken was the full time manager who I was replacing, and Bob was a horse shoer and our weekend manager. Carl's crew told me that Bob lived in our barn apartment and on Saturday morning I knocked on his door and offered to feed the horses for him. He came out screaming mad and told me that he didn't need me to tell him how to feed. I hadn't told him how to feed, but only asked if he needed help since I had nothing to do. He reeked of alcohol and I realized I had been set up by Carl's crew. Weeks later someone told me that Bob drank hard every weekend and everyone stayed clear of him because he was a nasty mean drunk.

Tim arrived from the Philippines and Jim from L.A. the day before the sale. Howard, a friend of Noels drove in from Texas. I had studied the sales catalog and we were ready to go shopping. Tim wanted to invest $150,000 in horses and I was excited.

It was hot and humid in Ocala, but we walked around the barn area and looked at every horse I had marked in the catalog. When we had looked at my list of horses Tim, Jim, and Howard all went into the air conditioned sales pavilion, but I preferred to stay outside and watch the young horses as they were brought into the paddock area, before they were walked to the sale stage and auctioned off.

When I look at a horse as a racing or pinhook prospect I like to sit quietly and notice who grabs my attention. I have had tremendous success with this slightly unusual approach. Most buyers and their agents are nervous and busy running around at a sale and taking notes while I sit. I call it getting out of my own way so that I can clearly listen to my intuition. An outstanding horse will grab my attention every time.

I proved my method once in Argentina, and I had no doubts that it was superior. Alberto and I were at an impressive Thoroughbred farm just outside of Buenos Aires to look at their yearling crop. The crew brought each yearling out, one at a time to show us, and it took most of the day. I was so happy to be out of the city that I was only half watching the horses and mostly playing with my dogs. Hours later after we had seen all 100 of the yearlings, Alberto asked me to pick the top two. I told him who my picks were and he laughed. One had the best pedigree of the bunch, but the other had no pedigree to speak of. The following year when the horses had all run, these two colts were the best of the group by far, and had both won stakes races.

I was very confident in Ocala sitting under a tree and waiting for a horse to grab me. We bought six really nice yearlings at the sale and Tim had two homebreds. I started with a stable of eight. The horses we bought were exceptional and the homebreds were nice too.

A week after they arrived Tim and Jim were getting in their car to go back to the airport and fly home when Tim casually announced that by the way, Howard will be living in the house with me. If I had been operating like a person who had some self-worth, I would have immediately said, "No way, that is not the deal we had." Instead I said nothing. I had known that this deal was too good to be true and here was the proof.

Howard was retired military and a pilot who had lost his pilot's license in the U.S., but flew for Tim in the Philippines. I suspected that he lost his license because he was an alcoholic. I disliked Howard from the moment I was introduced to him. He kissed Tim's ass and acted like a servant, but I could sense that it was all part of his game. We disagreed on every subject. He wanted to start a puppy mill on the farm. I informed Tim that puppy mills were cruel and inhumane, so we couldn't possibly be involved.

With my usual survivor's mindset I decided to make the best of the situation and just deal with Howard. I think he was attracted to me at first, and the mere thought gagged me. Tim had asked him to teach me how to use the computer so that we could communicate by email. Howard would get behind me as I sat in front of the computer, and put his hand on top of mine to show me where to move the mouse. His touch gave me the creeps, but I took it in stride and learned fast so that he wouldn't have an excuse to touch me.

Howard didn't like dogs in the house and told Tim that they should stay outside in the dog run. My dogs had never been in a dog run and I couldn't keep them in a cage, especially in Florida heat. We finally agreed that I wouldn't give the dogs the run of the house, but keep them in my room. This was so, not what I had imagined my life in Florida would be like.

I couldn't hide my distain for Howard and within a week we were at war. He was as useless as Alberto in the barn. The first time he walked one of my fillies down the aisle way in front of the barn, he turned her right into a wheel barrel. She hit her hind legs and then bolted forward, and I grabbed her from Howard or she would have been a loose horse. I emailed Tim and told him that Howard was too green to help in the barn and I needed to hire a groom. He agreed that we couldn't risk hurting the horses and told Howard to stay out of the barn.

I hired a groom and started breaking the horses. They had all been raised as sales prospects and were easy to break. Carl's riders seemed to hate me still, although we hadn't spoken ten words to each other, and they didn't even know me.

Howard sought revenge in the house. He started spying on me. When I used the phone to call friends in California, I had to go in my room and close the door, and then in my bathroom with the door closed, and then in the shower with that door closed. Still, he would manage to hear parts of my conversations. He rummaged through my dresser drawers and once found a fresh vomit stain on the carpet from the dogs before I did, although my bedroom door was closed.

Tim called me and asked why I hadn't been answering his emails and I told him I hadn't received any emails. Suspecting that Howard was screwing around, I searched his desk and found a file named 'Susan's emails.' He had deleted my email messages on the computer and then printed and hidden them from me.

I was getting very depressed in Florida. People weren't nice to me and I was sharing a house with a dreadful man. Karen and I were still having sessions on the phone once a week and she asked me why I didn't leave. At first I didn't see it as an option since I had committed to breaking these horses and getting them to the sale. She pointed out that Tim had broken our agreement when he put Howard in the house with me. I wasn't a quitter and didn't think I could leave in the middle of a breaking season.

The horses were all galloping beautifully on the track. Since Carl's riders wouldn't ride with me, I needed to hire a rider to get the horses going together, in company. The only rider I could find who would work for me was, Kenny, and he was young and very green.

I only planned on putting him on the easiest horses but he couldn't even ride them. He would lose his stirrups six times every lap around the track. I left him alone on the first day, and the second day I told him that if he relaxed his knees and let his weight fall down into his feet and ankles, he wouldn't lose his stirrups six times every mile he galloped. I didn't expect a thank you, but I was shocked when he started yelling at me. He screamed that I was the terrible rider and everyone was talking about me and how useless I was. I asked him who had broken these eight horses and had them galloping beautifully in only five weeks if not me? Kenny quit that day and stomped off still yelling at me.

Living in Florida was like going back in time, and I didn't fit here. Carl Roley had a son, Michael, who had made headlines before I arrived in Florida. Michael had a history of drunk driving and had already been arrested three times in Ocala. One night he was driving drunk with three friends in his truck when he hit and killed a young black boy walking along the road. The dead boy, Eugene McBride, was only thirteen years old and had been an honor student and a star athlete at his high school.

Michael was out on bail when he fled to Brazil with a fake passport. After six months in Brazil he came back to stand trial in Ocala. A Marion County jury acquitted him of DUI manslaughter and vehicular homicide. His only defense was that he had been playing chicken with the boy. There were no skid marks to indicate that he had even tried to avoid hitting the boy, and his blood alcohol level was .14, almost double the legal limit, an hour after the murder.

Michael came from a wealthy white family and had killed a black boy while driving drunk, and he was found not guilty of murder. I was absolutely shocked that a man who already had three drunk driving arrests could be anything but guilty of murder, after he ran over a black boy while drunk. I knew that life was different in the South, but this was an outrage.

The NAACP quickly organized a peaceful protest in a church in Ocala. I was sick with the horror that a rich white man could murder a black boy, break bail, flee to Brazil on a fake passport, and still be found not guilty of murder. I attended the protest and was the only white person in a crowd of over 300 protesters. Tears ran down my face as the boy's mother and sister spoke to us about forgiveness and pleaded with us not to riot in Ocala.

After the protest dozens of people shook my hand and thanked me for my support. They didn't care that I was white or from California. Even through the sadness, anger, and despair, I felt love that night and I joined the NAACP. I wanted to be as brave and strong as these people and vowed to always stand up against racism.

Howard continued to drive me crazy at the farm. He had a couple of horses of his own in Texas and was sure that he was a good horseman with valuable opinions. The previous manager had a great feeding program, and as a result, all of the mares were fat and dappled. Howard wanted to earn points from Tim by saving money, so he found some cheap grain and informed me that he was changing the feeding program to save money. I refused to make any changes since all of the horses looked fabulous, so Howard brought Tim into the argument. Tim sided with me, but it was a lame victory. I had survived eight years of living with a want-to-be horseman who thought he had valid opinions and I couldn't do it again.

I started hating Florida. The only horse person who had been nice to me was a young black boy, Kiely, who worked for Jim, a trainer and pinhooker neighbor. Kiely had dreams of being a jockey and Jim had promised him a job as a rider, but for the last six months he had been only feeding and cleaning stalls. One Sunday Kiely didn't want to go to church with Jim, who was a born-again Christian, and in a rage, Jim choked him. When I heard this story I was again outraged. Kiely was very small, weighed less than 100 pounds and was being treated like a slave. He was extremely athletic, and could do a series of front and back flips from a standstill with the ease of a super athlete. I had my pony, Gus, with me in Florida and told Kiely he could ride him. Gus was the first horse he rode in Florida and he couldn't thank me enough. Carl Roley stepped in when he heard that Jim had choked Kiely, and hired him as a rider to get him away from Jim. Kiely went on to become a good jockey in the Midwest before he died from injuries suffered in a racing accident.

I felt myself becoming very depressed. The mere sight of Howard nearly made me throw up. Tim finally moved him out of the house and into the barn apartment, but I still saw him on the farm. Howard had to be in charge and would invent ridiculous rules for me. One such rule was that I had to park in a straight line in front of the barn. It didn't matter that my car was usually the only car in front of the barn. It drove Howard crazy that I parked at an angle so he drew lines with paint and made parking spaces in front of the barn. The clearly defined parking spaces only made me protest more so now I would park parallel to the barn and across two of his spaces. This would make Howard so mad that he would shout at me I am the COO! This was as close to humor as I got in four months.

Lance and I had not really discussed our relationship when I left for Florida. My last night in California that I spent with him wasn't very comfortable. He had no electricity or water because he hadn't paid the bills. He laughed it off like it was a joke and he had forgotten to pay the bills, but it wasn't ringing true. I had no intention of being committed to a drug addict, and I saw him going downhill fast. To this day I wonder what possessed me to leave my two cats with him.

Lance and I talked on the phone a couple of times a week and he always told me the cats were fine. I had left them with a twenty pound bag of cat food and they were both easy to care for. About a month after I left California I got a call from Tina, the friend who had set me up with Lance. She told me that Lance was in jail and asked what she should do with my cats. I wanted them with me in Florida ASAP. Tina was wonderful, and she quickly organized transport for the two cats to fly to Florida. She warned me that Lance had not taken care of them and they were both very thin. I picked them up in Ocala two days later and was shocked at their condition. They were both extremely skinny and sat on my lap in the car all the way home. They couldn't take their eyes off me and I could see that they had suffered with Lance. I felt so terrible for letting them down. I had completely failed them and promised they would never ever be hungry again.

Finally I just couldn't take it anymore and wanted to leave Florida. I had some money saved but didn't want to go home to California without a job. I called my old friend, Jude, and he agreed that I should give notice and come home. He needed a trainer at Pomona race track for his two-year-olds for the next six months and hired me.

I gave notice to Tim and found a good trainer to send the horses to in Ocala. The new trainer met Howard and quickly banned him from her barn.

Chapter 30

Pomona

I was delighted to leave Florida and started my drive back to California on January first. My radio was blasting and I laughed when I got a speeding ticket as I drove away from Ocala. I couldn't get away fast enough.

Our trip was uneventful and not difficult even with the three dogs and two cats. I think they all wanted to go home too.

I arrived in California a week before my horses were due to ship in to Pomona and needed to find a place to live. Tina was also looking for a house so we decided to become roommates. I had known her in Santa Ynez when she was married to a rider at Silent Oaks Farm. Back then she was a mother and had a part time job as a waitress. I knew that she had left her children and husband to live with Mike, a trainer in Arizona. Mike was an abusive crystal meth addict, and I had heard that Tina was also doing meth. She told me she had broken up with Mike and he had just gotten out of jail for abusing her. Since she had done such a wonderful job of quickly shipping my cats to me in Florida I didn't thing she was doing meth anymore. I told her before we even looked for a house, that I wouldn't want Mike to be in the picture, and she assured me that she was finished with him.

Tina found a little farm to rent in Chino, only a fifteen minute drive from the track in Pomona. The farm was completely fenced for dogs so we were happy. The house was old, but at least it was in California. Life was good again, I had a training job and all of my animals were together and safe.

Jude's horses shipped in to Pomona and his rider, Bret, came with them. Bret was from New Zealand and was a good hand. He had broken all of the horses at Jude's farm and I expected him to be annoyed that I had been hired to train at Pomona instead of him. If he was bothered he never let it show. We got along great from day one. I was careful not to step on his toes. Since he knew the horses so well, I asked him to help me make up the set list. Bret and I would gallop the horses in sets and only he knew which horses should be paired together. We had so much fun galloping that people thought we were a couple. He had a wicked sense of humor that I appreciated. He was married, and we were just two riders who rode well together.

Lance had written me a long apologetic letter, when he was in jail for not paying child support. He was sorry that he hadn't taken care of my cats and admitted that crystal meth was his problem. He had gotten clean in jail and wanted to have a life without drugs. He planned on reviving his veterinary practice on the track and wanted me to be in his life again. Bret and Lance lived in the same apartment complex near Santa Anita and were friends.

I had been spending time with Lance since I got back to California and he did seem to be doing better. He didn't have a vet truck yet but was doing some vet work out of his car. He was spending at least three nights a week at my house.

One day an old girlfriend of Lance's called me to confirm that Lance and I were not seeing each other. Before I could answer that she was mistaken, she told me that she had just spent the night with Lance and he had fucked her three times. I told her that yes, we had broken up.

I immediately called Lance and asked him why he would sleep with another woman when he was dating me. His only answer was that emotions ran high and he had sex with her. I asked him if his emotions had run high three times and hung up on him.

For the next couple of days I was quiet at Pomona. I was as disappointed in myself as I was Lance. Bret asked me what was wrong and I finally told him what Lance had done. When I told him my sad story we were both in stalls, tacking up horses, and were talking over the walls. When I got to the part of the story about the woman telling me that Lance fucked her three times Bret feigned disgust and said, "Oh my God Susan, not three times!" This was so funny coming from Bret, with his heavy New Zealand accent, that I collapsed laughing. I realized I had made a mistake, but there was no point dwelling on it. For weeks Bret would find ways to put the number three into a conversation, and we couldn't stop laughing.

I was free of Lance and would stay that way for life. He went back to crystal meth, spent time in jail for abusing a woman who he bit in the face, and lost his veterinary license.

Bret and I did a fantastic job with the Jude's horses and had them all breezing 3/8ths of a mile before they shipped into Santa Anita. I stayed on at Pomona and freelanced horses for a few weeks after Jude's horses shipped out, but it felt too dangerous and I didn't want to get hurt. Pomona is not an A rated track and the track was only 5/8ths of a mile. I had all the horses I could get on, but many of them were sore and so working around tight turns wasn't safe or fun.

Tina had become a nightmare of a roommate. Although she agreed before she moved in that Mike would never be near our house, he was there all the time. She had a young Australian Shepard puppy that wasn't house broken and she wouldn't clean up after her dog. I would come home in the afternoon to find broken lawn furniture from a fight with Mike.

Tina desperately needed a job and Jude let me hire her as a groom at Pomona. She was good for two days and then started complaining that she didn't want to be a groom, she wanted to ride. We didn't need another rider, but I told her she could take my pony, Gus, out with our sets. It is always nice to have a good pony with young horses and I thought this would make Tina happy. Two days later she was complaining that she needed to be paid more if she was going to ride the pony all morning. I had to let her go. We had a good, happy, crew and Tina with her endless complaints and high drama didn't fit in.

One day Tina exploded at home and told me she was moving out. I was thrilled she was leaving but I hid my feelings. She ranted and raved for hours about what an impossible bitch I was. I was so happy that she was leaving that I didn't even pay attention to her rant.

Chapter 31

Pala

I was ready to leave Pomona and wanted to go back to San Luis Rey Downs. I found a cute little farmhouse to rent in Pala, only twelve miles from the track and moved in. My house was one of three on a twenty acre farm. The back of the property bordered Indian land with miles of trail riding and a beautiful mountain. I had a huge grass pasture for Gus and a barn.

The landlord's son, Chris, lived in another small house very close to mine, but he seemed friendly enough. The only other negative about the farm is that it bordered a busy road and was not fenced for dogs. I would have to know where my dogs were every second to keep them out of the road and safe.

The farm was a good place for us. We had miles of new trails to explore and a mountain to ride on. One trail took us to Medicine Rock, a sacred Indian landmark. I never saw anyone else on the trails and it felt like my own private paradise. The dogs were thrilled to out on trails again and so was I. We spent hours on the mountain every afternoon.

I went back to San Luis Rey Downs and was hired by Fabio Nor as a rider. He had a big stable of mostly older horses from trainer Neil Drysdale. Fabio was from Brazil and I had to be careful not to step on his Latin ego, but usually we got along fine. Neil had sent his own riders from Santa Anita and I was the only local rider and the only American in the barn.

We had one young horse in the barn that a fantastic rider, Nuno, rode. His name was Fusiachi Pegasus and he was a terror. This young horse was like none other. He was huge and powerful even as a two-year-old he had a mind of his own. It would take Nuno ten minutes extra just to get him to the track in the morning because he would duck into barns along the way and refuse to leave. Once he got out on the track he would stand on his hind legs in the middle of the track and stop traffic. Fusiachi Pegasus eventually won the Kentucky Derby and I don't think he would have ever gotten there without Nuno.

Fabio eventually lost Neil's horses and I went to work for another trainer at SLRD. Phillip had mostly young horses that needed to be broke and prepped for an upcoming two-year-old sale. Phillip was friendly but I had some doubts about his ability to break and train racehorses. He was a Cal Poly graduate and he thought his degree made him a horseman.

Phillip did his own groundwork on the young horses in the round pen and wanted me to do the first rides. If you know your horse, and have done your groundwork properly, the horse should already be comfortable with a saddle and know how to stop and turn before the rider gets on. Walter had taught me well, and I could do things in the round pen on long lines that most horse people hadn't even thought of. My horses never bucked and my first rides were never rodeos.

I told Phillip that I had no problem doing first rides, but I wanted to do my own groundwork. Phillip was insulted and said no. I asked him if I could long line each horse just once to get to know him before I got on and he said no. I understood that this was his barn and he was in charge, but I thought he was being unreasonable. I wasn't comfortable trusting his groundwork. Phillip asked me if I could suggest another rider and I told him to hire Mary Kay.

Mary Kay was a friend of mine and I had gotten her a job riding at Cedar Hills. When I broke a horse, I would take him to the track a few times until he knew how to behave, before I gave him to another rider. If he didn't behave on the track, he wasn't broke enough to pass on to another rider. I felt that my reputation as a horse breaker was riding on every one of my horse's butts, and I made sure they were safe and well broke. When I did pass him on to a rider I would tell them everything about the horse so that the transition was smooth. I had done this for Mary Kay at Cedar Hills and I assumed that she would have the same level of integrity that I did.

Mary Kay rode very different from me. If I had a horse with a problem, like he didn't want to turn left, I would fix it and teach him to turn left. Mary Kay did what Walter called stealing rides. Instead of fixing problems she would avoid them. If her horses didn't want to turn left she would only go to the right. When she handed her horse off to the next rider she would say nothing. An honest rider would have warned other rides that the horse won't turn left.

One morning I was on a 'Mary Kay broke' colt for the first time in the arena. We did a few laps to the right and when I turned him left he reared and fell into a fence post, crushing my knee. I was furious because Mary Kay didn't tell me he wouldn't turn left. After I got hurt I watched Mary Kay in the arena and saw that she never took her horses to the left because they would be going toward the open arena gate. In typical Mary Kay style, she avoided teaching them not to go out the open gate, and only went to the right.

I was diagnosed with a torn MCL and torn cartilage on what was previously my good knee. I had two knee surgeries and the summer off. I had learned from my experience at Cedar Hills that I needed to stop, rest, and recover because no one else was going to look out for me.

My Doctor was very good and the first surgery went well. I have always hated physical therapy. I have met too many physical therapists who were useless and I didn't trust them. Immediately after my surgery a therapist put an ultrasound machine on my still bandaged knee, and caused me so much pain that I screamed. He thought the machine might have shorted out so he got a different machine and made me scream again. When I told my doctor what had happened, he was angry because he hadn't ordered ultrasound, and he told me the pain was from the fluid in my knee post-surgery. When I told my doctor that I hated physical therapy and had no trust or respect for the therapists, he asked me if I would prefer to run instead. I jumped at the chance. To make it even better, he told me I should run on s, and the beach would be best.

I went to the beach in Del Mar every day with Chance, Gummy, and Star, and we ran. Workman's comp was sending me checks that covered my rent and food, and I had been ordered to run on the beach. In my whole life I had never had a paid vacation and I loved this.

Since I was now a regular on the Del Mar Beach, I met the other beach regulars. One handsome man had caught my attention because he went for long walks every day. His name was Dave and we said hello every day but that was all. I was too shy to talk to him and I assumed he wasn't very interested in me.

Gummy was up to her old tricks of looking for men for me and she met Phil. Phil was another regular on the Del Mar Beach and Gummy liked him because he shared food with her. She would sit on his lap until the food was eaten and then do a cute little twirl and skip and run to me. Phil was very friendly, but I wasn't interested in him because he sat for hours on the beach and drank beer. He never walked or swam, only drank for hours.

One day Phil was sitting very close to me after Gummy invited him and Dave walked by. Dave knew Phil and he stopped to talk. When Dave spoke to me, Phil put his arm on my back, like I was his. Phil had never touched me and I couldn't believe he was playing this game. I could see that Dave got the message that I was with Phil, but it was a lie. Although I didn't want to be touched by Phil, because of my lack of self-worth, I didn't feel like I could do anything. I sat in angry silence and then moved away from him after Dave left.

I knew that if I wanted to meet Dave I would have to make the effort now that he thought I was unavailable. The next day when I saw him on the beach I started a conversation and soon we became friends. He lived in a little beach house very close to our beach and was a surfer. Gummy loved him and stopped looking for other men for me.

Dave and I started dating and we were a good match. He was a true beach person like me, and loved the sand and sun. We went for long walks and swims in the warm summer ocean. I was having the most wonderful summer.

I found two young dogs on a country road between Pala and Temecula and wanted to help them. They had crossed the road in front of me once, and the young male dog stopped to look at me before his sister hustled him out of the road. He looked very friendly and as our eyes met, I could see what a good natured, happy guy he was. Both were very thin with horrible looking coats. Every time I saw the two dogs over the next couple of weeks they looked worse. Finally I saw them on a day that I had time to help and I parked on the side of the road. The young male dog was easy and jumped into my car more than ready to be rescued. The girl dog was in charge and very weary of me. The boy was in bad condition, extremely skinny, and his front legs were without hair and swollen. His skin looked like elephant skin and he smelled septic. The young girl dog was in a little better condition, but she would not get near me, even when her brother was sitting in the car. I thought it would be cruel to separate them so I took her brother out of the car and went home to get tranquilizer. I was back in twenty minutes with a can of cat food laced with tranquilizer and the young girl dog ate it. Forty-five minutes later she collapsed in a thicket of poison oak. I couldn't leave her there so I had to climb into the thicket and pull her out. I took both dogs home and a generous vet friend, Carl, spayed, neutered, and cleaned them up. They both had mange but it was easy to cure. I named the boy Anthony and the girl Daisy.

Anthony was always happy go lucky and grew up into a 120 pound dog. Daisy was very serious for a young dog and was devoted to Anthony. If she sensed danger, she quickly got Anthony to a safe place. She was terrified of gun shots and would take Anthony into the barn to hide if she heard a shot. Years later in an x-ray, we found a pellet from a gun in her hind leg.

My knee healed from the first surgery, but I was still sore and went in for a second surgery. Two days after the surgery, I was out taking a short walk around the farm with Dave when Anthony ran into my knee. He was huge and uncoordinated and was playing with Daisy, when he just hit me at the worst angle. I screamed in pain and then Chance jumped on Anthony to kill him. Chance didn't like Anthony to begin with and was sure that we didn't need him. Now that he had hurt me, Chance wanted him dead. I knew that Chance was in a rage and had to be stopped so I jumped in and separated them. My knee was mangled and I had torn my ACL. It took another surgery to clean up the torn ACL.

I have never been good at resting when I need to heal. I get depressed if I can't ride. Gus was such a good safe horse that I really didn't think I was taking a big risk by going on a trail ride. I saddled him up, climbed on the fence, swung on, and we were off to the mountain. The dogs were ecstatic and the weather was perfect. I found that riding wasn't as painful as walking and was enjoying our trail ride when I made the mistake of taking a new trail. I had Chance, Gummy, Anthony, Daisy, and old Star with me and the trail became very steep. I had to get off Gus and lead him up the steep incline. It was so steep that he couldn't walk but was taking lounging jumps to get up the hill. To turn around and go down the steep mountain would be even worse than continuing to climb. I still had my knee bandaged and was envisioning a helicopter rescue. We finally made it to the top, but Star had attempted to follow us and couldn't. She was still at the bottom of the hill and crying. The hill was way too steep to take a horse down and I planned on taking a different route home, but couldn't leave old Star stranded. I knew I would have to climb back down and help Star but there was nothing to tie Gus to. I was just getting ready to tie my reins behind the saddle and tell Gus to go home when a truck drove up. I had never seen a person on these trails until now, when I needed help. The driver of the truck was a geologist and he had a bowl and a gallon of water for the dogs. Even Gus took a sip. He held Gus for me while I climbed down the hill and rescued Star. We all survived and made it home safely.

I loved my little house and my mountain but the landlord's son, Chris, wasn't happy with my new dogs, Anthony and Daisy. I tried to place them but everyone wanted big goofy Anthony and not Daisy. Daisy was sweet and shy and it would take a special person to see what a dear she was. I didn't have the heart to separate them since Daisy's life purpose was to take care of her brother, so I kept them. Chris told me that he had seen the two of them months before and he shot at them to get them off of his ranch.

I was learning to dislike Chris. I thought he was a heartless jerk to shoot at starving puppies. Anthony and Daisy were still outside dogs and slept on my porch or in the barn and did no harm. Eventually I house broke them and invited them inside, much to Chris's dismay.

Chris smoked cigarettes and I was finding cigarette butts around my house, mostly near the windows. I didn't think that he was interested in me enough to be a peeping tom, but why else was he smoking outside my windows? If he was just taking a quick look inside to see that the dogs had not damaged his house, he wouldn't have been at the window long enough to drop a pile of cigarette butts.

Dave and I were getting along really well. He was romantic and fun and we both loved the beach. Chance, who had no friends besides me, even liked him. Chance was ball crazy, and Dave would throw him tennis balls until he was exhausted.

I never get jealous, but Dave had an old girlfriend, Patricia, who I found very annoying. She was one of those girls who always needed help and wasn't afraid to ask for it. Dave was a good friend to her and helped her time and time again.

After suffering through years with Alberto and never being a priority in my own relationship, I couldn't tolerate being second to Patricia. I wanted to be the most important woman in my boyfriend's life and could settle for nothing less.

One morning Dave had spent the night at my house and I got up early to feed the animals, make coffee, and pick up the newspaper at the gate. I thought that we could drink my delicious organic coffee with real cream and honey, and read the paper together in bed. This was a rare treat for me because I was always at the track in the mornings.

When I came back to bed with the coffee and newspaper Dave was on my phone with Patricia. They were planning a yard sale to get rid of everything Patricia had in storage on L.A. She wanted Dave to rent a truck, drive two hours to L.A., bring all of her things back to Del Mar, and have her yard sale at Dave's house. Most people just open the door of their storage space and sell without so much effort. They talked and talked and talked, and I was getting really angry. I drank my coffee and read the paper alone as they talked. Finally I could take it no more and I unplugged my phone.

Dave was furious that I could be so rude as to unplug the phone, and I was hurt and angry that he had ruined our morning by bringing Patricia and her needs into my bed. I knew that Dave was a wonderful man but I couldn't be second and we broke up.

My workman's comp vacation ended as the summer ended and I was ready to ride. I went back to SLRD as a freelance rider and worked at a farm in Temecula in the afternoons. After getting hurt twice in accidents that shouldn't have happened, I was more than ready to start my own business again.

Walter had warned me that I now knew too much to work for most people. It was hard for me to work for what I considered to be idiots, especially when my safety was on the line. I could be agreeable up until it got dangerous, and then I would say no. My biggest fear, which is shared by many riders on the track, was that I would end up in a wheelchair.

When I was new on the track I thought that accidents were just bad luck. Since then, I had seen many trainers making bad decisions and risking horses and riders out of ignorance. One morning at SLRD a trainer wanted to work a three-year-old filly that I had sold him, but his Argentine rider refused to work her. A group of owners were at the track waiting to watch this horse work. The Argentine told the trainer that his horse was too sore to work and he got off the horse. For a macho Argentine man to take off a horse, surrounded by a group of owners, she had to be dead lame. The trainer found another rider and told him to work the horse and he demanded a strong, fast work. This trainer was a good talker but knew nothing about legs. I was on the track as the horse attempted to work a half mile and fractured her knee. I was so upset that I cried all morning. I had sold the poor horse to this idiot trainer, and I felt that I had a hand in her demise.

Paulette was another trainer at SLRD who I considered to be an idiot. I had done some freelance riding for her and was shocked at her lack of knowledge. One day she told me to work a horse a half mile and as I walked out to the track she loosened my bridle three holes so the bit was way too low and very uncomfortable in my horse's mouth. She lectured me on the long walk to the track about how a horse needs to hold the bit up himself. Even young 4-H kids know that if a bit is too low it bangs on the horse's teeth. After the work, Paulette asked me why I only worked four furlongs. She had sent me out to work half mile and there are four furlongs in a half mile. Paulette had really wanted the horse to work five furlongs and she thought that there were five furlongs in a half mile. I just said, "Woops" like it was my mistake.

Paulette was very wealthy and played by her own rules. One week she had three horses break down and die on the track. It is illegal for a trainer to have needles and syringes on the track, but Paulette had set up the storage area in her horse trailer as her own personal drug store. After she killed three horses in a week, someone made an anonymous tip to the CHRB (California Horse Racing Board). A crew of investigators was sent to SLRD and they went straight to Paulette's drug store in her trailer. I watched them carry out dozens of boxes of illegal drugs. Her horses were all blood tested to prove that she had been administering the drugs to her horses. Trainers get busted for having one needle or one syringe on the backside. Over a dozen boxes of banned drugs, needles and syringes was unprecedented.

The investigation results were kept very quiet. Paulette was eventually suspended and banned from entering any track for six months and fined. Her horses were still allowed to run and she only had to put her assistant trainer down as trainer to get around the suspension. Her money was probably influential with the CHRB. Her horses did stop dying on the track at SLRD and were better off after the 'drug store' was shut down.

I got some horses in to train and set up my barn again. My friend, Arlene, in Santa Ynez called me and wanted me to come up to the Valley and meet a farm owner in Los Alamos who was looking for a trainer. I made the long drive and met Lotty at her farm. The farm was beautiful with big green pastures and oak trees for shade. Lotty was very wealthy and had studied bloodlines. She showed me all of her horses and it was obvious that she couldn't look at a horse and see what I could see. Some of her favorite horses with super bloodlines didn't look like racehorses to me, and others that she didn't like because their pedigrees weren't as fancy, did look like potential racehorses.

I entered into a training agreement with Lotty in true Susan style without considering myself. Lotty was an attorney and she drew up an agreement that suited her and didn't consider me. I was so anxious to fill my empty barn that I would have agreed to anything. She sent me five horses and I trained them almost for free. One day she was scheduled to come down and watch her horses gallop, but she had to cancel at the last minute. Her husband was a pilot and he was flying her to SLRD, but one of their planes was down, and wouldn't you know it, it was the plane with instruments. It took that statement for me to realize that I was being taken advantage of. She was fabulously wealthy, owned the Disney hotel, and couldn't pay me my normal training fee.

Lotty was in the beginning of a lawsuit against Equitrol, a feed supplement that controls flies. She had put every horse on the ranch on Equitrol and essentially fed them poison every day. After two years on this program, she had a ranch full of problems. Many of the horses showed neurological symptoms, others had skeletal problems, and her young horses all acted like they had attention deficit disorder. She won her lawsuit and then fired me. She had given me these fucked up young horses to train to show proof in court that her horses couldn't run.

After suffering through at least a dozen of Lotty's horses who had no ability and no brains, there was one that looked like a runner. His name was Cheroot, and he was a big dumb, fast horse. This was the only horse I wanted to keep but Lotty was convinced that she was ready for a big name trainer and couldn't be swayed.

Cheroot ran bad ten times for the new trainer but always in short distance races, known as sprints. I had wanted to run him long on the grass. Finally he was entered for a $25,000 maiden claiming, going long, and I wanted to claim him. I had an owner looking for a horse to claim but he wouldn't go for Cheroot because he thought I was being a girl and missed the horse. I told him that I didn't even like the horse, he was as dumb as a post, but fast and sound, but he still said no. Cheroot ended up earning over $500,000 running long on the grass. I wish I had been able to claim him myself, but $25,000 was a big number for me.

I was still living in my little house in Pala when a small dog that looked like a young Pit Bull appeared on the farm. My old Dalmatian, Star, had died a few days before and this young dog must have known I had an opening. I am not a Pit Bull fan and this dog didn't look hungry. Her weight was good so I told her to go home and I let the other dogs chase her away. The next day she was back, and I thought that maybe she had been dumped. Pala was part of an Indian reservation and dogs were always being abandoned. I gave her a big bowl of food and watched her inhale it. She wasn't hungry, she was starving. I felt terrible for telling her to go home when she didn't have a home. She must have slept in the woods behind my house that night and it was cold. I picked her up and saw 100 fleas on her tummy. She was shivering but needed a bath to kill the fleas. I gave her a warm bath inside, put her on my couch, covered her up with a soft blanket, and gave her a little pillow for her head. She instantly fell asleep and looked so cute I had to kiss her. She woke up with a start and looked around like she didn't know where she was. I kissed her again, tucked her in, and told her I was sorry I was a day slow in helping her. She made cute little puppy sounds and went back to sleep. I named her Amy. She was an English Staffordshire, not a Pit Bull. Amy was the sweetest little dog I was ever to know and a constant source of amusement for the next thirteen years.

Chris was furious that I had yet another dog and I was ordered to move out in thirty days. I would miss my mountain, but it was hard for me living so close to a busy road with five dogs to keep safe without a fence.

Chapter 32

Rainbow

I found a house in the little town of Rainbow to rent. The house was in bad shape, but on a beautiful piece of property, way out in the country, with a distant ocean view. I had a huge fireplace and lots of room for the dogs. The house was at the end of a dirt road and there was no traffic, so everyone could be safe without me being vigilant 100% of the time.

The house was big, more than I needed, and was attached to a granny flat. The flat had just been rented by Candace and her boyfriend Rick. They were very friendly and liked dogs. Candace was a school teacher in Temecula and Rick was an artist.

I bought some portable fence panels and put a small corral in, close to my house, for Gus and my new riding horse Con. I had bought Con, a big handsome gray gelding, the year before as a racehorse prospect and formed a partnership. He won a race at Santa Anita by seven lengths, but then the partners got stupid and wanted to run him over his head in Northern California. He had broken his maiden for $32,000 which was cool, since we only paid $5,000 for him and could have won again for $20,000. The partners wanted to run him for $62,500 and I was outvoted. Running him in such a tough race broke his heart and he never ran well again. I was in Florida and had left him with my friend Ben to train, thinking that Ben was honest and I would still have control. I was wrong on both counts. Con eventually fractured an ankle but with time off had healed, and was now a very handsome riding horse.

I loved the peacefulness of my new house. The sound of traffic has always driven me crazy and finally it was gone. Now I could hear birds again. The horses were close and we had new trails to explore.

The dogs were thrilled to be free and safe. Amy was like a little munchkin dog and made us all laugh. At night she would sleep so deeply that she could fall out of bed and not wake up. The first time she did it, I heard the loud thump of her body hitting the floor. I was still half asleep in the middle of the night and saw her body very still on the floor and thought she had hit her head and was dead. She was fine, but in such a deep sleep that she had not woken up even after she fell out of bed. After that incident I lined her side of the bed with pillows on the floor.

I had never seen the dogs as happy as they were in Rainbow. I had driven them a little crazy in Pala, never letting them even walk in the direction of the busy road. Anthony and Daisy would go off on adventures every morning while Chance, Amy, and Gummy waited at home for me to finish at SLRD. When I arrived home each day, usually around noon, the dogs would all run down the hill from the house to the horse corral to meet me. Amy would run so fast that she couldn't stop and would jump the last bit of the hill and land in my arms. If I wasn't braced to catch her we would both fall down and laugh while I hugged her hello.

It was spring with lots of new spring grass for the horses to graze on. After a ride I would sit on Gus and put a halter and rope on Con and let them eat grass. The dogs would play around us and Amy's antics would make me laugh out loud. It was easy to see that Amy had never been in the country and didn't know how to do simple things, like jump across a stream. One day the dogs were running circles and jumping a little stream, but Amy didn't want to play that game because she was afraid of water. Finally after watching the fun for a while she couldn't resist, and when she jumped the little stream she fell in. The stream was only two feet wide, but she missed and landed with a big splash. The game stopped and everyone looked at her like 'what is wrong with her?' She had such a sad distressed look on her face that I told her not to worry, this could have happened to anyone. I was to tell that many times over the next years.

Instead of playing such 'dangerous' games, Amy started inventing her own games. She would carefully dig a hole in the soft spring dirt, and when everyone was looking at her she would jump back with a wild look on her face, like there was a monster in the hole. This would cause all of the other dogs to investigate, but of course there was never anything in the hole. If she timed her 'jump back, there is a monster in the hole' wrong and no one noticed, she would start over. She didn't dig holes like a normal dog. Instead, she would use only one leg to dig with big sweeping strokes.

One day I was in the house and heard the dogs barking frantically. It was a strange bark and all of the dogs were doing it. I ran out of the house to see everyone in a circle around Amy, who had a four foot long harmless gopher snake in her mouth, and was swinging it in circles. Amy was having a great time twirling the snake in circles and her friends were telling her to stop. I made her drop the snake and peace was restored. We all looked out for Amy but she didn't always listen to us.

Amy was as far from an aggressive bully breed as a dog could be. I saw a medium size dog on a leash pin her in less than a minute and she didn't even try to fight back.

It seemed like I would never get away from drunks in my life. There was only one other house close to ours. It was a tiny ramshackle building that resembled a house and two men and a Mexican family lived there. I had not met them yet when a cop knocked at my door one day. He asked me why I had given a man permission to camp on the neighbor's property. I had no idea what the cop was talking about. The drunks next door had a friend with a small trailer, and they told him he could park on the neighbor's property and then blamed me.

It wasn't long after that incident that they had a chance to blame me again for something I had nothing to do with. They had two male dogs not neutered and a female dog in heat. A woman friend of theirs left her white German Shepard, also unneutered, with them for a week. When I saw three intact male dogs and a bitch in heat, I knew they would have problems. The males fought all week and the German Shepard had a bite on his neck. I will always feel guilty that I didn't intervene. I noticed a big stain on the Shepard's neck and his neck looked stiff, but I was keeping my distance and did nothing. When the Shepard's owner came to pick up her dog she took him to the vet and had him euthanized. She said that his neck was too infected to ever heal, and that her vet told her that only a Pit Bull could have injured her dog that severely. She wanted me to pay her vet bill because Amy, an English Staffordshire not a Pit-bull, had attacked her dog. This was utter nonsense so I told her so. I told her she was an idiot to leave her dog with drunks who had a bitch in heat. She was angry and got in her car and tried to run Amy down, but Amy jumped into some trees along the road and was safe. I was so fed up with drunks that I called 911, gave them her license plate number, and reported that she had tried to run my dog over and was driving drunk. I never saw her again.

My training business was growing at SLRD and I usually had at least twelve horses. I met a man who wanted to get in as a partner on some racehorses. Victor had owned Quarter Horses and run them at Los Alamitos in the past, but wanted to own Thoroughbreds now. Although Victor was a cowboy, I was attracted to him. He was recently divorced and an alcoholic. I attracted screwed up people like a magnet and should have been on my guard but wasn't. Victor lived on a small ranch in Temecula and started visiting me at home. He never arrived without bringing my favorite dinner, vegetarian pizza. The dogs all liked him and I thought he was wonderful. We bought a couple of horses together and saw each other almost every day.

There were some huge red flags that I totally ignored. One day we had just returned to SLRD from Santa Anita and had a horse, Fly Me Faster, in Victor's trailer. He had a cowboy style, three horse slant load trailer that I didn't like. I went in the trailer, untied the horse, and because of the bad design of the trailer needed someone outside to put the ramp down to let me out. Fly Me was huge, close to seventeen hands, and wanted to get out of the trailer as soon as he was untied. I had a shank on him but he was jumping and pawing and suddenly frantic to get out. I shouted at Victor to open the door. I knew he was right there waiting to open the door for me, but he didn't open it. Fly Me was jumping on me now and I was terrified and screaming, "Open the door! Open the door" and still the door stayed closed. I was scared and trapped in a corner with a huge horse in a panic and nowhere to go, except on top of me. Finally Victor opened the door and I had to turn the horse loose as he jumped over me. I was screaming mad and yelled, "I hate this fucking trailer" and Victor laughed. Four other trainers had come running when they heard Fly Me jumping in the trailer and me screaming. They all just looked at me, surprised that I wasn't seriously hurt. Later when I calmed down, I asked Victor why he hadn't opened the door, and he told me that he didn't hear me screaming. He did have a hearing problem, but the trailer was rocking back and forth with a 1,000 pound horse going nuts. There is no way that he didn't notice that.

Victor and I dated for six months when he asked me to bring my horses and dogs to his ranch and move in. He had a portable barn business and was doing well, or so he said. His house was tiny modular home, but the horses had a nice big paddock and the yard was big and almost fenced in for the dogs.

The first big red flag came up on the day we moved in. Actually there were two red flags that day. Victor had agreed to completely fence in his yard to keep my dogs safe and he told me it was finished. I let the dogs out of my car thinking they were safe and a few minutes later I saw them a half mile away in a big dirt field. Victor had to admit that he hadn't finished fencing the yard.

An hour later Victor was driving my car taking boxes to his storage shed. He had just gotten in the driver's seat, started the car, and was inching away from me. I needed to tell him something and since he couldn't hear well, I put my hand on the open driver's side window to get his attention. My intuition strongly told me not to put my hand in the open window, but I did it anyway. Victor smiled and had a sick expression on his face as he looked me in the eye and closed the window on my hand. I screamed in pain as the electric window crunched all four of my fingers, and Victor sat in the driver's seat and smiled. Victor's neighbor, Jason, a good friend and roping partner, heard me scream and came running. When Victor saw Jason he opened the window and couldn't stop laughing. At that moment I saw clearly that he was a sick fuck, but I had nowhere else to go.

Victor had sold his bedroom furniture before I moved in so that my bed would be ours. When his wife left him she took most of the furniture and there was an empty room for my office. I was not even completely moved in yet and I wanted to move out. Since I had just paid all of my bills at SLRD, I had no money and moving wasn't an option.

For the next nine days I slept in my bed with Victor and always put Amy in the middle. His touch repulsed me and sex was out of the question. I couldn't tell him that he was a sick fuck so my plan was to endure until I could afford to move out. I knew it wouldn't be easy to find a rental with two horses and five dogs.

On the tenth day of living at Victor's house, my intuition was telling me to read his emails. I have never invaded anyone's privacy by reading their emails so at first I ignored my intuition. Throughout the day I couldn't lose the thought, that I should read his emails. In fact the feeling grew stronger. Finally, at the end of the day I sat down at Victor's computer and read his emails and was shocked. He was emailing seven different women and flirting with all of them. They were from different dating websites, some he had met and others he was planning to meet. I really didn't care because I was so finished with him as a boyfriend, so I decided to have some fun.

I started printing out the emails from each of the women. Some of the dating sites were easy to access and I answered his emails for him. Posing as Victor, I told several of the women that I couldn't wait to 'meat' them. One of the women lived in Idaho and had plans to meet Victor in a few days. He told me that he was building a barn in Idaho and would be gone for the weekend. I waited until he was packed and walking out the door to tell him that I knew the barn in Idaho was really Shirley from match.com, but I didn't care, so he should have fun. He denied everything even with a stack of printed emails in my hand, but I just smiled.

I had been sleeping on my couch in the living room for weeks. It wasn't uncomfortable, but the dogs weren't happy. They were used to piling on my big bed and snuggling at night. Now they had to sleep on the floor. I was getting very depressed and thinking that I must be a real loser. Here I was without even a bed, sharing a house with a man I detested.

Victor went out every night pretending to attend an Alcoholics Anonymous meeting. He would come home hours later, waking us all up, and then take the phone into his bedroom. I could hear him talking to a woman about the sex they had that night. He would say, "Was it good for you honey?" It just seemed like the epitome of stupid for me to be sleeping on my couch instead of my bed, with Victor sneaking around every night. I would have been thrilled if he stayed with her and gave me back my bed.

I finally confronted him and told him to cut the shit, stop the lies, and stay with her. He was wrapped up in the drama of sneaking around and having sex, and I burst his bubble when I told him to go. He finally moved in with his honey and I got my bed back.

Victor's ranch was in Winchester, a little town just outside of Temecula. It was on a dirt road and all of the neighbors were cowboys and their wives. They hated me on sight because of my connection to Victor. They all knew him well and despised him. Had they taken time to know me they would have realized that I was on their team.

One day, I answered the house phone and spoke to a man calling from Idaho. He demanded to know who I was and I told him I was a trainer who lived in Victor's house. He warned me to get away from him. He had ordered a barn from Victor, paid the down payment of $16,000, and was still waiting six months later for his barn to be built. Victor had not answered phone calls or faxes for weeks. The man had finally received a fax from Victor's office, supposedly written by an employee that stated they were sorry that they could not build the barn in the near future. The fax went on to explain that Victor had been kicked by a racehorse, airlifted to a hospital, where he was now in a coma. I told the man it was all a lie, I had talked to Victor that day. As I listened to this outrageous story, my mouth dropped open and I had to sit down.

Victor and I had three horses in partnership, and I was sick to learn that my partner was even lower than I had given him credit for. So far he paid his share of the bills on time, and I now realized the money was coming from his barn 'stealing' schemes.

The neighbors talked to me just enough to talk shit about Victor. The closest neighbors were Jason, Victor's roping partner and his wife Violet. They shared the property with Victor and told me the previous year Victor was losing the ranch so they bought it, and allowed him to put the small prefab house that I was living in on the property and pay them rent. The barn, arena, and main house were no longer his. No wonder they hated me, Victor told me the barn was his and I had moved my office into the empty barn office. I even bought flower boxes and decorated the barn with beautiful flowers.

I stayed in the little house alone for nine months and saved money, while looking for a rental. Victor was still paying his training bills and he paid the rent on his little house to Violet and Jason. By now, I knew that most of what came out of Victor's mouth was a lie and wasn't surprised when he told me that he was selling his property and it was in escrow. I would have thirty days to leave. Since I knew that he didn't own the property and escrow was in his imagination, I wasn't very worried. I did crank up my search for a rental but still found nothing. A week before my deadline to move out escrow fell through.

Chapter 33

Lake Hodges Again

I finally did find a rental property that would accept the dogs and horses at Lake Hodges. The rent was reasonable and the landlord liked dogs, even five of them.

As I was moving out of Winchester Victor stopped paying his training bill. It quickly got up to $5,000, and I had to file a complaint with the Stewards at the race track. If an owner doesn't pay a trainer, the Stewards can suspend his license. We had a hearing with the Stewards and I produced the unpaid training bills. Hearings with the Stewards are limited to official racetrack business. Victor told the Stewards that he had not paid his bill because I owed him money. This was the first time I had heard this total nonsense, and he went on to say that I had lived in his house and trashed it. He had to buy new carpets and paint the house when I left. I had left the house clean and it never had carpet, was all hard wood floors. The Stewards reminded him that the hearing was only for official racetrack business but Victor wouldn't shut up. He told them that I hated his horse trailer and wouldn't let him haul his own horses in it. This was true but so what? He finished with a story that I had run up a $700 bill with AAA. The Stewards didn't believe a word he said and ordered him to pay me or lose his license. He wrote a check for $5,000 on the spot. Losing his license would be a humiliation he couldn't bear.

The story about the $700 AAA bill was true. My car had died shortly after I left Winchester and I needed it towed to my mechanic, over 100 miles away. Victor had given me an AAA card, and when I ordered the tow I was told that because he had used up his allotment of tows for the year, he would be charged by the mile. I smiled and told them that wouldn't be a problem. When the car was repaired and ready to come home, I ordered another AAA tow to return it to me. I was tempted to have it towed to New York and back but couldn't risk my little car in a practical joke. It had been hard to keep a straight face with the Stewards when all three of them told Victor they had never even heard of a $700 AAA tow bill.

Victor and I had three horses in partnership together, Evening Majesty, Gerry's Reality and Ben. Evening and Gerry were already out of the picture and retired from racing. Evening was my riding horse and Gerry, who was built like a Quarter Horse, was in training to be Victor's roping horse. Victor had told me that Gerry was doing well in training but had spur cuts on his shoulders. He told me this with the same sick smile he had when he shut my hand in the car window.

Ben was bought from Lotty at a public auction and had been affected by Equitrol. He was a big handsome chestnut horse and extremely intelligent and athletic, but had a knee problem and only ran two races before he went lame. Victor and I had brought in a third partner, Earl, and we were all disappointed when he went lame.

Victor demanded that I give him Ben so that he could run him at Los Alamitos in cheaper company. Los Alamitos is a Quarter Horse track that does run a few Thoroughbred races, but they are all sprints. This plan made no sense since Ben was not a sprinter, and a horse with a bad knee would never survive a 5/8ths mile track with tight turns. I made it my priority to protect Ben at all costs.

I wanted Ben retired now, before he became a statistic at Hollywood Park. He was lame and I needed to prove that publicly. I entered him in a race at Hollywood knowing that he would be a vet scratch. The State Vet examines every horse on the morning of his race and if he is found to be unsound, he is officially scratched by the vet. A vet scratch was my goal.

I brought Ben out of his stall at Hollywood Park to jog for the State Vet on the morning of the race, and the vet saw that he was lame. Since I had never entered a lame horse (and wouldn't) the vet asked me if I wanted to warm him up and then try again, but I said no thank you.

I now had an official vet scratch to back me up and I called a Thoroughbred retirement farm to organize Ben's transfer. I explained the situation to the manager and swore her to secrecy. I only told the third partner, Earl, that Ben was retired and didn't tell him where the horse was.

Victor went ballistic when I retired Ben and wouldn't tell him where he was. I loved Ben and couldn't turn him over to the monster that I knew Victor to be. I wish this could have been the end of Victor in my life, but that was not the case.

Life at Lake Hodges was a bit of a challenge, but I was happy to be far from Victor and his neighborhood. I had hired a man to put a fence up around our big yard for the dogs and they were safe and happy.

Lake Hodges has lots of empty lots and it has always been acceptable for horse people to put portable corals up, as long as the other neighbors don't mind. The neighbors next door to me were a young couple with a three-year-old boy and were thrilled that I wanted to put my horses on the empty lot between us.

My house was directly across from a house on the other side of a narrow road and way too close. I introduced myself to my neighbor, Jim, when I first moved in and could sense that he already disliked me. I had a sick feeling that it was happening again, someone was ready to hate me and didn't even know me.

Jim fulfilled my expectations and hated me. He didn't like the dogs, although they rarely even barked, and he didn't like that I was using the empty lot next to my house. The lot had not been touched for years and had weeds as tall as me, but he told me that his teenage kids played there all the time.

Jim had lived at Lake Hodges for over twenty years, and told me that as a landowner, he had the right to tell me to get my horses off the empty lot. He called my landlord and complained about the horses and dogs. My landlord came out and met the dogs for the first time and was impressed. Anthony now weighed over 120 pounds and sensed a problem with the landlord. He was so tall that when he walked next to me his head touched my hand. As I walked around the yard talking to the landlord, Anthony glued his head to my hand, like 'don't take me away from her.' The landlord told me that Jim was a troublemaker and a liar; he didn't own his house but had rented it for twenty years. He then said that he could see how much Anthony and the other dogs loved me and that I should just try to get along with crazy Jim.

I told the other neighbors that Jim didn't even own his house as he wanted everyone to believe, and that my landlord knew his landlord. This totally blew Jim's cover and his credibility in the neighborhood.

I made a point to be extra friendly with all the neighbors and invited their children to pet the horses. They told me several times that Jim had knocked on their doors trying to gather support to evict my horses from the vacant lot. The friendly neighbors would always come to me and warn me that Jim was at it again.

My old pony Gus and newly retired Evening were my riding horses at Lake Hodges. To get to the trail I had to walk my horse a short distance and cross a fairly busy road with the dogs, and then I could ride on a trail shared by hikers and cyclists. I was always careful crossing the road and would have three dogs on leashes in my left hand, and two loose dogs under my verbal commands, and my horse's reins in my right hand. It was a far cry from what I would consider a peaceful and safe ride, but it was the best I could do at the time.

I had met Logan when I was still living at Victor's house, and we had been dating for six months when I moved to Lake Hodges. Logan was very kind and good with dogs. He lived in San Diego and drove almost an hour to visit us in Winchester, but now his commute was cut in half.

Logan is the only person I ever met who didn't fall for Amy's charms. He thought she was playing us with her adorable behavior. Amy was a very girly girl and loved to wear her monogrammed jackets and had a complete wardrobe with a jacket for every occasion. I had gotten tired of people asking me if she was a Pit Bull, so I started painted her nails with pretty pink nail polish. Now when people asked if she was a Pit, I would say, "Have you ever seen a Pit Bull with nail polish??"

One day we were out on a trail ride and I heard the rattle of a rattlesnake just off the trail. The dogs were all headed in the direction of the snake and I yelled," Leave it." Chance, Gummy, Anthony, and Daisy all responded to my command, but Amy had to investigate. She was bitten in the face by the rattlesnake and we were about a mile and a half from home. I always had my cell phone in my pocket and I called my vet friend, Carl, and asked him what I should do. He said that I should get her to a vet ASAP, even if that meant running home. I was riding Evening and there was no way I could get Amy on his back, so we all jogged home. Carl had called my vet and told him we were on the way with an emergency snake bite.

We arrived at Dr. Henderson's office forty-five minutes later, and they were waiting for us. Amy had already started to swell and wasn't feeling very good. The vet hooked her up to an IV line and started treating her immediately. He flushed out her wound and inserted a drainage tube and then noticed her painted nails. He asked me if I painted her nails. I defensively answered that she loved nail polish. I watched Dr. Henderson try not to laugh out loud, but he failed and couldn't stop laughing.

Amy came home that night and slept from the moment I carried her into the house. She was draining huge amounts of fluid and her entire body was swollen. I had a Bioscan that I treated the horses with and I used it to treat poor Amy. Bioscan is a light energy modality and speeds up healing. Amy suffered for only two days and then started to rally. A few days later she was fine and ready for her next trail ride.

Logan and I were getting along great except for one issue. He had an old girlfriend in his life, Judith, and they were still very close. From the beginning I could only think, not again! The Judith issue was weird and it just didn't feel right to me. Logan and Judith had been friends for fifteen years and had dated for ten years. The last five years they remained good friends and had an agreement to spend every Sunday together. I trained my horses every day and didn't have Sunday's off, but I still didn't like their arrangement.

Every once in a while it would rain on Sunday and I would be finished early at the track, but Logan could never change his plans. He told me that Judith was more of an obligation than anything else and he didn't enjoy spending time with her. On Sunday she would present him with a list of projects to do around the house and he would do her chores. I asked him if I took a Sunday off and he gave Judith plenty of notice could we spend one Sunday together, but he said no. We broke up several times because of the Judith problem.

I tried hard to find a solution, but was met with cement walls each time. I wanted to meet Judith, but Logan told me she would never agree to meet me. He couldn't cancel his Sunday without notice and he couldn't cancel his Sunday with notice. I knew that this was fucked. On Sunday afternoons I always had a sick feeling, the sad lonely feeling you get when you are lonely but in a relationship.

Logan and I talked on the phone every day and I could call him anytime of the night. This didn't seem like someone who had another woman. We dated for three years before I caught him in a lie and had to end our relationship.

One night we were talking on the phone at 8:00. We had a close relationship, and if I had plans I would tell him, and he always told me what he had going on. After we got off the phone I remembered something I needed to tell him, but when I called him back there was no answer. He hadn't told me was going anywhere so at first I thought that maybe he was just in the shower and hadn't heard the phone ring. I called him all through the night and he didn't answer until seven in the morning. It was obvious that he had been out all night and I asked him why he hadn't told me he had plans to be out all night. He answered that Judith had an accident, had fallen off her porch and landed on her face, and had been in the emergency room all night. Logan was very smart and I had never caught him in a lie before. However, he had forgotten that he had already told me the 'Judith fell off her porch and landed on her face' story two years before, to illustrate how clumsy and needy she was.

Logan and I broke up after three years of being together. I had ignored my intuition from the start and he had played me for a fool. I realized that only a girl with no self-esteem would have tolerated all those miserable Sundays. I had made training my horses my priority and a relationship was second, but still, I deserved more than this.

Logan and I stayed friends for a few years after we broke up until I caught him stealing from me. We both sold on eBay and I had a camera that I wanted to sell. Since Logan was more knowledgeable about cameras than me, I asked him to sell it and offered him 50% of the selling price as a commission. The camera sold for $70, and a week later when he still hadn't paid me my $35, I asked him why. His reply was worth way more than $35. Logan told me that by asking for my 50% (that we had agreed on) I was acting like we were friends. I told him to keep the $35 and thanked him for showing me who he really was.

I could see that I was still a magnet for sick relationships with men and was tired of the fight. For a long time, I stayed away from relationships and worked on my people skills. My old style was only bringing me misery and the time for change was now. It was time to listen to my intuition and treat myself with love and respect. I had been acting and living like the daughter of alcoholics. Always prepared to 'pretend that he didn't really say that, or he didn't really do that.' I had become a master of the 'pretend it's not happening' game.

Logan and I had invested in two horses right before we broke up, Mythical Flyer and Sandy Sneakers. He wanted an owner's license and some fun at the upcoming Del Mar race meet.

Flyer was at SLRD with trainer Reggie Glat. I was looking at another horse in Reggie's barn when I saw Flyer for the first time walking on the hot walker. He was a big beautiful bay gelding and I couldn't take my eyes off him. Trying to remain casual and hide my intense interest, I asked Reggie who that horse was as I pointed to Flyer. Reggie was an old cowboy trainer and he spat on the ground before he answered, "Oh that piece of shit?" I didn't spit but I replied, "Yes. That piece of shit on the walker." Reggie told me that he had been beaten twenty-seven lengths in each of his last three races, and that I could have him for $3,000. Since he was drop dead gorgeous and I knew that at worst I could recoup the $3,000 by selling him as a hunter jumper, I wrote him a check on the spot.

I quickly walked to my barn and told the groom to bed down our best outside portable stall knee deep in straw for my new horse. I went back to Reggie's barn and saw his pathetic stalls with barely enough straw to cover the ground and put a shank on Flyer and led him to my barn. At first he walked slowly with his head down because he thought I was taking him to the pool. Reggie swam most of his horses because it was cheaper than paying a rider to gallop on the track. As soon as we got past the pool, Flyer put his head up and got interested. A few yards later when he was sure he wasn't going to the pool, he started dancing and prancing on the lead. When we got to my barn I lead him into our best stall that was bedded down for a king, and Flyer stopped, looked at the deep straw and then looked at me like 'is this really for me?' I turned him loose and watched him. His eyes were huge, like he couldn't believe his good fortune. I loved him from that moment on and knew we would be inseparable forever.

Flyer and I were a great team and I could read his every thought. He was super, super sensitive, had a sense of humor, and was very smart. On that first walk together, he reminded me of when I was in high school and would cut classes and escape for the day. It would be a beautiful spring day and I just couldn't force myself to sit in a classroom another minute, so I would walk out the front door of the school. At first I would walk very casual and slow as if I wasn't really just walking out the door and ditching school. I would walk about a 100 yards and pick up my stride a little, and then turn the corner and run! My horse was boarded only two miles away and once I was out of town and safe, I would enjoy my walk to the farm and then ride all day.

I sold half of Flyer to Logan for $1,500 and gave him a super deal on training fees. I agreed to charge him 50% of real cost, instead of 50% of my day rate of $75 per day. I would be working for free, but this didn't concern me.

I started training Flyer and he was a dream to gallop and work. He was so sensitive that I couldn't even carry a whip on him without him worrying about it. I watched videos of his old races and saw that he ran in the lead until the 3/8 mile pole and then, when the rest of the field caught up with him, he would slow down to a stop. Horses would pass him like he was going backwards. He was brilliant until the pressure was on and then he quit. In the videos it looked like he stopped because he couldn't breathe, like he was cutting his own air off. The way he stopped was so dramatic that it wasn't like he was thinking, 'oh I think I will stop now.' It was more like, 'oh fuck, I can't breathe.'

He was already fit and sound, so I entered him in a race at Del Mar. I wanted to see what would happen if we ran him without putting any pressure on him. I chose a new apprentice rider, Scotty Zeigler, and gave him the strangest instructions that he had ever been given before a race. I told him I didn't care where we finished, I wanted him to ride with no whip, and to be a passenger and leave the horse alone. If Flyer wanted to run at the end, he could hand ride a little. Scotty was young and enthusiastic and just happy to have a mount at Del Mar. He followed my instructions perfectly. Flyer broke on top and then settled back to the end of the pack. At the 3/8th mile pole he was last by fifteen lengths, waiting for Scotty to start hitting him. Scotty was riding without a whip. When Flyer realized that he wouldn't be hit, he started running. He made a most impressive stretch run and finished fourth that day. Scotty was so excited that even before he got off Flyer he was shouting, "It worked, it worked! I rode him just like you said and it worked!" Flyer validated me as a trainer, and I validated him as a racehorse. We were a perfect match.

When Logan and I broke up he wanted out of our partnerships. I told him that Flyer was "sittin' on a win" as they say on the backside, but Logan still wanted out. In a very generous deal, I paid Logan his initial $1,500 investment, and the training fees he had paid. No one was ever reimbursed training fees and I thought I was being over the top generous. Logan, however, wanted more. He wanted me to give him 50% of any projected earnings. I wanted to tell him to go fuck himself, but I laughed at him instead.

Flyer and I were a match made in heaven. Every morning when he saw me walking towards the barn he would start nodding his head up and down, happy to see me. When I got to the barn I would always say, "Good morning handsome" and give him a hug. Racehorses don't do tricks, but Flyer loved two tricks that I taught him. Before I got on him in the barn to go to the track, I always walked him around the barn a couple of times to loosen up. He would walk loose, with no shank, and follow me. Then he would stop at the hay stack on the corner of the barn, and let me climb up and swing on his back.

I made a mistake of showing a new groom Flyer's other trick one morning. After a horse is cooled out the last thing we do is to wash the dirt of their legs with a hose, and then dry them with a towel. I always did Flyer's legs myself because he wanted me to. When I was finished I would turn him loose and tell him to go to his stall. He would walk down the shedrow and into his stall by himself. The next morning, the new groom didn't know that I always washed Flyer's legs and he brought him in, hosed his legs and then turned him loose and told him to go to his stall. Flyer decided to run away instead of going to his stall and ran through three barns near ours before he came home. The poor groom was so embarrassed that he had turned Flyer loose and told him to go to his stall.

Flyer won his next two races after Logan got out of the partnership and over $100,000 in the next five years. He ran until he was eleven years old and won his last race, before I retired him to be my forever riding horse. I am still in awe of his beauty and can't look at him without smiling.

I bought Logan out of Sandy Sneakers and turned her out to heal a stress fractured tibia. This is not as ugly as it sounds because tibias do heal with three or four months rest. Dr. Paul had a friend who wanted to buy into a racehorse so I sold half of Sneakers to Nadeen. She was very wealthy and very strange. I was so hungry for owners that I tried to ignore her oddities, but it wasn't easy. She fell in love with Sneakers and even had personalized license plates for her Lexus with 'Sneakers.'

Sneakers first race for me was at Del Mar. I always stayed close to my horse and the groom on race day and as we entered the paddock I wanted to crawl under a rock. Nadeen was jumping up and down in the middle of the paddock yelling, "Sneakers, Sneakers." She was making so much noise that she spooked all of the fillies in the paddock and they all were looking at her. Nadeen then started yelling, "Sneakers I love you! Oh look, she loves me too, she is looking at me." She was too drunk to realize that everyone was looking at her because she was in the paddock jumping up and down and screaming.

I really had to stay focused on Sneakers because she had a bad habit of flipping over backwards, often for no apparent reason. I had the best groom handling Sneakers and I knew that together we could keep her feet on the ground. I got her saddled safely and she ran a descent race for her comeback.

After the race the groom and trainer always go out on the track to meet the horse and jockey. I was already on the track when Nadeen barged through security and ran out on to the track with a bag of apples and carrots for Sneakers. Security caught up to her, grabbed her, and practically dragged her off the track as they explained that Sneakers would be drug tested after the race and couldn't eat treats right now. The day after the race, the Stewards called me and told me in a nice way that if I couldn't get my owner under control, they would do it for me.

One day Nadeen went to SLRD in the afternoon to visit Sneakers. The backside was always quiet in the afternoon before feed time. My stable colors were pink and gray, easy to see. Nadeen went into my neighbor's stall whose colors were blue and white and started brushing his bay colt. The trainer, Tony, found her in his stall brushing his horse and politely asked her what she was doing. She told him all about Sneakers and how much she loved her. Tony knew Sneakers and asked Nadeen if Sneakers was a chestnut filly. Nadeen got all excited that Tony knew her horse, and she went on to tell him that she had personalized license plates and had decorated her living room in pictures of Sneakers. Tony told me later that he hated to do this, but finally had to tell her that she was brushing his bay colt, not her chestnut filly Sneakers. The next day Tony asked me if my owner was a little bit stupid and I could only laugh.

Nadeen was good pay but even weird about paying me. We eventually had four horses running in partnership and she wanted to pay me in advance. She didn't understand that racehorse trainers do their bills at the end of the month because there are so many incidentals to bill out. Runners had to be billed for the pony in the post parade, the extra groom for the paddock, shoeing, worming and travel expenses. I couldn't possibly predict with accuracy what my bill would be for each horse. Although I appreciated being paid, she made more bookwork for me because I had to do my bills and keep track of her deficit and then argue with her about why there were incidentals.

Just when I thought that Victor had disappeared he returned with a vengeance. One morning I saw an overweight, badly dressed woman wandering around SLRD looking lost. She entered my barn and asked me if I was Susan Bump and when I said yes, she handed me a huge envelope and said, "You have been served." Victor was suing me and Earl, Ben's third partner in a bogus lawsuit. His first complaint was that Ben had never been part of a partnership, that Victor had always owned 100% of him. His training bills had always been for 33% of the horse and he was clearly only messing with me. He had fifty-one other complaints about me in the lawsuit.

Although I knew the suit was ridiculous and could easily prove it, I still had to hire an attorney to defend myself. I was sick that Victor was once again in my life. The very thought of him made me shudder in disgust, like stepping in vomit with bare feet.

I made an appointment to meet with a lawyer in L.A. who was familiar with the racetrack and left the dogs at home on the day of my appointment. On the day of our meeting I could not focus on my horses. I felt tarnished by Victor's false accusations and was embarrassed to talk to anyone about the lawsuit. Now I had to drive two hours to L.A. and talk about it with the attorney. I was riding my last horse on this fateful day, a silly filly I had bought 50% of from John, my horse shoer.

John had not been honest about the horse and I already didn't like her. He told me she was galloping nicely at Golden Eagle farm, and it wouldn't take long to get her fit and ready to run. The truth was that she was barely broke and had no heart. She was scared of everything and could barely walk around the barn without spooking at water buckets. Because I was worried about my appointment with the attorney only three hours away, I wasn't focused and made the mistake of riding her with my cell phone in my pocket. We were still in the barn when my phone rang and spooked the filly. She immediately flipped out and started bucking and rearing but I was able to steer her into an empty stall. She bucked me off in the stall and my foot got hung up in the stirrup, which is every rider's worst nightmare. My groom, Adam, was in the next stall. I remember calling him to help me and knowing, that although if he acted quickly he could save me, he wouldn't put out the effort. The filly ran out of the stall dragging me, and now kicking at me and all I could do was cover my face with my arms. I was wearing my helmet and safety vest but I could still feel the kicks. I remember my head hitting the metal rails that lined the shedrow. My last thought was that no one here was brave enough to help me and that I was fucked. I must have been going in and out of consciousness because it seemed like I was dragged for hours and it was probably only minutes. The last thing I saw was an arm that looked blue like the sky, catch the filly in a smooth professional style, and turn her head gently and quickly to the left so that she had to stop. It was a move like Walter had taught me, and only an experienced horseman could have pulled it off.

When I woke up I was still on the ground in my shedrow. I couldn't move or open my eyes and I was scared. I knew people were around me, but I didn't know who they were until someone took my helmet off and put her hand under my head to keep it out of the dirt. Emily was a masseuse at SLRD and had given me a massage once when my back was sore on a race day. I instantly recognized her touch and said,

"Emily, is that you?" When she replied, "Yes", I told her I was scared and asked her to please not leave me. She said she would stay with me, but she didn't.

When the paramedics arrived I was unconscious again and woke up with someone touching my ribs. I awoke with a fright thinking I was being molested. I still couldn't move but now I was angry and I said, "What are you doing?" The paramedic answered that he was checking to see if my ribs were broken. I was scared and furious when the paramedics started asking me questions. They wanted to know what day it was, what time it was, and who the president was. I didn't have any of the answers and by now just wanted everyone to get the hell out of my barn and leave me alone.

I was strapped onto a stretcher and put in the ambulance under protest. I could speak now and expected to be listened to, but instead, everyone completely ignored me. In the ambulance I was furious and refused the IV. The last thing I remembered was the paramedic telling me that if I didn't stop fighting he would put the IV catheter in my neck.

I must have been unconscious at first in the hospital, because I heard someone moaning, and to my horror I realized it was me. My leg hurt, but I could move it, so knew it wasn't broken. A nurse asked if she should call someone and I gave her Logan's number. When he arrived I didn't know who he was. He told me later that I was staring off into space and not seeing anything. I remember that when he touched me it brought me back and I knew he was Logan.

Five hours later I was alert and pissed. I was ready to go home and wanted to be released immediately. They had done a CAT scan and were ready to release me, but were waiting for the doctor to sign me out. I wasn't waiting, didn't need anyone's permission to walk out the door. I sat up and only then noticed that I had an IV catheter in my arm and demanded that they take it out now. My arm was taped to a board and I hadn't noticed until then. Looking at the IV catheter and my arm taped to a board, made me furious and Logan quickly put my arm back under the sheet to calm me down. Finally a nurse and a doctor were both looking at me and the nurse said, "Admit?" and I shouted, "No!" I really thought she was asking me, so I must have been pretty messed up. I don't think they dared to keep me so I was released, and Logan drove me home.

I had a serious concussion, but other than that I was only badly bruised. The next day I was able to go to the track, but not ride. Everyone at SLRD was shocked to see me back so soon. There were three reasons I couldn't stay away. The first of course was my horses. I couldn't trust Adam, my worthless groom who hadn't helped me when I was hung up and being dragged, to care for them without me there. Adam never looked me in the eye after the day I got hurt. We both knew that if he had listened to me and run to the stall to help me, he could have caught the filly before she bolted out of the stall and nearly killed me.

The second reason I had to be at SLRD that day was to thank the person who caught the filly and saved my life. I had seen the blue arm, but not a face, so I still didn't know who it was. Logan was with me when I asked the group of horsemen who were gathered around me who caught the horse. I said, "Who caught the filly, I saw the blue arm but I don't know who it was. I have to thank him." They all looked at me like I had lost my brain. They told me that no one had caught the filly, there was no blue arm. I know what I saw and I saw the blue arm of a good horseman catch the filly, and bend her head around to one side so she would stop and I could get loose. Everyone insisted that no one caught the horse.

The third reason I was at SLRD that morning was to help Boo, a barn cat who had been injured and had done nothing but lie still for three days. I had been treating him with my Bioscan and couldn't miss a day. When I was unable to move I was thinking of Boo and I understood now why he wouldn't move. I realized that you can feel so damn awful that you just can't move. I had to help Boo. My trainer friend Wayne, Boo's owner, tried to talk me out of it but I said, "Boo needs me" and I treated him. Boo was much better the next day and managed to walk over to my barn and hang with me. What a pair we were!

The next few months were hell for me. The first thirty days I stuttered and had no balance or coordination. I was terrified of the horses in my barn. When I looked down my shedrow instead of seeing happy friendly faces I saw monsters with fire in their eyes. I knew that I used to ride them and now I didn't want to be near them. I had to touch them to check their legs each morning before my friend, Donny, galloped them, and it took all of my courage to walk into a stall.

My friend, Janice, saw me the week after I got hurt and I could see the shock in her face. I knew I wasn't myself, but I didn't think that anyone could see it. She told me later, that my face was frozen with no expression. Janice is a therapist and she did Thought Field therapy on me. It took only fifteen minutes and was a strange therapy with tapping and humming, but it worked. I lost the terror I had been feeling and could touch a horse without fear.

I still struggled with simple things like putting polo bandages on a horse to gallop in. Polo wraps have to be put on perfectly or they will come loose on the track, trip the horse and kill or hurt the horse and rider. I knew I could do polos with my eyes closed before, but now my wraps looked like a three-year-old child put them on. I would take the wraps off and try again but they would look just as bad or even worse on my second and third tries. It was so hard not to cry, but I couldn't let anyone see how messed up I was. Finally I would just pull all the wraps off and tell Adam the horse didn't need wraps today.

At home the dogs knew I was different and still watched over me, but from a distance. I was really depressed and couldn't snap out of it. I still had no balance and fell on face trying to climb over a small fence in my yard.

I was angry all the time but tried to hide it. I knew Adam had fucked up by not helping me. He was in the next stall and should have been in my stall in seconds, but he wasn't. I was also angry at John, the horse shoer who had sold me half of the filly and lied about how unbroken she was. I was looking to buy runners, not horses that weren't broke yet, and I would never have bought her if he had been honest. I felt sorry for the filly because I couldn't even look at her. I told John to buy me out and get her out of the barn. He got her out of my barn immediately, but it took three weeks of hounding him to get my money back, and that made me mad too.

It took months for my brain to feel normal again. Sometimes I couldn't find words. I would be in the middle of a sentence and forget a simple word like book. I preferred to not speak rather than let anyone see that I couldn't find words.

I had started riding again after three weeks. I had decided that when I could climb over the little fence in my yard without falling down I would be ready to ride. I had a picture of me that I loved, galloping a horse on the track. I didn't see the photographer taking my picture and he captured my joy of galloping in the photo, as I came around the turn smiling with the sun on my face and the horse's coat glistening. The picture was on my computer and I would look at it and tell myself that I could do that again.

This was the seventh concussion I had in my life and by far the worst. It was like the real Susan was gone and my replacement was a cardboard cutout. I remembered that I used to have a sense of humor and some wit, but my humor died. I didn't know if or when I would ever be myself again and that made me very sad.

I had a horse ready to run a couple of weeks after I got hurt, and although I always hauled my own horses to the races I didn't dare to drive my truck and trailer. I shipped the filly with a commercial hauler, Brian. After she was loaded he asked me for the out-slip, a signed departure form that he needed to take a horse out the gate. The out-slip should have been in my hand, but I had mistakenly put it in my tack box. I pointed to the box and told Brian that the slip was in the book. I used the word book instead of box, and although I knew I had made a mistake I couldn't think of the word box so I had to point and say, "It's in there." I was so embarrassed when Brian saw that I struggled with such simple words.

My filly ran an impressive third on the grass that day at Hollywood Park and everything started getting better after the race. I had stopped stuttering and my words came back. My confidence on the track was slowly returning. For weeks I would go out on the track each morning and have to ask the outrider if she thought I could do this. She would say yes, and I would say, "I was a good rider before, wasn't I?" and she would always say, "Yes you were."

Chapter 34

Valley Center

I had bought a house in Valley Center just before Lotty fired me, so I did have a peaceful place to recover. We were way out in the country at the end of a dirt road, where the dogs were safe and free again. I had my horses in the back yard and we had nice safe trails to ride on.

I bought a new helmet since my old one had failed to keep me safe. I always rode in breeches and the day of my accident I was wearing my favorite navy blue Golden Dress breeches. I sold them on eBay because I didn't want to ever wear them again. I also sold the saddle that I had been dragged by. I wanted nothing to remind me of that day.

I knew that I had been gone mentally for a while and was lucky that I made a comeback. Fear began to seep into me, where there had been only joy before. I didn't wear a helmet at home on the trails and if my horse stumbled or bucked a little, my first thought was always, oh no not my head.

I rode for three more years on the track until it was no longer fun. My last two months of galloping I was thankful at the end of each morning that I had survived. I knew that this thought pattern was deadly and I would crash soon, so I stopped galloping.

My last two years training I had some descent horses and a wonderful partner. Roy, was a financial advisor, and only invested his disposable income in racehorses. There was never any pressure for them to earn money. We claimed several horses together, some were good and some were bad claims.

Claiming racehorses can be very exciting. I would watch the entries, read the form, and when I saw a horse I liked on paper entered a race, I would drive to the track and look at him in the paddock. If I liked him in the paddock, I would put a claim in for him. In a claiming race any horse can be bought (claimed), but you have to drop your claim fifteen minutes before the race. After the race, the horse is yours even if he dies on the track. The object of the claiming game is to claim horses that you can improve on, and then win races.

Our best claim was P.T.'s Gray Eagle. Eagle was an old stakes horse who had gone down the claiming ranks to the lowest level of claiming $8,000. I told Roy I wanted the horse with or without him as a partner and he jumped in. In the paddock on race day I saw that Eagle had bad feet and glue-on shoes, and a very sore body, but his legs looked good.

I bought a Papimi machine from a chiropractor in Las Vegas to treat my horses. Papimi is electromagnetic pulsation therapy and most of the horses loved it. Eagle was my best patient. I worked on him every day and he wouldn't let me stop. My plan was always a thirty minute treatment and at the end of thirty minutes he would move his body towards me as if to say, oh just a little more, right here. I always made more time for the Eagle and it paid off.

Jockey Mike Smith was a P.T.'s Gray Eagle fan and he rode him for me. He was one of the first riders to use a foam tip whip and he told me he couldn't hit such a class horse. I respected Mike and was impressed with his sensitivity. Although we didn't win with the Eagle, we ran several seconds and thirds and went up the claiming ranks to claiming $32,000 when he was claimed from us. I hated to see him claimed, but it was always good to make a profit.

I had always struggled with profit in racing. In order to stay in business I had to make a profit. My challenge was to remain humane and honest and still make money. I always told myself that I could never risk injury to a horse or rider by running a sore horse. In the lower claiming ranks all the horses are sore. The Papimi machine helped a lot, but there were several horses that we claimed and then gave away because they could no longer run.

We claimed a nice filly for $10,000 who had tons of heart. I jumped her up to claiming $16,000 and she ran an impressive second, barely beaten. After that race she came up lame with a sore knee. I had just given away two of our claiming horses and I had to make money on this filly. The vet x-rayed the knee and found degenerative joint disease. There is no cure and she should have been retired. Financially I couldn't take another loss so I crossed my own line that I had drawn and told the vet to inject her knee. I entered her for $10,000 claiming and she won and got claimed. On paper the win and claim looked good, but morally it was bad, really bad.

I had become a real trainer and I didn't like how it felt. The filly's win wasn't fun. Instead of being excited as she crossed the wire and won, I was praying that she didn't break down. I saw her walk off the track with the claiming tag on her halter and didn't feel like a winner. An hour later I saw her leave the test barn and she was walking sore. I was a shit.

By crossing my own line of morality I lost respect for myself, even as everyone else gained respect for me as a trainer. I knew that this wasn't who I wanted to be.

The last horse Roy and I ran together was a gelding that we bought at SLRD. He was very thin and unhappy and this was my favorite type of horse to buy. I could always get them happy and eating and usually it would pay off. This horse was also very nervous, but he calmed down with me. After three months of hard work, I entered the horse in a cheap, $3,000 claiming race, at Santa Rosa, a long, eleven hour haul to Northern California.

On race day everything was going great until we got to the paddock. My horse was so nervous that he washed out, sweating buckets of sweat. His eyes were scared and wild and I knew we didn't have a chance. He ran terrible and after the race he looked petrified, with his eyes bugged out. I was sorry that I had even asked him to run, now that I could clearly see that he hated racing.

As we walked off the track we had to walk around the horse ambulance. Another horse in our race had broken down and could walk on three legs but refused to enter the ambulance. On the track we always tell each other not to look when a horse breaks down. I heard a voice in my head say loud and clear, "It's time to look." I turned my head and looked at the poor broken down horse. He had fractured a hind leg and was in a metal splint and hopping around in extreme pain. Our eyes met and locked and I saw his pain and fear. I couldn't look away. I started crying right there, standing on the track. For once I didn't care who saw me.

I walked back to my barn and cooled my own horse out but couldn't stop crying. I have always lived by the saying, 'If you are not part of the solution you are part of the problem' and I knew that I contributed to the horrors of racing. I saw clearly that this is not who I want to be. I called Roy two hours after the race and through my tears I told him that our horse didn't want to run, and I have to quit training now.

When I got home the next day I began selling and giving away my racehorses. None of them remained racehorses; I was able to get them all off the track. I knew for sure that I no longer had the heart to train racehorses. Part of me knew this was a good thing but still it was very sad.

I had started a tack company a few months before I quit training and was selling high end Amish tack. My business was growing and I was also selling on eBay. My plan was to hire sales reps and sell tack at tracks around the country. I had a really good lady in Northern California, a man in Florida and another in New York. At first it was exciting and I loved earning money from home. My reps were well stocked and would just mail me checks.

Eventually every one of my sales reps either disappointed me by not selling enough, or by stealing from me. I grew to hate the tack business. I was still shy, but forced myself to sell at Del Mar in the summer. Some mornings sales were wonderful and I sold lots of tack, but I still hated it. I rewarded myself with a swim at the beach every morning and that was all that kept me going back to the track. At this point I was liquidating my inventory and getting out.

I had been putting more time and effort into my eBay business and it was growing. I shopped at yard sales and thrift stores and found treasures to sell on eBay. This was a business I could do easily and it was fun. I didn't have to speak to any of my customers, everything was online. Most of my buyers were great, and I became a 'Top Rated Seller' with 100-percent positive feedback.

I still had my riding horses, Flyer and Axel at home and now I could trail ride in the mornings. Axel is a Mustang I bought from a groom at SLRD. His owner didn't have a car and used him to make beer runs to the liquor store about two miles away. I had seen him on the busy road crossing a bridge in traffic and he impressed me. He was a short chestnut gelding, only 13 1/2 hands, and very wide, with big intelligent naughty eyes, and a flaxen mane and tail. Axel was exactly what I had been looking for.

I loved being retired from racing from my first day of not going to the track. I soon realized that I had been a prisoner of my passion, racehorses. For the previous seven years I had not taken a single day off. My version of a day off was to come in a little late if I could manage to work all of the horses on the same day, and then give them all the same day off. Since the day after a work is the most important day to check legs, I still had to be at the barn, but not quite as early. Often, if I was running a horse, my 'day off' would be race day instead.

Mornings at home were my favorite. I got up very early, fed the horses, dogs and cats, and then went for a trail ride. Now I had time to give my ponies' baths, comb out their manes and tails, and just be with them. I mucked my paddock at first light and always thought that I must be the only person who enjoyed mucking. I loved the quiet of the morning, only broken by birds singing and my dogs' rough housing.

I have always loved gardening but couldn't keep up with my yard and flowers when I was training. I would try to keep everything weeded and pretty, but there just weren't enough hours in the day and would hire a good gardener for a day or two to get caught up. Now, I could do it all myself and I loved every minute. I would be listening to the birds sing, watching hawks fly over me, enjoying my dogs and flowers and think that life couldn't get any better than this.

There were so many changes in my life when I stopped training. My neighbors Lorie and Frank didn't adjust to the change well. When I was busy at the track, I had no opinions on little things at home. The truth was that I was so focused on my runners that little things, like where we put our trash cans for pickup, or what the other neighbors were doing, weren't important to me.

Lorie and Frank were raging alcoholics and very stupid, hillbilly type of people. Their English was peppered with double negatives and their thoughts were always simple. Lorie and I were friendly, but not really friends because I didn't like her. She fed my horses for me when I was at the races and I helped her with her horses. I made feeding very simple for her, by measuring out the grain and setting aside the flakes of hay, so that she only had to throw the feed over the fence. A blind idiot could have fed my horses in less than a minute.

Even though Lorie had owned horses for many years, she knew very little about caring for them. She had two Tennessee Walkers, and I often felt sorry for them. Frank always rode his horse, Titan, while drunk, and Lorie rode her horse, Nash. Titan was a wonderful horse and didn't like Frank at all. He was fat and sluggish although they fed him very little. I suggested that they test his thyroid and pointed out that he had classic symptoms of low thyroid. They refused to call a vet out to pull blood on the horse so I offered to pull his blood and drop it off at a vet clinic to save them the call charge. They would only have to pay a $40 lab fee to check Titan's thyroid. They refused my offer to help the horse. A year and a half later Titan, who had a wonderful disposition, became angry and aggressive with Lorie and Frank. He was chasing them both out of his paddock, so they finally called the vet who found that his thyroid enzyme levels were upside down. Poor Titan was hungry because they only fed him one tiny flake of Bermuda hay per day and had been doing that for years.

My Axel, the Mustang, didn't like going out on the trails alone and would walk as slow as he possibly could. Mustangs seem to be more herd-oriented than other breeds and to make him happy I started riding with Lorie. With company Axel was fun and lively, but I had to endure Lorie. She worked as a butcher and had nothing but negative stories to tell me on our rides. She hated her job and complained for hours that she had never been promoted to manager. Often she was drunk and slurring her words but in typical Susan style I endured. After a ride I always felt like shit, and wondered why I put myself though that, and then would remember I did it for Axel.

Lorie and Frank fought with everyone who lived near them. Neighbors Kathy and Gary, who lived at the top of our hill, had built a decorative vinyl fence along the side of the road. Unfortunately, the fence was built on top of our water lines. Lorie wanted to sue them and expected me to join in the lawsuit; after all, she had fed my horses for years. At first I agreed that the fence should not have been built over our water lines, but the more I listened to her, the less I wanted to be involved. She thought that she could sue without a lawyer and would represent herself. I could just imagine her standing up in court speaking in double negatives with me there as a witness, nodding my head in agreement.

I pointed out that starting a fight with our neighbors wouldn't be a smart thing to do. She and I both had loose, unlicensed dogs, and lots of them. Anyone who wanted to get even with us would only have to call Animal Control.

One day Lorie and I were riding and our neighbor Gary drove by and stopped to talk to us. He apologized for placing the fence over our pipes and explained that he would cover any damage caused by his fence to our pipes. I told him that I was good with that, but Lorie said nothing.

A few days later Lorie knocked on Gary's door and told him that she and I would be bringing a lawsuit against them if they didn't move their fence. I knew nothing about Lorie's threat, but the next time Gary drove by me, I waved like I always do and he didn't wave back. I went to Gary and Kathy's house, knocked on their door and asked if we had a problem. That is when I found out that Lorie had lied about me supporting her. She had also named another neighbor as being in support of her lawsuit and I knew that to be a lie.

I tried to have a conversation with Lorie and asked her why she lied, but she wouldn't speak to me. In truth I thought that Lorie not speaking to me was a gift from God. I had been suffering through trail rides with her to please Axel, and now I was free.

We went for months without speaking. Whenever she or her husband drove by me, I smiled and waved. They gave me dirty looks, but I continued to smile. In fact I smiled bigger and waved harder just to screw with them.

It wasn't long until they chose to turn our disagreement into a bigger fight. They decided that we should put our trash cans at the bottom of the hill so that the big trash truck didn't tear up our old dirt road. I explained that I couldn't fit the new giant size cans into my car and I couldn't lift them into my truck. Although they drove right by my house to take their cans to the bottom of the hill, they didn't offer to help me.

I began putting my trash cans at the end of my driveway and Lorie was furious when the garbage truck turned around in her driveway. Interesting fact was that her driveway wasn't even on her property but encroaching on another neighbor's property. She stopped to talk to me one day and told me that I better tell the trash company not to turn around on her driveway. I just smiled real big and waved at her hoping she would drive away.

The next week she was waiting in the dark at 6:00am for the trash truck. As the truck backed into her driveway to turn around she started screaming at the poor driver and waving a big stick at him. The trash company called me later that day to inform me that they could no longer pick up my trash because Lorie had told them they weren't allowed to drive on our street. I informed them that Lorie didn't own the street and the supervisor on the phone told me that she had screamed at their driver and threatened him with a stick. I asked him how his driver could be scared of a short drunk woman with a stick and he laughed. I told him I would circulate a petition in the neighborhood and prove that Lorie was the only one with a problem. He agreed, I got all the signatures that I needed and life went on.

Lorie and Frank seemed to be in a full time drunken rage now and aimed their venom at me. One morning I was working in the yard on my flowers enjoying the early morning quiet. Lorie's horses Titan and Nash started nickering to me every time I walked near my haystack. I knew they hadn't been fed yet and were hungry. At 10:30 the horses still hadn't been fed and were nickering constantly to me. They wanted food and didn't understand why I couldn't feed them. I can't ignore hungry animals and I knew that Lorie and Frank were both home. I finally called them and, since they never answer their phone, I left a message that their horses were hungry. A short while later, they drove past my house, both of them hanging out of their truck window screaming at me. By then I was inside and they didn't even see me, but were screaming at my house. In what was to be their unique style of attack they both screamed as loud as they could in unison, but saying different words so they drowned each other out. I did hear, "Fucking psycho bitch."

An hour later I had errands to run and pulled out of my driveway and headed down the dirt road in my little Saab. I only drove a half mile when I met the crazies. Frank was driving his truck and he stopped in the road and left his truck parked diagonally across the road so that I could not pass. They both got out of the truck and started their screaming match again only this time in my face. It was the most ridiculous attack I have ever witnessed, because they were so busy screaming they didn't even realize that neither one of them could be heard. They finally stopped for a second to take a breath and I calmly told them they were both acting like stupid drunks. I had my cell phone in my hand when Lorie said, "Let's go Frank, she is calling 911." Instead of leaving, Frank reached into my car through the open window and knocked my phone out of my hand. I picked up my phone and he did it again. I hadn't been at all frightened, until now. My window was open because I wasn't scared. I thought they were stupid loud drunks, but I didn't think I was in danger. They were acting like drunken idiots and I felt like a spectator. Frank was a big, overweight man and he leaned on my car door so that I couldn't get out. He then reached into my car and hit me in the face. I smiled and said, "You really are stupid aren't you?" My old style of never letting anyone know that they had hurt me had kicked in. Lorie was now screaming at Frank to leave me alone and get in the truck. They finally drove off and I called 911.

If I had known that the Valley Center cops were completely useless I would have at least tried to defend myself. I thought the bruises on my face would be enough evidence to have Frank arrested for assault. A cop arrived two hours after I called 911 and did nothing. I told him my story and I had to tell him to take a picture of my bruised face. He told me that he couldn't arrest Frank because it would be my word against his.

The cop turned his report into Lt. Blackmon, an investigator with the Sheriff's Department in Valley Center. I called the police station many times over the next few weeks to request an appointment with Blackmon, so that I could tell him the history behind the assault and show that the problems were escalating. We set three appointments and he cancelled all of them. Finally seven weeks after I was assaulted Blackmon told me he had finished his investigation. I was beyond furious. How could they even call it an investigation without ever speaking to me, the victim?

I wrote a scathing letter to the Editor of the local paper detailing my assault and the lack of response from our local police, especially Investigator Blackmon, who hadn't even taken the time to speak to me. The day before my story was published Blackmon called me and asked to meet and re-interview me. Since he had never interviewed me I said, "Do you mean that you want to interview me for the first time now that the case has been closed?" I couldn't hide my disdain and lack of respect for this man.

Blackmon and his partner came to my house the next day and we talked in my dining room. I have only two chairs in my dining room, I sat in one, Blackmon in the other, and his partner sat on a little plastic step stool that I keep in the kitchen. I was hoping the stool would break and he would land on the floor. They wasted my time going through the motions of investigating a closed case. Blackmon told me that the District Attorney had asked him to interview me, but when I called the District Attorney they said the case had been closed a month ago, and they had made no requests.

Jill was Lorie's best friend and I knew her because she lived close by and we sometimes met on the trails. She was on a trail ride and came to my house two weeks after Frank assaulted me and asked me what happened to my face. I said, "Like you don't know" and she replied that she had heard that Lorie and I had a fight on the road, but that was all she heard. When I told her the entire true version of the story she seemed shocked. She later went to Lorie for verification and Lorie told her that she, not Frank had hit me.

I told Jill that I would take no more abuse from her friends and that I was armed with my gun, had gotten a concealed weapon permit, and carried pepper spray at all times. I knew that Jill would run to Lorie and warn her about the gun. The pepper spray was true but I invented the story of the concealed weapon permit, knowing it would get back to Lorie within hours.

Lorie and Frank had been running me off the road whenever we met and after Jill told them about the gun, they stayed on their own side of the road for a while.

My peace at home was shattered by drunks. I could hear them throwing their empty beer bottles into already full trash cans of bottles and the noise made me cringe. Was my entire life to be influenced by drunks, I wondered.

After Lorie and Frank assaulted me, I couldn't stand the sight of them. I would involuntarily shutter every time I saw them. I relived the assault thousands of times in my head and each time had a better way I could have reacted. The trucks they drive are diesel and easy to hear from far away, so it was easy for me to disappear from their sight. I would hear them in the distance and step into the garage or behind a tree and watch them drive by my house. Most of the time, they would flip me off as they drove by my house, even though they didn't see me.

Unbelievably, Lorie and Frank still rode their horses on a trail that begins on my property. If we met on my trail on my property they would scream at me, usually so loud and distorted that I couldn't make out the words. I didn't want to close my trail to other riders. After telling Lorie and Frank several times in emails that if they wanted to ride on my property, they would have to be polite to me, I put no trespassing signs up. The signs read "No Trespassing, Lorie and Frank Zubov." They were once again infuriated with me and tore my signs down. I made the signs with cardboard and stakes so it was easy to replace them, but my patience was wearing thin. One day I was on the trail and Lorie tore my signs down in front of me, spewing venom and so drunk that I had no idea what she was even trying to say. I warned her that I would call 911 and report her for trespassing and still she wouldn't leave and she wouldn't stop yelling at me. The cops arrived an hour later and did nothing once again. A week later I called the cops again and reported her for trespassing and again they were too late to do anything.

I had decided to fight back. I couldn't live in fear of crazy drunk neighbors forever. Moving away would be admitting defeat and that was not an option. The third time I called the cops I finally had a cop respond who believed me and seemed to be on my side. I explained the history behind my complaint and my latest encounter with Lorie. I had just finished a perfect trail ride on a Sunday morning and was still on my horse at the corner of my property watching my dogs play with Lorie's dogs. The sun had just come up, the birds were singing, and all the dogs were happy as I sat smiling at my good fortune on my beautiful Flyer. I heard someone talking and since Lorie and I didn't speak, at first I didn't know anyone was talking to me. Lorie was in the road, had gotten up early to harass me, and now yelled, "Stop yelling at my dogs, bitch, or we will beat you up again." I had not said a word to any of the dogs and have never screamed at her dogs. I said nothing, just looked at her, like you sick fuck, and rode down to my paddock. As soon as I got away from her I started shaking uncontrollably. I called 911 and reported that a crazy drunk neighbor had threatened me. The cops arrived and for once believed me. I don't know what they said to Lorie and Frank but it was effective. From that day on, when they drove by my house they looked straight ahead, like naughty school children who have been reprimanded.

The friendly cops suggested that I make a case against Lorie and Frank and back it up with solid evidence. Although tape recordings and videos probably wouldn't be allowed in court, at least the responding officers would have proof that they could use as threat to Lorie and Frank. He told me that when they lie to the officer he can then respond with my recording. Since that day I always have my recorder in my pocket and turned on whenever there is a chance that we will meet.

When I moved way out here in the country I naively believed that my neighbors would all be nature lovers and live in peace. It took a cop to explain to me that many people prefer the country so that they can do drugs and drink and act like hillbillies.

My closest neighbors Gary and Patsy lived in a rental house next door with their two young children. They were white supremacists, flew a Confederate flag in their front yard, and had parties that lasted for three days. I was still dating Gary, who was black, when they moved in and they hated me. I had never been around white supremacists and had to do a Google search to see if the Confederate flag meant what I guessed it stood for.

The neighbor's son, Charlie, was only ten years old and a good kid. He told me that he had already flunked two grades at school and didn't like going to school. He loved horses and always wanted to help me brush them and muck my corral. I noticed that he missed a lot of school days and he told me that his mother couldn't get out of bed after parties to take him to the bus stop, which was only a mile away. I felt so sorry for Charlie and probably should have called social services, but the foster care system is so bad that I may have made his life worse, instead of better. As far as I could tell he wasn't abused. I did take the time to tell him over and over what a great kid he was. I intuitively knew that something big would go down soon and I told him that whatever happened he had to remember that I knew he was a good kid.

I abhor racism and go out of my way to expose it. Now I was living next door to white supremacists.

Another family of white supremacist lived only a half mile from me. Jim, his wife Stacey, and their two young daughters were best friends with my next door neighbors. They all drove dune buggies on our dirt road that had been modified to make more noise and sounded like Harley motorcycles. The children and the parents zipped back and forth to each other's homes littering the road and my front yard with beer and soda cans. I was trying hard to endure and might have succeeded if I didn't have horses.

Gary and Patsy, next door, owned a small excavating business that they ran from their home. Often at night, I would be awakened after midnight when Gary illegally dumped loads of rocks and dirt on their rental property. The sound of rocks being dumped from a commercial dump truck was so loud that my horses would get spooked and charge around their paddock. I would have to go outside to settle the horses down and make sure that they weren't hurt. I had Axel, Flyer, and another Thoroughbred, Copain in a big paddock in my back yard. Axel was always sensible, but the Thoroughbreds would be so scared that they would run into the fences.

One night I finally realized that dumping boulders at all hours of the night couldn't be legal. I knew that my property was zoned agricultural, not commercial, and assumed that the neighbors had the same zoning. My first call the next morning was to Tom, the property manager of the rental house next door. I had already called him to complain several times about the three day parties and the trash lining our road. I told him that that it was illegal to run a commercial trucking company from an agricultural zoned property. He lied and told me that agricultural zoning and commercial zoning were identical.

My next call was to the zoning department. I placed a formal complaint and emailed them pictures of the commercial dump truck and piles of dirt and boulders that had been dumped. I called them back every few days asking when they would begin their investigation, but the department had been cut back to one man and he couldn't even give me an estimated date.

One night the party next door got crazier and louder than usual and my horses got hurt. I knew that parties didn't last for three days without the help of crystal meth and plenty of alcohol. The party guests were yelling at me even though they couldn't see me. I could clearly hear them shouting, "You fucking nigger lover, I want to fuck you in the face." My horses were running crazy in their paddock from the noise of the yelling and dirt bikes, and I quietly sneaked out onto my deck in the dark to check on them. I called Tom, the property manager, and held the phone up in the air so he could hear what I had to live with. He heard them clearly and told me that it wasn't his problem. The yelling and dirt bikes went on for hours. I continued to sneak outside to check on the horses and could see them running around and around their paddock.

I was crouched behind my hot tub on the deck when I heard the drunken partiers urging their dogs to fight. It was clear that the dogs didn't want to fight, but after several minutes I heard growling and then a dog fight broke out. The thought of such scummy human beings making their dogs fight turned my stomach and I started to tremble. I called 911 for the fourth time that night and reported that the white supremacists were now fighting dogs and if they didn't get out here now, I would break up the dog fight myself. The dispatcher told me that an officer was on the way. When the cop car pulled into their driveway the drunks quickly ended the dog fight.

The cop came to my house and I couldn't hide my fear. I told him what they had been yelling at me and that I had a black boy friend and I was scared. He told me he was going to leave and then come back with his lights off and sit nearby in his car, so that he could hear the racial taunts himself. The drunks started with their despicable chants as soon as they thought the coast was clear. The cop heard what he needed to hear and broke up their party. He then parked in front of my house until every last one of them was gone.

The next morning when I went out to feed the horses, both Thoroughbreds were injured. Flyer had a swollen ankle and Copain had a swollen hock, and they had lost three shoes during the night. Axel, the sensible Mustang, looked tired but he wasn't hurt. I put bandages on the horses, filled them with Bute and called the shoer while I was boiling mad inside. I had failed to keep them safe. This was my only job, keeping my animals safe, and I had failed, let them down, and I couldn't let it happen again.

I walked next door and banged on Gary and Patsy's door at 6:30 a.m. Little Charlie answered the door and I told him that I needed to speak to his father. He told me that he was still asleep and I said, "Wake him up, this is important." Gary heard me at his door and walked stumbling and still drunk out to speak to me. I informed him that two of my horses had been injured last night, and this shit was over. He apologized for hurting the horses and said that it wouldn't happen again.

That night, just before dark I heard the loud dune buggy from the other white supremacist family in front of my house again. The horses were charging around their paddock because of the noise, and I went out into the road and flagged the dune buggy down. The neighbors' two young girls were driving it and I calmly told them that my horses had been hurt the night before and were scared of their noisy dune buggy, and now I wanted them to turn around, go home, and never come back.

Minutes later the girl's father, Jim, raced to my house in his pickup truck leaning on the horn. He parked in front of my house and got out of his truck in a screaming crystal meth rage. He was yelling, "You bitch, I'm going to kill you, you fucking bitch." I couldn't risk letting my dogs out because they would surely have bitten this screaming maniac and knowing how useless the justice system is, I decided not to risk their safety. Instead, I went outside alone and told him to get off my property. He would not leave and was in such a crazed state that I had no doubt that he was on crystal meth as he continued to threaten me. I called 911 and had to yell into the phone to be heard over his rants. I held the phone up in the air and asked the 911 operator if she could hear Jim threatening to kill me and she said yes. She told me that she would have an officer sent out immediately and I asked her to stay on the phone with me. Jim suddenly stopped yelling and said, "I will leave now but I am coming back and I am going to kill you, you fucking bitch." He got into his truck and drove to his house, which I could see clearly from my front yard. He left his truck running and ran into his house for less than a minute, and then got into his truck and headed back to my house. Now I was really scared, I told the 911 operator that he was coming back and I thought he had run into his house to get a gun since he had just told me that he was going to kill me. The operator sarcastically asked me how I knew he was coming back, and I answered that I could see his truck on the road coming towards me. She told me to go into my house and lock the doors. I thought she was a useless idiot at this point. If a crazed crystal meth addict knows where I am and wants to kill me, how easy it that? I told her no, that I would not wait for him to find me in the house; instead I would be across the street hiding behind a horse trailer.

Jim came back and I heard him park in front of my house again. I was too scared to move and was shaking like a leaf, hiding behind the horse trailer. The moon was so bright that I was afraid that he would see my shadow trembling and I tried to stop shaking, but I couldn't. I heard my dogs barking and I knew he was walking around my house looking for me. After ten minutes of my dogs going crazy in the house, everything got dead quiet and I thought he must be looking for me outside. Finally the cop arrived and found me behind the horse trailer. He told me to go back to my house and I refused and told him I wasn't moving until he captured this man who was threatening to kill me.

A few minutes later the cop saw two men walking down the road toward us and he acted like a cop at first, yelling, "Put your hands up, shut the fuck up and put your hands in the air." He then ordered me to go back to my house, and I wish I had ignored him and stayed outside.

Lorie and Frank had called a short truce and told me that they had seen everything that night from the beginning, when I calmly told the little girls that they couldn't scare my horses and must go home. Lorie told me that the second I was in my house the cop and the two neighbors started laughing, like they were all old friends.

The cop knocked on my door and told me that Jim had not come back to my house to kill me; he was only going to visit Gary next door.

When the cop had arrived he asked me whose truck was parked in my front yard, and I had told him it was Jim's truck. When I asked the obvious question, if Jim came back only to visit Gary, why was he parked on my property, 100 yards from Gary's house, he ignored my question. I was already feeling like I was living an episode of the *Twilight Zone*, when the cop said that Gary and Jim both wanted to talk to me and could they come into my house and sit down. I reminded him that thirty minutes ago, in a drug induced rage, Jim threatened to kill me and the cop said, "Well that is your word against his." I reminded him that it was all on the 911 tape and he ignored me again. I told him that I would not allow the men into my house and I wanted Jim arrested, and I planned on getting a restraining order against him. He wouldn't arrest Jim and I could see that they must be friends and probably the cop was a white supremacist too.

The next morning I went to the court house and got a restraining order against Jim. After the unbelievable lack of response from the cops, I realized that I was completely on my own and would have to defend myself. I went to a gun shop and bought a 38-caliber Smith and Wesson hand gun and bullets. When I got home, I loaded the gun and put it in my nightstand drawer close to my bed. I vowed never to run and hide again. Next time they could bring it on, and I would kill them if I had to.

A week later a cop knocked on my door and served me with a restraining order from Gary and Jim. They had gone to court and told ridiculous lies about me. The lies were all easy to prove. The most ridiculous lie was that I hung out at the bus stop and threatened their children. The bus stop at the end of our road is a major stop for children within a three mile radius, and I had always seen at least six cars dropping off children. It wouldn't be difficult to confirm that I had never been at the bus stop.

I didn't know anything about the hearing process of restraining orders and did Google searches to find information. I should have hired an attorney, but I thought that with the 911 tape as solid evidence the hearing would be a breeze. I called the police station and asked for a copy of the 911 tape for court and was told that it had to be ordered by the court. From that statement I understood that I had to ask the judge in court to procure the tape and that was my plan. I called an attorney as back up and she couldn't be in court with me, but advised me to ask for a continuance. She told me that the law states that I would be granted one continuance.

I had asked Lorie to come to court as a witness but she refused. Thinking she was too busy to give up a day to help me, I asked her if she could write a statement instead. Although she had already told me that she had seen and heard everything now she said, "I didn't see nothin'."

On the court date I wasn't surprised to see that Gary and Jim had let their hair grow out. They were not skinheads on that day, but both had very short hair. What did surprise me was that they had brought their friend, the responding officer, in as a witness for them. I had a sick feeling that I was fucked.

I asked the judge for a continuance and he said no. I told him that I understood that by law I had a right to a continuance and he still said no. I asked him if he would order the 911 tape so that he could hear the threats to kill me and he said no. I was fucked, the court system was fucked and corrupt, and it was a damn good thing that I owned a gun.

Although I had lost in court and wasn't granted a permanent restraining order, there were some good changes on my street. The dune buggies were gone and my horses stayed quiet. After the court date I called the zoning office again and told them that this was more than a zoning issue. I told the zoning commissioner that I had a black boyfriend and the neighbors in violation of the zoning laws were white supremacists who hated me, I lived alone, and had been threatened. The very next day I saw the zoning commissioner next door and he called me later to tell me that he had given them thirty days to shut down.

My victory was bittersweet. Of course I was beyond thrilled that the white supremacists would be leaving. I felt shell shocked, like I had seen too much. Predictably Lorie had lied and refused to help me. I was deeply unsettled to see for myself how corrupt the cops and the court system were. No one even listened to the damning evidence on the 911 tape.

I didn't want this negativity to seep into my soul and I tried hard to find some positives that I could cling to instead. I had remained honest when everyone around me was lying, this was good. I knew that now that I had a gun I could protect myself and my animals, and no one would ever fuck with us again. I was through with being a victim.

I had seen Lorie, the cop, the judge, Jim and Gary for who they were and I had to let that be their problem, not mine. I knew that the Universe would deal with the scumbags and I had to stay in my own peaceful place. It wasn't long before Lorie got breast cancer and Jim lost his pool cleaning business after a knee injury.

With the white supremacists gone, life at home went back to normal. I stayed busy with my dogs, cats and horses and loved working on eBay from home. I had to go out to shop for items to sell, but most of work was on the computer. My animals loved having me home so much and my office became their hang out. I always had at least three dogs in beds in the office and one or two at my feet. The cats had beds on the windowsills.

Gummy's old body was worn out and she had become frail. She still was the alpha dog and had never been challenged. One day I was in the horse paddock and heard her scream and I ran up to the house to find her having a seizure. I held her until her body became still and a few minutes later she seemed fine. Her eyes were brighter than normal and she was more aware. For two hours she felt great and even ate a big dinner and then she screamed again. I held her poor old body and knew that this was the end. She tried hard to stay with me until I told her it was okay to go. Her body was spent and I couldn't watch her suffer. I was sobbing and hugging her as she looked into my eyes and then her heart stopped. We all missed our Greta Gumdrop dog and no one stepped up to be the alpha dog.

Chance died soon after Gummy. He had a tumor on a hind leg that had to be removed and he never fully recovered from the anesthesia. I knew he loved me and protected me but he didn't kiss me until the day he died. Close to death he was finally able to let his guard down and show me the affection that I had always known was there.

Anthony had died a year before with a heart condition which is common in large breed dogs. His sister Daisy was devastated and lost without him. She had devoted her life to taking care of her big goofy brother. The two of us mourned him and cried for days. The dogs had always argued about whose turn it was to sleep on the living room couch and Anthony had always won. He was so big that he took up the entire oversized couch. After he died no one wanted to sleep on the couch. We all missed him terribly.

I had never seen two dogs as close as Anthony and Daisy. They had survived living as wild dogs after they were abandoned and their bond was tight. One day we were all outside and I heard shots being fired. I saw Daisy go to Anthony who was sleeping, nudge him to wake him up, and then herd him into the house. Once inside she started trembling with fear. She had been shot when she was a stray puppy in Pala and was terrified of gunshots, but still got Anthony into the house where she knew they were both safe. I hugged her and told her she was a wonderful sister to take such good care of her brother, but she could let me help too. I told her that when she was scared she should come to me. The next time she heard shots she put Anthony in the house again and then ran to me. I loved being a dog mom.

Scooter had become part of our family when I was still training at SLRD. He had an owner and lived in a big house up on a hill above the track. The first time I saw him he was asleep in the guard shack and I thought he belonged to a security guard. I asked Ed at security where the beautiful dog had come from and he told me that he didn't like his home and preferred hanging out at the gate. He was a big Collie mix and would sleep at the gate, not paying any attention to other dogs or their owners, as we all passed through the gate. After months of hanging out at the gate, trainers started to complain that he was spooking their horses. By then Scooter was bringing his friend, Molly, with him and they would quietly walk through the barn area of SLRD to get to the gate. I never once saw them do anything that would spook a horse, but a lot of trainers like to complain. Security would call the dog's owner and tell her that her dogs were at the gate again and she would come and pick them up. Eventually she got tired of picking her dogs up and told Security that if they couldn't find a home for her dogs she would euthanize them.

I hadn't met Molly but everyone knew I was crazy about Scooter so Security asked me if I would take both dogs. I felt guilty that I really only wanted Scooter, but I couldn't separate him from his friend, so I took both of them home. Once they were at my house, it was obvious why they didn't like their old home. I couldn't get either of them to enter my house; they were both terrified of walking through the door. My small back yard was fenced so finally I gave up on getting them in the house and I put two rugs outside for them to sleep on. They both looked at the rugs like, what are they for, and then walked away and slept in the dirt. In the morning both dogs were gone. I thought they had jumped my fence, but later I found a hole in the fence where they had chewed through the metal mesh. I looked everywhere for them and several people at SLRD helped me search and put signs up. We called all the shelters, but the dogs had vanished. Three days later I was headed out on a trail ride and Scooter came walking home. I was so happy to see him that I jumped off my horse to hug him, and he never left me again. We never did find Molly and I will always feel guilty that I hadn't really wanted her in the first place. I am sure that I would have loved her once I knew her.

Scooter was a rogue of a dog. I wanted him home and safe, but he was a vagabond who wouldn't be contained. I replaced the chewed up fence with a heavier mesh that he couldn't chew through and thought that I had him under control. I left him in the yard and went to the track and when I returned home he was in the garage. He had torn apart my wooden gate in the yard and let himself out. I was able to put the gate back together with stronger screws and the next day when I came home the gate was shredded into a million little pieces. I still wasn't ready to accept that I couldn't control this dog, so I replaced the gate with a vinyl gate. Silly me, I thought it looked sturdy. Scooter carefully took one slat off of the gate so that he could come and go as he pleased. By now I realized that I was never going to win this battle. I left the slat off the gate and gave up.

Scooter hated being alone and had to be with people. Neighbors told me that as soon as I left for the track in the morning, he went to their houses and waited for me to come home. I didn't think that he would enjoy going to the track with me. I took Gummy, Chance and sometimes Amy with me to the track because they understood the rules and still wanted to go. Because I had to be 100 percent focused on my horses until the track closed at 10:00, the dogs had to understand that they would be ignored until then. They had dog beds in my tack room, and I used a dog gate instead of shutting the door so that they could see out. They were always happy just to be there and slept until the track closed.

I began taking Scooter to the track with me in the mornings, and he was thrilled. He had some weird ideas that I never did figure out. In the parking lot, he couldn't walk on the white lines that defined parking spaces. He made us all walk around the lines, and anyone watching us must have thought we were a family of nerds. Once we got to our barn, he took the biggest dog bed and went back to sleep.

Most of my dogs were getting old, and I didn't feel as safe as I had when Chance was alive. Chance was never completely sane, and he would have shredded anyone who he perceived as a threat to me or the other dogs. This was a liability at times, but I felt protected.

I got online looking for a Dalmatian that I could adopt and couldn't find one. Instead, a picture of a Jindo at a shelter in Los Angeles kept jumping out at me. A Jindo looks like an Akita and although I didn't know it then, they are the most popular breed in Korea. They are known for fighting to the death to protect their owners. For days, every time I got online to search for a Dalmatian I saw the Jindo. Intuition was telling me this was my dog but I didn't want to hear it at first. I knew nothing about the breed and still missing Chance, I really wanted a Dalmatian. I was without a Dalmatian for the first time in thirty years.

I finally read the bio on Henry, the Jindo, and it broke my heart. He was only three years old and had lived in the shelter for two years. I called the shelter to see why he hadn't been adopted. They told me that a shelter worker wanted him for herself but hadn't been able to rent a house with a yard for him. Her friends had finally convinced her that she was doing the dog a disservice by keeping him in the shelter for years. On the phone they warned me that he had some weird quirks and would need a good handler. When I told them that I was a trainer they were thrilled.

I drove to L.A. the next day and met Henry. It was obvious that one of his problems was the shelter worker who had wanted to keep him. She brought him into the waiting area to meet me and he freaked on the slippery linoleum floor. He panicked and was slipping and sliding when the kennel worker grabbed him and hugged him, which freaked him out even more. He escaped from her grasp and scampered off the slippery linoleum. The girl looked at me, thinking that I would bail after this display, but she was wrong.

I took Henry for a short walk around the city block, which he didn't enjoy because he wanted to get back to his kennel. Since I am not a city person I wasn't enjoying walking around a block in Los Angeles either. I was already sure that I wanted this dog, but the kennel worker insisted that I walk him around the block three more times to be absolutely sure. She told me that he wouldn't be a good protector and that once when a man approached her on the street Henry hid behind her. After seeing how out of tune she was with this dog I didn't listen to anything she had to say about him. I was listening to my intuition now, and I knew that Henry was my dog.

I brought Henry home and he was so messed up it was heartbreaking to witness. Living in a kennel for two years had nearly shut his brain down. He behaved like a prisoner who had been in prison so long that he had become institutionalized. When he was outside in the yard and I called him in, he would come in and then stand near the door. An hour later he would still be standing near the door. It was like he didn't have thoughts of his own and was waiting for me to tell him what to do next.

I bought him a new dog bed that was 'his' and he thought he should guard it. At least his brain was working and deciding to guard his bed seemed like a healthy thought. I bought him some toys and two more beds so that he could make decisions. He had to think about which toy to chew on and which bed to sleep in. I stayed very quiet around him and praised him all the time.

Henry wasn't house broken yet but he did have definite ideas about how to pee that he learned in the kennel. He would sacrifice a dog bed or blanket and wad it into a ball and then pee on it. That way all of the urine would be soaked up in the blanket and not on the floor. I could see how this worked for him living in a kennel with a cement floor. After I watched him do this once, it was easy to suggest to him that it would be better to go potty outside and housebreaking him was a breeze.

Henry was not a natural trail dog and not very interested in becoming one. For the first month I kept him on a long expandable leash on our rides and never turned him loose. He didn't complain, but it was never the highlight of his day. Eventually he was safe to turn loose and he accompanied us on trail rides occasionally, when I really begged him to come with us. For the longest time he wouldn't venture off of the dirt roads that wind through the avocado grove. The other dogs loved to play in the leaves under the trees, but not Henry. Once we turn for home he would decide that he should bolt and ran home instead of staying with us. I understand that this is an after effect of being in a kennel for so long. Something in his brain clicks and he must get home now.

I love Henry and he is the dog I count on to protect me. Once he settled in at my house his breeding became evident and I could see why Jindos are so popular in Korea. The first time someone knocked on my door, I knew how it felt to be protected by a Jindo. All the dogs were barking and Henry just did a low throaty menacing growl. We all just looked at him like, 'where did that come from?'

I always know that if I am in danger Henry will be there. Lorie, my crazy drunk neighbor, got a new dog, a young aggressive Rottweiler who made the mistake of growling at me one day. I thought I was alone in the front yard with the growling Rottweiler, but like magic, Henry was there and chased her away. She never growled at me again.

I dated a man for a short time who Henry didn't like. The man put his arm on my shoulder one day, and again out of nowhere, I heard the low throaty growl. With Henry around I am safe, and Henry is always around, like magic.

Life had gotten peaceful again and I was enjoying my dogs, cats and horses. One day I was out shopping and drove home on a back road that I usually avoid because it makes me carsick. I was driving very slowly as I passed by a small rundown farm. I have always looked at animals that I drive by, and this farm caught my attention every time I drove by. I had a feeling that the animals weren't happy there and needed help. I had never seen anything, it was more of a strong feeling and I couldn't report my 'feelings' to Animal Control. It was 103 degrees that day and I was hot and thirsty and wanted to get home, when I saw what looked like protruding ribs on one of the horses. The horse was standing under a sycamore tree and at first I thought that I must be mistaken, and was probably only seeing shadows from the tree. I did a U turn and took another look and still wasn't sure so I did yet another U turn. This time I was sure, and there was another horse that also had ribs and hip bones protruding.

I parked my car at the nearest house and knocked on the door, but there was no answer. When I walked near the fence line of the farm every animal on the farm made a noise to ask for help. The horses nickered, goats brayed, chickens and birds squawked, all in unison. I knew they were begging for help and I wouldn't turn my back on them, but needed a minute to decide how best to proceed. Knowing that I would be breaking the law if I trespassed to help them, I played it safe, and first called 911 to report an animal emergency. The dispatcher connected me to Animal Control and they weren't the least bit interested in helping these animals. I explained that when I got out of my car and looked at them they all made noise like asking for help, it was 103 degrees, and none of them appeared to have water and the horses were dangerously thin. I could see from the road the horse's water troughs were over-turned and empty. I reported that I could smell the rotting carcass of a dead animal from the road, and still Animal Control couldn't tell me when they would be able to respond to my call.

I had just finished reading the amazing book, *'Conversations With God'* by Neale Donald Walsch. I loved the advice he had written, that when in doubt, ask yourself, 'What would love do now?' I calmly asked myself, what would love do now, and I was halfway over the fence in a heartbeat. Love would help these animals and damn the consequences, of this I had no doubt. The animals were frantic when they saw me approach. I ran to a hose and turned it on but there was no water. I was trying hard to stay grounded and think. The level of despair of so many desperate animals was overwhelming me and I was crying, but a voice in my head said help them, and I couldn't turn back. I found a bull in a small corral with half a trough of filthy green slimy water, but I couldn't find a bucket. The animals were all frantically screaming at me as I ran around the unkempt farm searching for a bucket. Finally, I found a small metal feed scoop and I scooped tiny amounts of water out of the filthy trough and ran first to the horses. They drank the few sips I could offer of this green stinky slime and wanted more. My heart was breaking and I couldn't stop crying as I ran back and forth from the bull's trough with this stupid little scoop of filthy water, giving everyone just a few sips of the foul smelling water. I could see that this would take forever and I would run out of water before I could help all of the animals.

I called Jill, a neighbor and crazy Lorie's best friend, because I knew she was an animal lover. She told me she could be there in fifteen minutes with buckets of water. I dashed home to fill my containers with water and Jill, her husband Tom, and I, all went to the farm together with twenty-five gallons of water. With clean water, the three of us we quickly watered every animal on the farm. There were rabbits in cages without water and a dead rotting rabbit in the back of one cage. When we poured water into the cage of chickens, turkeys and ducks they all fought to be the first to get a drink. Some of the animals had water, but it was even more filthy than the bull's water and undrinkable. Finally everyone had water and we were leaving just as a truck pulled into the farm.

I had been thinking that for every animal to be in such bad shape the owner must have died several days ago, but I was wrong. The owners were a young couple, Mary and Jason and they were not happy to find us on their property. They had calves and other animals in their truck and said that they were returning from a petting zoo at their church. Jill spoke to them first and calmly told them that their animals were all desperately thirsty and hungry. Jason started yelling at his girlfriend and called her a fat lazy bitch and told her this was all on her. She said that she had been late for work at the Wild Animal Park in Ramona and did not have time to give her animals water that morning, but they were all fine and she smiled. I interrupted her and said, "Fine? You call this fine?? Look around you! Your horses are skeletal and dying of thirst! How can that be fine?" Mary smiled at me and told me I didn't know what I was talking about. At this point I lost my temper and told her she was a fucking idiot who shouldn't be allowed to be near an animal if this was the best she could do. Jill, Tom and I all left the farm but it was far from over.

When I got home I immediately got on the phone and called Animal Control again. I called every hour, for five hours, and they still hadn't been out to check on the animals. Three days later, they finally made an official visit to the farm and found everything to be fine. I nearly exploded when they told me this on the phone. I asked if they had seen the very thin horses, the skinny young kittens, and the dead rabbit carcass. They only repeated that everything was fine and added that I didn't know what I was talking about.

Again, I felt like I was living in a bad episode of Twilight Zone. I wrote a letter to the editor of the local paper that was published, depicting my experience at this farm on Lilac Road in Valley Center. I urged people to be aware, especially during a heat wave and to help animals that need help.

An old woman, Loralie, in Valley Center read my letter to the editor in the local paper and called me. She had a friend who had asked her to help a herd of miniature horses on a property that was on Lilac Rd adjacent to the property where I had watered animals. She told me that she had been there the night before and seen twenty- four emaciated miniature horses with no water or food. She was going back to the miniatures now with some friends to clean their filthy water tubs and get water to them. She said that the water tubs were so dirty that they smelled like sewage and the poor little miniatures couldn't drink. She had met the caretakers and they told her everything was fine. The caretakers were Mary and Jason and the horses were owned by their neighbor, an attorney.

I was on my way to help Loralie and the other women, and as I drove past the farm where I had watered animals the week before, I was shocked to see them all without water again. The water troughs were tipped over and the horses looked even worse than they had two weeks before. I parked my car, got out and all the animals called to me again. I was standing on the side of the road with my cell phone calling 911 when a woman stopped and asked if she could help. I told her that these animals are all very thirsty, this is the second time I have been here, and I have already called 911, but didn't expect Animal Control to help. Caroline climbed through the fence with me, and this time the water was working, so we quickly watered all of the animals. Again, they were all desperately thirsty. It was very hot and the kittens were even skinnier than before and screaming for food. I picked one up and was reaching for the other kitten and was thinking of running to my car and saving them. Just as I grabbed the second kitten Mary and Jason arrived. They recognized me immediately and told me I was trespassing. I told them that their animals were once again thirsty and miserable. Mary smiled and told me they were all fine, that Animal Control had been there and said they looked really good. There was something very wrong with these people who could inflict such suffering on animals. The system that was designed to protect the animals was turning a blind eye.

Caroline and I walked back to our cars parked along the road and were leaving as a cop pulled in. I had a sick feeling that things were about to get a whole lot worse. I turned the recorder on in my iPhone and told the cop I wanted to record our conversation. He spent the next ten minutes telling me that I could be arrested for recording him and that I had to turn it off. This was a lie and I had every right to record him, but I turned the recorder off. Jason walked across the road and told the cop that he wanted me arrested for trespassing. I told the cop that I was only watering desperately thirsty animals that Animal Control had ignored. I had called them many times and they could only tell me that the animals were fine. The cop told me I had broken the law, and I replied that I answered to a higher moral authority than the law. Three times he told me I had broken the law and three times I repeated that I answered to a higher moral authority than the law. I could see that this would go on forever, just like his lecture on not recording him, so I broke the circle of repeated sentences by saying, "Well then, I guess that makes me a vigilante, doesn't it?" By then Caroline had driven away and the cop asked me to identify her. I had her contact information, but I told the cop that I wasn't a rat and I wouldn't give it to him. He cited me for trespassing but let me go.

When I got home I called *The North County Times* and they were very interested in my story. They sent a writer and a photographer out the next day and did a story that made the front page of the Sunday edition of their paper.

I was suddenly a headline story and my phone didn't stop ringing. All I wanted was for Animal Control to step in and do their job. I had knocked on doors of the neighbors around Mary and Jason and got the same story from all of them. An attorney, James, who was a complete prick, owned the miniatures, his wife had left him, and he didn't care if the miniature horses died. He had hired Jason and Mary as caretakers, and seven of the miniatures had already died of dehydration and starvation. Neighbors had watched the horses die and done nothing. Mary's own animals had looked like shit for years but no one had done anything about it because of her ties with James, the attorney. Animal Control had been called countless times, but they were also afraid of messing with a nasty lawyer.

I wasn't about to give up my fight to save these animals just because I had been arrested. I called my trainer friends around the country and asked them to call Animal Control and ask for the status of the case on Lilac Rd and they all did. My friends reported back to me that Animal Control was very concerned that this case had gone national. I also contacted PETA and every rescue group I could find on the Internet.

Animal Control finally got interested in these animals, now that they could no longer be hidden. They opened an investigation and stated that, at first they found nothing wrong, but later found a dog that needed grooming, and now they were investigating. At the end of their investigation nine months later, they gave Mary notice that they planned on seizing two of the miniature horses because she had not complied with the Animal Control orders to give them food and water. The morning that Animal Control arrived with a horse trailer to pick up the horses they were gone. A man in Valley Center had called Animal Control to report that James, the owner, had offered him $500 to make the miniature horses disappear. Instead of taking the money, he went to the police. Animal Control concluded their investigation after nine months and charged Mary with six counts of animal cruelty.

During the nine months that it took Animal Control to investigate, I was busy fighting the trespassing charge. I had thought that trespassing was as minor as a speeding ticket and didn't realize that maximum penalty was six months in jail and a $2,000 fine. I hate courts and I had already seen how corrupt the Valley Center Police and Animal Control were, and I didn't expect a fair deal from a corrupt legal system.

I couldn't afford an attorney and was assigned a Public Defender at my arraignment as I plead not guilty. I was told to call the Public Defender's office and speak to my appointed attorney within the next three weeks before my first hearing. I called my attorney, Lacey Martz, at least twelve times before she finally called me back the day prior to my hearing. When we finally spoke, I told her that I had an organized legal file with all of the information about my case, including pictures of the emaciated animals and would like to meet with her to go over it. She didn't want to meet me and told me to email the file to her. I sent her twenty one documents via email.

On the day of my hearing, Lacey and I met for the first time, only thirty minutes before I was to go into the courtroom. She told me that she had read all twenty-one of my documents and that I should plead guilty, since there were no witnesses and it would be my word against Mary's. Within the twenty-one documents that she claimed to have read, there were thirty-three references to Carolyn, Jill, and Tom, my three witnesses who were on Mary's property with me. I wish I had stopped right then and called her a fucking liar. Instead, I stayed calm and told her that there were in fact three witnesses and I would not plead guilty. I didn't ever think I would get a fair deal in court but to have a Public Defender whose first sentence to me was a lie, was more than I could wrap my brain around. I felt sick, betrayed and scared.

After I was arrested Loralei called me and offered help and support. We met for lunch and she brought five other supporters with her. It felt so good to have someone on my side. My three witnesses, Jill, Tom and Carolyn, had all refused to help me. Jill told me that she didn't want to be involved, which made no sense since she was already involved. She told me that she couldn't afford to help me financially or emotionally, although she is very wealthy. I had Carolyn's phone number and had left several messages but she refused to return my calls. I had been feeling very alone and scared. The women with Loralei were all very kind and they assured me that they would support me until the end of this ridiculous case.

The next day I went to Loralie's house to see three of the miniature horses that she had rescued from the herd of twenty-four who were starving and dying. She and her friend, Hazel, had each taken three horses. Loralei showed me pictures of them before she took me to their corral and I was prepared to see emaciated animals, but still I was shocked at their condition. These poor little animals were nothing but skin and bones. You could count every rib, and their spines and hips, and even shoulder blades stuck out with no flesh on them. Their skin was covered with fungus and sores and they had lost most of their hair. They had given up on life and were all standing absolutely still, hanging their heads with dull glazed eyes. I went to the saddest little mare, put my arms around her neck and told her I was sorry that humans had failed her. I cried and tears were running down my face uncontrollably. I had never seen such an example of inhumanity and a failed, useless, Animal Control system. I had been demanding help from Animal Control for over a month and they had looked at these poor dying animals and said they were fine. I wanted to scream but cried quietly instead. I could see that they had suffered more than I could even imagine. I will never forget the dull sad eyes on these nearly dead little horses. Their spirits were broken after months of suffering. They were patiently waiting to die.

Loralie was 72 years old when she rescued the three miniature horses and her friend, Hazel, was 83 years old. Their bodies were old but these two horsewomen still had fire in their hearts. They both had the vet out to look at the little horses and began a feeding program that would get them back on their feet without killing them. I visited the miniatures many times over the next few months and never saw them when they weren't eating.

Loralie had worked for many years as a paralegal and she spent hours helping me organize my case. We put together a large legal file with pictures of the starving animals and pages of the discrepancies that we found in the police report. As we began finding lies in the police report, I gained confidence.

On the night I was arrested, the cop told me that since he knew nothing about horses, he wasn't even going to enter the property to look at the animals and would leave that to Animal Control. As soon as I drove away, he went on the property and reported that all of the animals looked fine and none were lame. One horse had a bad case of rain rot, which is a fungus that horses get, usually in climates were it rains a lot and their hair stays wet and un-groomed. There is no reason except neglect that a horse in California would ever have rain rot in the summer. The ignorant cop reported that he did find one horse with 'ring rot,' but he was still shiny and muscular. It would be impossible for a skinny horse covered with fungus to shine, yet the cop who examined the horse with a flashlight deemed him healthy. His entire written report made him look like a total idiot, which he obviously was. Again the cards appeared to be stacked against me and Mary and Jason were being protected.

After I had seen Hazel and Loralie's starving horses Hazel and I went to the local newspaper to expose this cruelty that the police and Animal Control so desperately wanted to hide. I had written several letters to the Editor, David, but had never met the fat fuck. David was very overweight and sitting in his office chair when we arrived. He was so fat that I had trouble not looking at the fat that hung over his socks when he crossed his legs and his ankles were exposed. Hazel knew him well and did most of the talking. She explained that she and Loralie had each taken three of the nearly dead miniatures, but there were still over a dozen of them starving and without water in the pasture on Lilac Road. We invited David to come with us and see the animals for himself. By the looks of him he rarely got out of his chair and he refused to accompany us to the farm.

Crazy seemed to be a place I was trapped in, and after our visit to the local paper, Hazel called David and told him not to use any of her statements or pictures. David did eventually go to the farm on Lilac Road and wrote a four page story about the 'poor victimized' owners. When I read the story I was shocked, angry, hurt, and confused. David spent most of the four pages attacking me and called me a vigilante who climbs fences and interferes for no reason. He described the owners as twenty year Valley Center residents and church goers. In his long story that started on the front page, he reported that as a Vigilante I had organized a group of people who were preparing to rescue all of Mary's animals at night. He said that I had a website but he couldn't supply the link. By the time I got to this part of his story I was fuming. I had never, even as a joke, said or written anything even close to this nonsense. I counted sixteen lies in David's biased story. Nine months later when Mary was charged with six counts of animal cruelty, David wrote a tiny little story on page three.

The North County Times was a bigger paper than David Roth's little local joke of a paper, and they at least had stayed near the truth. A North

County Times reporter was at my arraignment and reported that I had pled not guilty and was accompanied by an entourage of supporters.

My many supporters gave me hope throughout this ordeal. Kerri was an old friend who became my main supporter. She never left my side at my court appearances. Her steady calm demeanor helped me stay grounded even when I was shaking inside. Another friend, Patricia, drove two and a half hours to be with me in court and she was as strong as Kerri. Many of the other supporters were new friends who either knew Loralie or had read my story in the paper.

My court case dragged on forever, and I continued to catch my attorney Lacey in lies. Finally Lacey decided we should request a trial and I decided she needed to be fired. I had been speaking to Bryan Pease, who is a well-known animal rights activist attorney. He was too busy to represent me but he sent me to Sarah, who would represent me pro bono, since she too, was an animal right activist. Bryan also hooked me up with two other attorneys who were activists, and suddenly, I had four attorney's helping me from the sidelines.

Maria was one of the attorneys that Bryan had hooked me up with. She had worked as a District Attorney and her first question to me was, "What is their offer?" When I told her that there was no offer, in fact Lacey had just told me that she wanted a trial, she laughed. Maria told me that it is Lacey's job to go to the D.A. and get an offer. I politely emailed and called Lacey and reminded her that she had told me the D.A. had not made an offer and I asked her why we didn't have an offer. Within two hours Lacey called me back and said that the D.A. had offered to change the charge from misdemeanor trespassing to an infraction with a $50 fine. I just wanted this farce to be over and I was overjoyed with the offer.

Lacey was a nasty little bitch whose lies I had documented and I had already spoken to her supervisor. She was not happy with me taking control of my own case and making her perform her job. At our next court appearance she arrived late, and when she entered the courtroom she walked to me and whispered, "Would you come outside and speak to me." I answered, "Yes" and stood up to wait for her as she spoke to the bailiff. She turned around and yelled, "Outside" like I was a bad dog who hadn't followed her command. I didn't want to lose control like she had, so I said nothing, smiled and then walked very, very slowly to the door. We were outside only for seconds and I told her I would accept the offer from the D.A. After court I again called Lacey's supervisor and complained. This time the supervisor said, "Didn't I read about you in the paper? When I replied, "Yes, that there had been stories about me and the starving animals" she said, "You just keep doing what you are doing." I could hardly believe my ears and for the first time I thought maybe there are some people in the system who are not corrupt.

This long ordeal was nearly over and I had only one more court appearance. Mary had lied in court and told a judge that I had threatened her in order to get a restraining order against me. Sarah, the attorney Bryan had sent me, had met me, taken the folder that Loralie and I had put together, and was ready to defend me. I had been staying in contact with Animal Control and knew that they had completed their investigation months ago and it had been sent to the District Attorney. Now we were waiting for the D.A. to decide if charges would be pressed. I called and emailed the D.A. every few days. The day before my restraining order hearing I finally got an email from the D.A. stating that Mary had been charged with six counts of animal cruelty, and had been notified by mail. Sarah and I were thrilled at the perfect timing of this news.

I went to court with Sarah to represent me, with my entourage of supporters in tow. As usual Kerri was glued to my right side and I tried hard not to shake visibly. Mary had an attorney and I could see that they were confident. Mary, Jason, and a friend who had been at the farm the day I was arrested all testified against me and all said that I had threatened Mary by saying, "I am going to hit you now." Mary was the last to testify, and although Sarah had given the judge and Mary's attorney a copy of my email from the D.A., they appeared to be unaware that Mary had a pending criminal case. Mary's attorney asked her what I was doing on her property when she first saw me and Mary answered that I was giving water to her horses. The attorney asked her what I did next and she answered that I watered the goats, rabbits, and then the chickens. At that point, the judge interrupted and asked Mary if she was aware that she had been charged with six counts of animal cruelty and was incriminating herself. Mary answered, "No, that it isn't true." The judge assured her that it was true and then her attorney asked for a short recess. They went outside in the hallway and a few minutes later asked my attorney to join them. After conferring with both attorneys Mary refused to drop the restraining order against me and continued to incriminate herself on the stand. The Judge

interrupted her two more times to warn her that she was incriminating herself and anything she said today in court could be used against her. She insisted that she wasn't incriminating herself and continued her story of how I gave water to all of her animals and then lectured her on the care of farm animals. Finally after she testified that I had threatened her by saying, "I am going to hit you now," the judge said he had heard enough and ordered her to stop talking and go back to her seat. He addressed the court and said that he did not find it believable that I had stood in front of her and said, "I am going to hit you now." It was over! Someone had finally called Mary on her lies and seen the truth.

I was so happy to be over this life-changing ordeal. I had gone from nearly being a recluse, to the front lines and at first it was very uncomfortable. The supporters who came out to help me touched my soul with their kindness. I have always felt alone and had never fit in when suddenly, at age 52, I had found my niche. My supporters continually reminded me that I had done nothing wrong, the laws are wrong. It can't be a crime to come to the aid of suffering animals.

I had never felt love or respect before I was arrested. At court, with Kerri on my right side and Patricia on my left side, I knew what love felt like. Kerri was fighting a life-threatening sickness and felt like shit, but still she was there for me. Patricia took a day off work and drove two and a half hours to stand by my side. This is what love and true friendship feels like.

My other supporters, most of them new to me, were also amazing. They respected me for having the courage to climb that fence and help the suffering animals. To be surrounded by a dozen like-minded people was a powerful gift.

Since my arrest I have become an activist. I was so moved by the power of positive energy of a group of like-minded people and I couldn't go back to being a social recluse. I chose the causes that felt powerful to me and protested in solidarity with the Egyptians as they ousted Mubarak. I spent hours reading every news story about their revolution and wanted to be as brave as they are. The story of the protesters who made a human chain at Tahrir Square to protect their fellow protesters made a powerful impression on me. Would I be brave enough to be part of the human chain?

I marched with Occupy San Diego in the huge 2,000-man strong kick-off protest. Talk about positive energy flow! After the march I was able to walk around and talk to complete strangers. In a million years I would never have guessed that I would ever be capable of fitting in and actually enjoying people.

I joined the San Diego Animal Defense Team and rarely miss a protest against puppy mills. Janice, their founder has this Martin Luther King quote on each email she sends us;

> *"Never, never be afraid to do what is right, especially if the well-being of a person or animal is at stake. Society's punishments are small compared to the wounds we inflict on our soul when we look the other way."*
>
> *- Martin Luther King*

In the end it all comes down to love. When I didn't love myself, I was a magnet for disrespect and lived one painful drama after another. I found myself the day that I answered 'what would love do now?' and then climbed the fence and helped the suffering animals. It was like meeting myself for the first time, and I saw a person who I respected and loved, and it was me.

THE END...

or is it the beginning?

Books that Change Lives

COMING SOON TO AN ONLINE BOOKSTORE NEAR YOU:

"Learn to Speak Marketing" by Myles Bristowe, Chief Marketing Officer (CMO) at CommCreative in Boston, MA

"Monica Loves the Movies" by Steve Wolfson of Harbor View Farm

"Angel Gabriel - A True Story" by Joy LaPlante

Originally published in 1999, but just released to the Amazon Kindle Store in the summer of 2013.

This is the true story in the aftermath of Comair flight 3272 which crashed in January, 1997. Don't miss this incredible story as told by Monroe, Michigan resident Joy LaPlante. Only $2.97 in e-book formats.

BUSINESS BOOKS

"GETTING SEEN: The Ultimate Guide to Creating the Most Important Document of your Life – Your Resume" by *James Hale*, founder of Path Choices

Do you want to stand out among all the many job applicants? Want to give prospective employers the answers to the questions they are seeking. Let professional career guidance expert James Hale take you by the hand and teach you the proper way to set up your resume and present yourself on the job interview. This outstanding resume book, which ranked in the top 3 of two business categories on Amazon last fall, is available in **Kindle format through Amazon ($4.97)**, as well as **all e-book formats through Smashwords.**

HEALTH / WELL-BEING

Sleep Great for Life - *by Rich Nilsen.* **"The Solution** to One of Life's Greatest Health Risks."

Learn the 15 steps for a solid and secure sleep foundation, and then start applying the secret key to great sleep for life. "Sleep Great for Life" will help you overcome your insomnia so you can start reaping the benefits that come from a great night's rest. It available exclusively in Kindle format through Amazon ($4.97), and Paperback here from All Star Press.

This is a must-read for anyone who suffers from insomnia one or more times per week. This book is rated 5 stars on Amazon. Order today in Paperback or download "Sleep Great for Life" to your eReader today!

The Road to Recovery: **Overcoming and Moving Beyond Your Grief**

This easy-to-read ebook is a tremendous comfort and resource for anyone who has suffered the loss of a loved one. It was originally written and distributed free for the Sept. 11th families. This book is **rated 5 stars** on Amazon. Download "The Road to Recovery" to your Kindle eReader today! Only $2.99.

CHILDREN'S BOOKS

"Goodnight, Boone" by Yogi Collins.

This is a children's story focused around the popular town of **Boone, North Carolina in the nook of the Blue Ridge Mountains.** Author Yogi Collins grew up in Boone, NC, and while she loves that the High Country is filled with interesting and quirky people, she is also fascinated by how people end up in this little slice of heaven. A television producer/writer by trade, Yogi again lives in Boone, now with her husband Dan and two incredible kids. This is her first book.

CHRISTIAN / SELF-HELP

"Quiet Spaces: Hearing God's Call in a Noisy World" *by James Hale*, founder of Path Choices

In this powerful book Hale teaches you how to incorporate your calling into your day job. A **45-day easy-to-follow devotional is included** in "Quiet Spaces." Learn to hear God's call in your life with this great teaching guide from James Hale. Now only $5 for this important, life-changing book.

"I Am Not a Syndrome – My Name is Simon" by Trisomy mom Sheryl Crosier

Read the gripping story of baby Simon Crosier and his parent's fight for respect from the medical community. Born with

Trisomy 18, a genetic disorder, Simon touched the lives of so many people. Proceeds from this wonderful, pro-life book supports *SOFT – Support Organization for Trisomy 13, 18 and Related Disorders.*

12 out of 14 Five-star Ratings on Amazon.com!

"The House that Richard Built – Life Lessons from a Carpenter's Son" by James D. Smith (Kindle)

God has told us that He has "plans for you: plans to prosper you, plans to give you hope and a future." (Jer 29:11)

If God has these great plans for you, wouldn't you want to build the awesome things that He has in store? The House that Richard Built will take you on a life-changing journey into the world of a master carpenter! Some of the things you will learn in this powerful life guide: What it means to "measure twice and cut once," what to do when the roof comes crashing down, how to ensure you're building on the right foundation, how to focus so you hit the nails, and much more!

All Star Press digital publications are available wherever

e-books are sold.

Are you ready to become an author?

Become a published author and sell books with the help of All Star Press. Contact President Rich Nilsen at allstarpress@verizon.net to discuss your needs as an aspiring author. Our focus here at All Star Press is helping authors publish for both print and e-book formats for the Kindle, Nook and tablets. With our experience in marketing, All Star Press helps authors successfully promote their finished work with a detailed marketing plan.

All Star Press has a business model that is very beneficial to aspiring authors. We are not a 'vanity press' that charges authors fees up front to produce their work. **We only make money if the author makes money.** As a real book publisher All Star Press has a vested interest in the success of our authors.

In this day of ever-changing technology, understanding the e-book industry is key. Every day our team is analyzing the market and learning the best practices for targeting today's e-book readers.

The simple truth is that most authors are not marketers. Marketing your book effectively is not easy for the overwhelming majority of writers. Let All Star Press help you sell more books by reaching your audience in new ways.

Let All Star Press help you make your dream a reality.

Visit allstarpress.com today

www.ingramcontent.com/pod-product-compliance
Lightning Source LLC
Chambersburg PA
CBHW071944110426
42744CB00030B/283